JUST CALL ME

# Andi

I0874932

# JUST CALL ME *Andi*

## *SPORTS STORIES from a TRAILBLAZER*

ANDRIA PETRILLO

ECW

Copyright ©Andria Petrillo, 2025

Published by ECW Press
665 Gerrard Street East
Toronto, Ontario, Canada M4M 1Y2
416-694-3348 / info@ecwpress.com

All rights reserved. No part of this publication may be reproduced, stored in a retrieval system, or transmitted in any form by any process — electronic, mechanical, photocopying, recording, or otherwise — without the prior written permission of the copyright owners and ECW Press. The scanning, uploading, and distribution of this book via the internet or via any other means without the permission of the publisher is illegal and punishable by law. This book may not be used for text and data mining, AI training, and similar technologies. Please purchase only authorized electronic editions, and do not participate in or encourage electronic piracy of copyrighted materials. Your support of the author's rights is appreciated.

Editor for the Press: Michael Holmes
Copy editor: Carrie Gleason
Cover design: Jess Albert
Cover photograph: © Darren Goldstein (dsgphoto.com). Courtesy Bell Media.

To the best of her abilities, the author has related experiences, places, people, and organizations from her memories of them. In order to protect the privacy of others, she has, in some instances, changed the names of certain people and details of events and places.

LIBRARY AND ARCHIVES CANADA CATALOGUING IN PUBLICATION

Title: Just call me Andi / Andria Petrillo.

Names: Petrillo, Andi, author.

Identifiers: Canadiana (print) 20250228149 | Canadiana (ebook) 2025022819X

ISBN 978-1-77041-793-9 (softcover)
ISBN 978-1-77852-479-0 (PDF)
ISBN 978-1-77852-478-3 (ePub)

Subjects: LCSH: Petrillo, Andi. | LCSH: Women sportscasters—Canada—Biography. | LCSH: Sportscasters—Canada—Biography. | LCGFT: Autobiographies.

Classification: LCC GV742.42.P48 A3 2025 | DDC 070.4/49796092—dc23

This book is funded in part by the Government of Canada. *Ce livre est financé en partie par le gouvernement du Canada.* We also acknowledge the support of the Government of Ontario through the Ontario Book Publishing Tax Credit, and through Ontario Creates.

PRINTED AND BOUND IN CANADA

PRINTING: MARQUIS 5 4 3 2 1

Get the ebook free!* *proof of purchase required

Purchase the print edition and receive the ebook free. For details, go to ecwpress.com/ebook.

*To Mom, Dad, Jon,*
*and the incredible teammates*
*I've had in my life and career;*
*thank you for all the assists*
*throughout the years.*

"Sometimes just being yourself is the radical act. When you occupy space in systems that weren't built for you, your authenticity is activism."

— ELAINE WELTEROTH,

*More Than Enough: Claiming Space for Who You Are (No Matter What They Say)*

# CONTENTS

# FOREWORD

I have a real problem with Andi Petrillo.

I know, I know. This is the foreword for *her* book. I'm supposed to be nice. But hear me out.

You see, both Andi and I are in the extremely fortunate position of having careers hosting major sporting events on television. Lottery-winner lucky, both of us.

But when I host something — say a World Junior Hockey Championship or a Masters golf tournament — I like to tell my bosses I need plenty of time to prepare. And recover.

"It's mentally exhausting doing a pregame show and a couple of intermissions, plus having to powder my giant forehead constantly," is how my whining usually goes.

I'll take off a week to prep before the event. ("Doing in-depth research, don't bother me.") And then disappear somewhere like Turks and Caicos for a week after. ("The nation needs me looking fresh and rested.")

So, imagine my shock and dismay when I watched Andi host a huge Canadian men's soccer game one February night in 2022 on OneSoccer, then woke up the next morning to see her hosting the Beijing Olympics at some inhumane hour on CBC.

And here's the rub: She does this kind of thing regularly — jumping from sport to sport, network to network — tirelessly and seamlessly.

Andi's energy, drive, and professionalism is . . . let's just cut to the chase . . . selfish and mean-spirited.

It has ruined my entire cushy routine. Now when I beg my bosses for (unwarranted) time off, I have to hear, "But Andi Petrillo covers all these events without ever taking a br—"

Don't "But Andi" me, you soulless (yet factually accurate) suits!

It gets worse. In the Canadian sportscasting age known as B.A. (Before Andi), I had a run where misguided (and easily bribed) voters handed me a few Canadian Screen Awards. Then Petrillo comes along, and the awards ceremony becomes an annual "Clap for Andi" night.

One year, during Covid, the ceremony was held online (like everything else in our lives at that time). The nominees all pop up in our little computer screen boxes. And guess where Andi is? At the freaking spa.

*"And the Canadian Screen Award for Best Sports Host goes to . . . Andi Petrillo!"*

I'm staring at my little screen camera, fake-smiling, trying not to sob like I usually do when I lose. Meanwhile, Andi is in a robe, surrounded by candles, about to get some sixty-minute agave-Thai-honey-butter body wrap.

Infuriating.

And now, this. The last straw. The only remaining thing I had over Andi was that I'd written a few books. I introduce myself to people at parties as "James Duthie, anchor/author." (They smile uncomfortably, pretend to need a drink, and scurry away.) All Andi had was the anchor part. I would remind her of this every time I texted her: "Hey A. Nice work on that interview with McDavid. There's a great chapter on him in *Beauties*, the book I *authored*. Like, I wrote it. Myself! It was a lot of words."

Now that's gone too. Because freakin' Petrillo has written a really entertaining, inspiring, and important book about following your dreams, breaking down barriers, and the changing landscape of sports and sports broadcasting. Oh, and also falling in love with a giant soccer goalkeeper. (I'm a sucker for the romantic parts.)

So yeah, Andi's an anchor/author now too. I should loathe her for doing this to me. But the problem is, my nemesis is also my good friend.

I began watching Andi in her early years hosting with Maple Leaf Sports and Entertainment. You couldn't help but be impressed by her presence, her smooth delivery, and her obvious passion for sports. So, when she called me asking for career advice a couple of times, I was happy to oblige. (You'll read about these later — I demanded she include them in the book to make me sound generous and thoughtful.)

Truth is, she didn't need my advice. Andi was going to make it, no matter what I or anyone else told her.

This is her story. The story of how a proud Italian-Canadian "tomboy" grows up to relentlessly chase down her dream of being a sports broadcaster, leaping over hurdle after hurdle to become a star (she won't say the "star" part in the book, so I will).

We went for a drink on a patio a few summers ago. She told me she was leaving TSN. I was thrilled for her because I knew it meant a ton of other great opportunities would be headed her way. But sad for us because she made our network better. And because she's a great teammate — as warm and likeable off camera as she is on it.

I just wish she wouldn't work so hard and keep making me look lazy and spoiled. (Which I am. I just don't like everyone knowing.)

I guess I just have to keep writing more books, so I can stay ahead of her . . . *at something.*

JAMES DUTHIE

## CHAPTER 1

# WILD CHILD

I was seven years old. I wasn't in a particularly good mood that day despite being outside with my friends. I was wearing a dress. And I loathed it. My father had just come back from visiting family in Italy, and they'd sent him home with gifts. One was a dress for me. I was a tomboy. Not as widely an accepted term these days, but in 1987, that's what we used to describe girls who did all the things boys typically did. I liked playing sports, I liked getting dirty, and all my friends on my street were boys. But there I stood, with a dress on. The game that day was to sit on a skateboard and see who could roll down the driveway the fastest. Nobody was keeping time, I don't think any of us knew how to anyway, so we judged speed by our eyes and made guesses that always caused an argument. I had a plan. I would sacrifice my speed, and so my ego, by putting the destruction of the dress ahead of victory. When it was my turn, I grabbed the hem of the dress and jammed it around the wheel of the skateboard. My first run succeeded in getting it dirty. Not good enough. The second run twisted it up really good, to the point of fraying. Third run, success. The dress ripped. I stepped aside and started taking deep breaths. I was reaching into my chest to conjure up convincing tears. Once I felt my eyes were wet enough, I ran across the street and into my house.

"Ma! My new dress is ruined!" I shouted hysterically.

"How so? What did you do?" She was not impressed.

"I was playing, and it got caught under the skateboard wheel."

"Got caught or you put it there?" she said, eyes narrowing. She was onto me pretty quickly.

I gasped. "No way! It was an accident. I liked this dress!"

*Ugh, why did I say that last bit? I went too far. Now for sure she'll know I'm lying.*

"You never liked that dress. You hated it the second I put it on you. You did this on purpose," she said. "That's it, it's time you learned how to behave properly. I'm signing you up for modelling classes."

Now, before you go judging my mother, she would've done the same to a son. My mother always behaves with splendid propriety. If her parents signed her up for finishing school as a child, she would've had the same reaction as other kids being told they were going to Disneyland. I always joke that my mother acts like she's a descendant of the Queen.

I gave a petulant yet confused reaction to my mother's punishment. I was miffed I got busted, but where was I going? What did she want me to do?

She signed me up with the Eleanor Fulcher Modelling Agency, which also taught self-improvement. Right before I was to start, I got lice. My long beautiful golden-brown hair had to be chopped off. Splendid start to the "new me."

The modelling bit was a disaster. I didn't want to dress up, and I hated the fashion show we put on. But there was an acting component to the lessons, which I loved: I got to ham it up.

In my adult years, I learned that Eleanor Fulcher is an ambitious person who ventured into a business world that wasn't easy for women. To be a female entrepreneur in the 1960s was very bold.

Fast-forward seventeen years, and I was doing my own venturing into a world that was just as tough for women — sports broadcasting. Much to the delight of my mother, I did grow into loving dresses, spa days, and developing proper manners. But the wild child never left.

## CHAPTER 2

# FOR THE LOVE OF FAMILY

I am the daughter of immigrants. I am a proud second-generation Canadian.

My upbringing was blessed by being in a country that afforded me a good life, while honouring the homeland of my relatives.

I am Canadian. I am Italian.

But how can you be both? Easily.

I grew up with heavy Italian accents all around me. With the exception of my cousins, who like me were born in Canada, every other member of the family spoke broken English. They reminisced about the hard times in their small Italian village; they shared stories of love and laughter. They even found a way to look back on their poverty and share stories of their tough youth in a cathartic way with us, the next generation, that softened the pain they had felt while living it.

My maternal grandfather, Matteo, grew up with no running water. On their farm in Abruzzo, Italy, they would go outside to do their business. One night, as a little boy, he had an upset stomach. He woke up in the middle of the night, slipped his little feet into his father's big shoes, and clomped outside to relieve himself. Half awake, half in dreamland. Shivering, he made his way back to bed and eventually fell back to sleep. The screaming woke him in the morning. Someone had pooped in their father's shoes! Matteo sheepishly admitted his mishap. His little body wasn't big enough to clear the back of the shoes. He thought he was relieving himself on the soft, absorbing dirt, but his aim landed his business right inside the heel of his father's homemade footwear. He took his beating. It wasn't pleasant. He would laugh about it when he recounted the story to me. "You see," he would say, "we didn't have shoe stores the way you have them now. My father had that pair, and that was it. He spent forever cleaning them. I was a little boy. I made a mistake. So, my father hit me. But it's ok." However, I could see he was transported back to that night. Reminded of the no running water, the lack of food, and the lack of clothing. He never wanted his kids or his grandkids to feel the pain that comes with that kind of struggle.

My maternal grandmother, Angela, grew up in similar circumstances. The eldest of ten children, she became an adult before losing her first tooth. She helped raise her siblings and worked on the farm. She didn't own her first pair of store-bought shoes until she was seventeen. A boy she was dating bought them for her. Beautiful red shoes. Up to that point in life, my grandmother and her siblings wore homemade shoes fashioned from rubber from discarded tires or wooden clogs carved by their father. She would only wear the red shoes when she went out with her boyfriend. No other time. She didn't want them to become ruined. And after every wear, Angela would take great care to clean them and would then give them a little kiss before putting them back in their original box and storing them under her bed. One day, there was a party in the village. Angela wasn't allowed to go. Her boyfriend wasn't available to escort her, and her mother said it wouldn't be a good look for her to attend a party without him. But one of her sisters, Ida, was going, and she wanted to borrow the beautiful red shoes. Angela had a fit. No one was to touch her shoes. "But come on," Ida pleaded. "You're not going to the party, and I don't have those kinds of shoes. This isn't fair." Angela squinted, eyes turning black (a frightening look I would come to know well as a rebellious grandchild), and she gave one last warning not to touch the red shoes.

A few hours later, after farm chores, Angela made her way inside. Ida had already left for the party. Something didn't sit right with Angela, so she ran to her bed, kneeled down, and pulled the box out from under it and quickly threw back the lid. As she suspected, the shoes were gone! Her blood began to boil. She felt a rage that couldn't be contained. She told her mother, "I'm going to that house party and I'm getting my shoes back!" No one stopped her.

When she arrived at the party, she spotted her younger sister dancing up a storm. She didn't care that Ida was having a good time; she also didn't care that there were people around to witness this sibling shakedown. Angela marched right up to her sister, and Ida, upon spotting her, went pale. Busted. Angela demanded she take off the shoes.

"Right here, right now? But I'll be barefoot!" Ida said.

Angela had zero sympathy. "I told you no. I told you not to touch them. You know how much they mean to me. Too bad, take them off."

The night ended miserably for Ida. For Angela, it ended with the ritual of cleaning her red shoes and kissing them goodnight. They were back in their box safe and sound.

My grandmother was barley five feet tall, but she was a firecracker. My grandfather was such a kind and philosophical soul. Having them by my side throughout life was a blessing.

They wed in Abruzzo, in a tiny church in the city of Sulmona. My mother, Eva, was born on October 18, 1954. But she almost wasn't. I have to take you back to July 26 of that year. The day of Saint Anne. Matteo was leaving the next day for Venezuela to work in the mines with his brothers. Jobs were scarce in Italy after the war. He didn't know when he would be back, but he would send money. The young couple wanted to spend their last day together. The weather was horrible: wind, rain, lightning, and thunder. They wanted to stay inside and be cozy, especially with Angela being pregnant. But Matteo's father, who was a hard man, insisted on fieldwork being done on the farm before his son had to leave. Angela and Matteo begged not to go out; it wasn't safe, and even the horse was being difficult. But the old man wouldn't budge. He insisted on going with them to get the job done.

They got in a few hours of work, and the weather worsened. They knew they needed to head back. All three stepped up into the wagon and that's when all hell broke loose. The horse was spooked by the lightning and thunder and bolted. Matteo and his father tried with all their strength to get the horse to slow down. Nothing worked. In fact, the harness and hitch came apart, the horse went loose, and part of the wooden hitch hit Matteo's father in the ribs, cutting him open. The whole time, all

Matteo could think about was his pregnant wife. He thought for sure they were going to crash and die. To save her, he pushed her from the wagon, hoping the earth would soften her landing. But the weight of her pregnant belly threw her off balance, and her stomach bore the brunt of the fall. She lay there in pain. Matteo continued to struggle to slow down the horse while his wife was on the ground suffering and his father was bleeding. Finally, he was able to calm the horse down. Immediately, he got his father and wife to the hospital. Angela was sent for observation, and the entire time she prayed to Saint Anne, the mother of the Virgin Mary and patron saint of women in labour: "Please save my baby. You are a mother, please don't take my child. If you save this baby, I will name her after you."

Thankfully, baby and mother were fine. Angela stayed overnight to rest. The next day, Matteo left for Venezuela. He wouldn't see his baby girl, his firstborn, until she was almost two years old.

You may be wondering, How is it your mother's name is Eva when your grandmother promised Saint Anne she would name her Anna? Cue Ida once again. My grandmother had been in labour for over twenty-four hours. Her father, known affectionately as Nonno Chico, knew the midwife had done all she could; it was time to go to the hospital. He had lost a sister in childbirth, and there was no way he was going to lose his daughter the same way.

After giving birth to her daughter in the hospital, Angela was very groggy because of all the drugs they gave her to deal with the pain. Being sedated, she was incapable of registering her newborn baby. No need to worry, sister Ida took care of all the paperwork. At this time, Ida was reading a book and had taken a shining to the main character's name: Eva. So, without any consultation from the parents (one was passed out and the other wasn't in the country), the baby was named Eva.

Don't fret, my grandmother more than honoured her promise to Saint Anne when she gave birth to my twin aunts. She doubled down and named them Anna and Rosanna. My grandmother could rest easy knowing she had appeased the saint.

My grandfather's time in Venezuela was hard. He lost a brother in the most devastating of ways. One day, while they were working in a mine, it collapsed. My grandfather became stuck under some rocks, and he watched, helplessly, as his eldest brother was buried alive. I can't even imagine the anger and sorrow he felt.

He toiled away for almost two years, sending just about all his earnings back home to the family. When he was finally able to return home, he met his daughter for the first time.

My grandparents knew their time in their homeland was coming to an end. If they wanted a better life, if they wanted to give their children a better life, it was time to go. On March 7, 1957, my grandparents left Italy for Canada. My mom was about two and a half years old, and my grandmother was pregnant. She didn't know at the time that she was carrying twins. In 1957, they didn't go to the doctor for regular checkups, and they didn't have ultrasounds or crazy gender reveal parties. The birth of twins was truly a surprise.

Whenever I'm having travel issues — delays, cancellations, layovers, etc. — I try to calm down by reminding myself that my grandmother travelled by boat from Italy to Halifax, Nova Scotia, and then took a train to Toronto, all while pregnant with twins and a toddler in tow.

Anna and Rosanna were born on June 25, shortly after my family arrived in Canada. My grandmother almost died. There was confusion. There was fear. My grandparents didn't know a word of English. My aunts ended up staying in the hospital for a few months. We later learned they were one of the first babies in Canada to receive a blood transfusion. On the twenty-fifth anniversary of the procedure, my aunts got a phone call from a medical student at McGill University who was doing a follow-up. They wanted to know about the quality of life of the babies who were saved by this fairly new medical treatment. That's how we found out what happened at the time of their birth. My grandparents never understood what was happening.

Canada gave my family hope. Canada gave my family opportunities. But man, it wasn't easy.

When my mother and grandparents arrived in Canada with other immigrants, they were "greeted" by people yelling at them. My grandfather didn't know what they were saying. Being a kind man, he assumed they were welcoming them. He later learned they were hurling insults, calling them filthy, worthless, and horrible slang names.

There were no luxuries during my mom's childhood. My grandparents worked shift work, and she was left raising her twin sisters at a young age.

My mother was also the leader of a few domestic rebellions. One such uprising was motivated by bags of potato chips. Being poor, my grandparents never bought junk food for their kids because it was considered frivolous spending. Although one time, while still trying to figure out the English language, my grandfather couldn't believe that a pack of cigarettes was five cents when they normally went for twenty-five cents. So, he bought a bunch of boxes, sat on the porch, lit one, and . . . it melted. *What the heck?* he thought. Lit another, and it melted. That's when he tasted chocolate. No wonder they were cheap, they were candy cigarettes! My mom and aunts were the happy beneficiaries of my grandfather's mistake.

But other than that fortuitous night, sweet and salty foods were a delicacy.

One night, my grandmother came home with a box of Humpty Dumpty chips. A whole box! Eva, Anna, and Rosanna were over the moon. Their joy was promptly quashed: "It's not for you," Angela warned. "It's for the kids who come on Halloween." Angela was working the night shift at the famous chip company's factory at the time. It was a big deal for her to bring a box home. It was a big deal to have something to hand out on the popular night.

Eva wasn't having it. She pulled her sisters aside.

"That's not fair, you know. We're their children. We should get those chips, not kids they don't even know." The twelve-year-old was very convincing to the nine-year-olds. She rallied the troops. It was time for a mutiny.

Eva said the only recourse for being so greatly disrespected was to eat all the chips. Anna and Rosanna nodded in agreement, not really understanding what they were about to do to their tummies. They waited for the perfect opportunity to pull off their plan. Their parents stepped out to run some errands, and that's when they pounced. In the front hall closet, on the floor in plain sight, were the mouth-watering ripple potato chips. Resolute in their cause, the three sisters sat down and began to eat. The box contained fifty small-sized bags. What began with excitement ended with painful stomach aches.

"I can't eat anymore," Anna groaned.

"Too bad," Eva snapped. "We have to teach them a lesson. We can only do that by finishing all the bags."

"Ok, but I think I'm going to be sick."

The two turned their heads towards Rosanna and noticed two very chubby cheeks. She couldn't swallow another bite but didn't want to upset her sisters, so she mushed up the chips and kept them in her mouth, like a cow chewing cud.

When my grandparents came home and discovered the empty bags of chips and children sick from too much grease and salt, they didn't get angry, they felt sad. They knew these were the types of treats they couldn't afford for their children.

But what they could give was love. We have a lot of it in our family. They taught compassion and hard work.

When more of our relatives started coming over from Italy, they would live with my grandparents for a bit before finding their own way. My mom and her sisters weren't just raised by a strong mother, they also had strong-willed aunts as role models.

So, it's no surprise that the three young girls grew up to be strong and confident women. My mother is an avid learner and strong-willed, which my father has always been supportive of. And in the 1980s, that was a big deal.

My father's name is Giuseppe. You can also call him Pepe or Joe.

In the '80s, especially in Italian culture, gender roles were very stereotypical. The women stayed home and raised the kids. The men worked and were catered to when they got home.

My father wasn't having any of that. He believed then, as he does now, in independence. He encouraged my mother to work, to have her own money, to explore her own interests. And when it came to me, he was very much involved in my upbringing.

When I was two years old, my parents took a trip to Venezuela to visit some relatives. When my grandfather went with his brothers to work in the mines, one stayed behind and built a life in that country.

After a long journey, I was cranky, and my mother wasn't feeling well. My father didn't hesitate to step in and take care of me. When he tried to soothe me by taking me for a walk in my stroller, men on the street relentlessly teased him. They taunted him by saying he was doing woman's work. He didn't care. He didn't feel ashamed. He walked to the beat of his own drum. The opinions of sheep never bothered him.

Like my mother, my father also grew up with very little. He's from the town of Baiano just outside of Naples, Italy. My father always told me: "Your mother comes from the mountains of Abruzzo. Hard-working people. I'm from the city where everyone works hard to swindle you!" My father is playful but very mischievous. A bit of a rebel. Perhaps he got those traits from his mom, my grandmother Antonietta. When her family didn't want her to marry a man named Raffaele (who would become my grandfather), she ran away with him, got pregnant, and came back defiant, knowing they would now have to bless the union!

She also had a love for soccer. She couldn't afford tickets to the Serie A club, SSC Napoli, but when she was able to save up some money, she would go and watch the local team.

And she wasn't a quiet spectator.

When my father was about eight years old, my grandmother got a ticket to a match but couldn't afford one for him. No problem, my father had become very good at sneaking into places.

Antonietta took her seat; her son found a perch not too far above her.

Their team was winning, and the goalkeeper was standing on his head.

A fan for the opposing team wasn't happy. "We need to take their goalkeeper out! He's stealing the game! Somebody run into him and knock him out!" the man yelled.

It was a cloudy day, so Antonietta had an umbrella with her, and she wasn't afraid to use it in ways other than its intended purpose.

Umbrella raised towards the man, she growled, "What did you say? You keep your mouth shut. Don't threaten my players or else you'll see what I'll do to you!"

"Ok, ok, ok, signora, no need to get aggressive," the man replied, not taking any chances testing her sanity.

My father watched all this from his "borrowed" seat. He was ready to jump into action if his mom needed him. But she didn't. Antonietta was tough.

My paternal grandfather was a lumberjack. He got injured on the job, hit by a tree, and cracked some ribs. He was in a lot of pain and couldn't work anymore, making the financial situation for the family all the more dire.

My father didn't have much growing up. He would often sneak onto other people's properties, climb up their fruit trees, and treat himself to a meal. His lunch was always interrupted by the owners chasing him off their land and cursing him for eating their produce. His breakfast often consisted of stale bread dunked in hot water to soften it, making it more palatable.

He started working at around nine years old at the local cinema, back when you had to load the massive circular film reel into position. Some movies needed two reels, and there were nights when little Pepe would fall asleep and be awoken by the screaming mob below. The first reel was over, and they had been staring at a blank screen for several minutes. They let their impatience be known, and at the back of the theatre, in his little nook, Pepe scrambled to appease the moviegoers by lifting one heavy reel off and replacing it with another. He would then walk home, late at night in the pitch black, all by himself.

Pepe needed to work to help the family. That meant school was done for him after he completed the elementary levels at age thirteen. He began to work with his brother-in-law, who was an ironworker. My dad was the last child to be born to Antonietta and Raffaele, so his siblings, and their spouses, were much older. His eldest brother, Nunzio, was twenty years his senior.

Many of their clients in the ironworking business belonged to the camorra (a Mafia-style organization), and my father would go to their homes to collect payment. Apparently, they were great clients who always paid on time.

Life was hard in Napoli. Almost every cent my father made, he handed over to his mother. Sometimes he would lie about the amount he made that week just so he could squirrel away some money for himself.

Finally, on March 12, 1966, at the age of sixteen, my father left for Canada. One of his sisters, Emilia, had married and moved to the Great White North. He wanted a better life too.

That's not to say things were peachy the second he started his life in Canada. He had to learn a new language and start working right away. But my father, a true Neapolitan, still found a way to sing his way through life. Pepe knows how to have a good time. He found a job as an ironworker and worked for the same company until the day he retired. He was good at saving his money; he was also a pretty good hustler at the local pool hall.

My playful side definitely comes from my father. Even after a long day of work, he was always up for a game of cards, bowling, or dancing. And he would sing through it all . . . still does. We even teamed up as a musical act one year. My music school put on a Christmas concert, and I chose to play "O Holy Night" on the piano while my dad performed the vocals.

My dad used to call me his little princess; he also called me his little devil — that's a book for another time! But he never treated me like a delicate princess.

Both he and my mom raised me to get myself out of the tower.

My parents met at a nightclub. They love dancing. In fact, they used to teach dance lessons at their local hangout, Momo's. I still have vivid memories of going on vacation with my parents, and when the local entertainment crew called on the hotel guests to get up and dance, my parents always ended up stealing the show. They would just look at each other, get up, grab hands, make their way to the centre of it all, and amaze everyone with a merengue, salsa, or cha-cha-cha; whatever the music called for. To this day, they go dancing with friends; although, more Epsom salt baths are being taken as well.

My parents were determined to give me an easier life than theirs. And they did. I wanted for nothing.

Even though I am an only child, our house was always full. Sunday lunches with the family, back when everything was still closed on Sundays, were the best.

We gathered around the table to devour anything from homemade pasta, pizza, polenta, and fresh vegetables from the garden to homemade wine. Yes, as a child, I was served watered down wine. Bless my grandfather, Matteo, who's no longer with us, but he firmly believed red wine is what made our blood red and strong. Thank goodness for the water because the homemade stuff was a little hit or miss!

Most of my mother's family is in Canada. A lot of my father's family is still in Napoli. And I've always had a strong connection with both.

In 2003, for my grandparents' fiftieth wedding anniversary, we all went back to Abruzzo. Walking alongside my nonno and nonna as they reminisced was special. I saw where they had lived, where they worked, and where they sat and read love letters from each other. Reliving their memories with them and seeing the beginnings of my mother's life was magical.

In 2015, we went back to Napoli for a family wedding. My father and I spent a day together, just the two of us, and we floated through the streets where little Pepe played, worked, and caused trouble. When I closed my eyes, I could hear the echo of young Pepe's voice bouncing off every pebble and brick.

I wouldn't be able to take the steps I take in Canada if they hadn't started walking in Italy first. That's why I say proudly: I am both Canadian and Italian.

## CHAPTER 3

# THE DAY I WENT MISSING

I wouldn't say I'm the type to make dramatic entrances, but I also wouldn't say I go unnoticed when I walk into a room. And that has to do with the fact that I come in two volumes: loud and louder. I've had my fair share of run-ins with librarians over the years.

There have been times when I've arrived at the studio, everyone working away in their cubicles or offices, and I start joyously saying hello to people or playfully teasing someone over something. I've had the occasional annoyed head pop up or office door close, but the majority of my co-workers join in on the conversation. Everyone knows when Andi has arrived. And sure, as an only child, I welcome being the centre of attention. When I was younger, during dinnertime, I would get up from the kitchen table and make my way to the adjoining dining room. Hiding behind the dining room door, I would tell my mother to pretend she had a microphone and to introduce me to the pretend crowd who was in attendance. My mother would always play along, and in her most announcer voice, she would boom: "And now, ladies and gentlemen, the greatest tap dancer you'll ever see! Miss Andi Petrillo!" And I would shuffle ball change my way back into the kitchen and do a little routine for my parents, my mom clapping and my dad giving me the thumbs up as he continued eating his dinner.

So maybe I do like dramatic entrances? Perhaps I'm just in denial.

But there's no denying I made the most dramatic entrance of all on my first day of school.

I was five years old and excited to be going to school. I remember being so proud of my uniform: a plaid skirt and sweater vest. And the shoes; I loved my shoes. While waiting for the bus, I kept looking down at my feet and being entranced by the loafers with the tassels on them. I kept wiggling my foot so the tassels would shake. My parents were at work, so it was my grandmother — Nonna — who watched me get on the bus. Michael, my mother's cousin's son, was also starting school that day. So, my nonna and his mom, Silvana, waved goodbye to us as we drove off.

When we arrived at St. Andrew Catholic School in Rexdale, Ontario, we all stood up to get off the bus. That's when this troublemaker, Rocky, said to me, "This isn't your school. You have to stay on the bus and get off at the next stop."

Oh, ok. I didn't know any better. So, I stayed on the bus.

Now, the events that followed get a little crazy. Things were happening simultaneously, so I'll do my best to keep things organized and easy to understand.

As the school bus pulled away, I remained silent and still excited to get dropped off at my school. When the woman driving the bus finally parked, my little eyes could tell we weren't at a school, we were in the parking lot of a strip mall.

"Excuse me, miss," I piped up.

The bus driver screamed with fright when she heard my voice. "What are you still doing here?!?" she yelled angrily.

"I was told you still have to take me to my school."

"You were supposed to get off with the other kids. That's the only school." This woman was not being gentle or sympathetic at all.

Panic was starting to set in. I was scared. I burst into tears, but this woman was hard. She didn't even flinch: "Well too bad. You have to sit there now until my break is over." And with that, she left the bus.

She would later tell the cops she hadn't seen me because I fell asleep.

Liar, liar, pants on fire.

As this exchange was taking place, Silvana said to my nonna, "I know you're nervous about today being Andi's first day of school, so why don't we walk over and see the kids in the yard before the bell rings? We can watch

Andi and Michael playing. We'll make sure they don't see us. We don't want to embarrass them."

The two ladies happily made their way to the school, which was within walking distance, and stood off to the side looking through the fence as all the kids were playing before the bell rang for school to start.

They spotted Michael right away. But there was no sign of little Andi. After searching with no luck, the women had to blow their cover and approach the school grounds.

Silvana called her son over. "Michael, where's Andi?" she asked.

"I don't know," he said, shrugging his shoulders.

"What do you mean you don't know? She was on the bus with you!"

"Yeah, but I haven't seen her."

Michael was young too. There was only so much information he could give.

Now, if you want to talk drama, if you want to talk theatrics, allow me to introduce you to my nonna. She immediately started freaking out and went after the first teacher she saw. She was all of five foot nothing, thick Italian accent, but she made sure everyone could hear her.

"My granddaughter is missing!" she screamed.

"Hold on, ma'am, she must be here somewhere," the teacher on duty said, desperately trying to calm her down.

"Don't tell me to hold on! Find her!"

They rang the bell early to have all the kids line up. Still no sign of Andi.

My nonna almost fainted.

As the school began their search for me — behind and underneath portables, in bathroom stalls, under desks — they finally realized they had to call the police. This was now a case of a missing child.

Meanwhile, I was crying hysterically in the school bus. That ugly woman had left me. When I got older, I figured out she had been in a bar drinking.

I cried so hard that I eventually fell asleep.

The cops arrived at the school. By now, my grandmother had become homicidal. She was willing to kill anyone who brought her bad news. At one point, the cops scoured the surrounding area and brought any piece of clothing they found to my nonna and asked, "Was this hers? Was she wearing this today?"

"You think someone took her? You think she's dead?!" My grandmother found another level of hysteria.

"Ma'am, we have to think of everything."

My grandmother was raving mad, but she refused to call my parents. She didn't know what she would say to them. Then she overheard two officers talking about possibly giving her a tranquilizer; that's how badly she was freaking out. My nonna jumped in on their hushed conversation: "You want to stab *me* with something? I stab *you* with something!"

I don't think those cops went near her again.

It was 1985, and there were no cell phones. So, it wasn't exactly easy to get ahold of the bus driver. To this day, I'm not quite sure how they found her, but I woke up to her charging onto the bus and grumbling, "You've caused a lot of trouble for me! You've made such a mess of things!"

We took off towards the school.

When we pulled up, one of the cops clearly wanted to play the hero, because he came onto the bus, scooped me up, and carried me out to my grandmother who, at that point, was dropping to her knees and thanking God. I was more than capable of walking out on my own, but hey, it added to the dramatic entrance.

Everyone believed the bus driver's story about not knowing I was on the bus because I fell asleep — except for one person.

My nonna believed me from day one; she knew I hadn't fallen asleep. She knew the bus driver abandoned me. The next day, when the bus pulled up, my nonna got on before me. She told the driver she believed her granddaughter over her and that this saga was far from over. Shortly after, the bus driver was fired.

Everyone in school knew who I was right from the get-go: The Girl Who Got Lost.

Things have changed since the '80s when it comes to school bus safety. A friend's father drives a bus and said that now the driver has to walk to the back of the bus and push a button before exiting the vehicle. This ensures that the driver has thoroughly checked for any kids left behind.

I could have used that safety feature back in the day; but then again, I wouldn't have had such a dramatic entrance into the educational system — where's the fun in that?

## CHAPTER 4

# AN ATHLETE AT HEART

Ever since I can remember, I've loved playing sports. When I was a kid, I'd be outside with my friends playing street hockey, soccer, baseball, soccer baseball, and any other crazy sport with ridiculous rules that we would make up.

My parents didn't put me in organized sports. Instead, I took dance lessons and piano lessons. I was put into swimming lessons as well and went through all the levels, including lifeguarding classes.

It was around grade 4 that I started participating in school sports. I was fast. Track and field was my first love. I was really good at sprinting and won the 100m and 200m dashes at every track event I went to. I anchored our 4x100m relay team.

I qualified for regionals, and it was the first time in over a year that I had lost a race. However, I still ended up on the podium with bronze in the 100m.

The next day at school, I brought my medal. My classmates thought it was the coolest thing. My teacher, Mr. Fleming, wore it around his neck at recess. He said he didn't want it getting lost or ruined, but I knew it was because he was proud of me and loved showing it off to the other teachers.

But then puberty hit, and I got hips. In fact, my body was growing faster than my bones — did you know that was a thing? I didn't but quickly found out it was. My pelvic and hip bones were in excruciating pain after every race. I would always collapse at the finish line clutching my hip bones.

It was around this time — grades 7 and 8 — that I started taking up team sports at school. I loved the camaraderie of it all — even though there were some girls on the team who annoyed me. We've all had those teammates!

When I was in grade 8, my school put on a production of *Joseph and the Amazing Technicolor Dreamcoat*. No boys wanted to play Joseph. They were too shy, and the few who did audition weren't that good. So, I ended up being Joseph! It was a snazzy production. When my designer aunt, Anna, learned I was the lead character, she wanted to help out with the set design and put together something incredible for a bunch of fourteen-year-olds.

We had many performances. We did a show for our school, for other elementary schools, for our families, and we did one in front of high school students. That last one was intimidating. Turns out, the drama teacher from the high school I was going to attend in the fall loved my performance. Right then and there, she offered me a role in the high school's performance the following year of *Little Shop of Horrors*. There are three narrators in that play, and she wanted me to be one of them. I was thrilled to accept.

School broke for the summer, and I enjoyed being a kid for a few more months before entering the big scary life of a high schooler.

A few weeks into the new school year, they announced basketball tryouts. I made the team. I was even named captain. But when I looked at my practice schedule and my rehearsal schedule, the two didn't jive. Damn. I would have to drop one. I knew right away I wanted to play basketball, but I felt bad letting my drama teacher down. She didn't take the news well. I don't blame her. I had committed to her first, but my love for sports was overwhelming. As the years went on, it wasn't lost on me that I eventually married my passion for sports with my passion to put on a show when I got into broadcasting.

The basketball team got off to a great start. But almost immediately my body started breaking down on me.

You see, I developed very young; I became curvy and "womanly" at a very young age. I began menstruating when I was only ten years old. This was stressful for me in locker rooms. I'd be the only one of my teammates changing in the bathroom stall, and I was always nervous someone would see a pad in my bag. I took to wearing spandex shorts under my uniform during that time of the month. A lot of young girls who get their period early leave sports because of all the stresses that come with being one of the few whose body is already changing. If you have an accident, it can be mortifying. And white shorts? Holy friggin' hell. Just kill me.

I remember hosting a panel for International Women's Day in March 2019. We were discussing the alarming rates in which young girls were leaving sports. Lack of support, both financially and emotionally, were mentioned. I suggested menstruation. The room went silent.

I proceeded: "Did you ever think that a young girl doesn't want to be teased by her teammates because she's the only one menstruating? It happens. Or what about uniforms? Some shorts are too short, too white, and in some sports like gymnastics and figure skating, where you have to contort your body wearing very little, it can be very stressful."

I was astounded by the number of women who came up to me afterwards to share their stories of feeling shame because they had their period at a young age and were uncomfortable around teammates and didn't like wearing certain uniforms.

Since 2019, more and more female athletes have become vocal about what they have to wear while competing. Obviously, at the pro level the concern isn't about shame around teammates anymore, it's more about the uniforms. In 2023, when soccer players on England's national team announced they would no longer be wearing white shorts, I shared the story on Twitter. A former Canadian national team soccer player reached out to me and said, "I'm still traumatized by the 2008 Olympics. We were competing for the first time in the Games, and I was so stoked. And whaddya know? I get my period the night before our first game. And what kits did Canada Soccer choose to have us wear? The ones with the white shorts. How am I supposed to focus on this huge match when all I can think is 'don't have an accident in front of millions!'"

Starting in 2024, the National Women's Soccer League has also done away with white shorts.

All of that is to say that by fourteen years of age, my body was far more developed than the other girls', and because of my changing hormones, I couldn't handle the type of training they were doing.

I sprained my knee — recovered. I tore ligaments in my ankle — recovered. Pulled my hamstring — recovered. The final straw was when I fell and broke my wrist. Just over the halfway mark of the basketball season, we were the best team, but my playing time was done. Years later I came across an American Girl Doll on crutches and wearing an arm cast, and I never related more to a doll!

I continued going to every practice and every game. I wasn't going to abandon my team. We went on to win the regional title — the school's first ever championship.

After my body healed, I joined the volleyball team, the indoor soccer team, and then the outdoor soccer team. I was in my zone. Was I the best player on my team? Of course not. But I was always a starter, and I was the captain of the majority of teams I was on.

I decided I wanted to play sports outside of school. For a while, I was playing in an outside volleyball league. I would wear the bruises on my hip bones with pride as I dove for balls left, right, and centre. I hit my peak height at thirteen years old — 5'4 — so there was no hope for growth and becoming an intimidating spiker. Instead, I revelled in my role as a setter and also as a libero.

At sixteen, I joined my first soccer team — the Vaughan Lightning. Wow, I loved those girls. A lot of them were also on my school soccer team, so we gelled right away on the field.

During the playoffs in 1997, disaster struck. I collided with a girl on the opposite team while battling for the ball, and my left leg buckled. It was my left knee. Having gone through so many knee sprains, I told my coach I was good to stay in the game. But I quickly realized this knee injury was different. When I tried to run, there was no power. It was almost like my leg wasn't there. I tried to push off it sideways, and the pain was excruciating. I had to be subbed off. At least we won the game.

The next day, my knee was the size of a melon. Again, because I had been down this road before, I told my parents there was no need to go to the hospital and get x-rays; I'd just ice my knee, and it would be good for next week's semifinals. My knee was still bad a week later, and my mother lost her mind: "There's no way you're playing! Stop this nonsense! If you want to go to the game to support your teammates, fine. But don't you dare even think of gearing up."

My dad pulled me aside and asked me what I wanted to do.

"I want to try. Just let me try. If it's no good, then I'll come off. But let's see how I do wearing my knee brace," I said.

My dad became my accomplice. I left the house wearing my team track suit; my mother made sure my uniform wasn't underneath or in my bag — my dad and I were careful to hide it in the trunk of the car when she wasn't looking.

I played in the game and was absolutely awful. No power in my left leg and slow as molasses. I was called for a few fouls because I kept pulling on the backs of opponents' jerseys; I couldn't keep up with them. That was the soul crushing part. I wasn't the most skilled player on the team, but I was the fastest. I could always rely on my speed. And now that was gone.

We lost the game. No finals and no chance at a championship for us. I sat in the car and sulked all the way home. My dad pulled into a side street before we got home so I could change out of my uniform to keep up the ruse with my mom. I cried the whole time I was changing at the side of the car, wincing in pain every time I had to move my left leg.

Some of you might be wondering, Did you ever play hockey? After all, many of you were first introduced to me as a hockey host. Hockey broadcasting is what I've been doing for the past twenty years of my career. And the answer is no. I played ball hockey and pickup shinny at the local rink sometimes, but I was never in any kind of organized hockey. My parents didn't have the work schedule that would allow them to meet the demands of a hockey schedule, and I was also quite content being driven around to my piano lessons, dance lessons, and swimming lessons. When I got older, I took myself to practices and games. I may not have played organized hockey, but as many of you know, my obsession for the sport runs deep.

Now back to my knee.

Like a true idiot in denial, I kept playing on my destroyed knee. Basketball season came around, and I was doing ok until I pushed off my left leg to move sideways, and I buckled. Would I stop there? Nope. Indoor soccer season came around, and I was doing ok until I challenged for the ball in a game. My pace was non-existent, so I stretched out my body by extending my right leg forward to get the ball. I hyperextended my left leg to complete this ballet-like move, and it was too much for my knee to handle. But this time, my knee made a weird sound. Even weirder than the snaps it had made before. While on the ground rocking in pain, I made eye contact with the ref, who said, "I heard something. It was loud. You need to come off."

I finally saw a specialist, and boy, did I do a doozy on my knee. Torn MCL, ACL, and cartilage damage.

I had reconstructive knee surgery at eighteen, and they took a chunk of my hamstring to recreate my annihilated ACL ligament.

I spent a few days in the hospital, and they were some of the most eventful days of my life. When I think back on my time in the hospital, I can't help but feel a pang of guilt for the old woman who was in the bed next to me. Allow me to explain.

The woman was very old. Poor thing was in a room next to a teenager who woke up puking after the anesthetic. My left leg was on a motorized device that gently bent and straightened my leg. It wasn't a loud machine. But no doubt annoying when you're trying to rest.

I was also hooked up to an IV with a self-injecting morphine pump and was saying some really strange things. I'm sure she *loved* listening to my weird ravings.

One night, I almost blew us up. I love my essential oils, and I told my mom to bring my diffuser to the hospital so I could burn my favourite scent. A little tea light was lit under the oil holder. When the nurse saw it, she freaked out.

"You can't have an open flame in here! The woman next to you is hooked up to an oxygen tank!"

Oopsie.

By the way, the puking, the gibberish talk, and the close call of things going boom all happened on the first day!

On the second night, tragedy struck, and then all hell broke loose.

My mom was with me as I ate dinner. I had to use the washroom, but because of the motorized device for my leg, I was using a bedpan. Yuck. One day was enough for me, and I refused to use it again. We asked the nurse if I could get a wheelchair so I could take myself to the toilet like a civilized human being. She said it was imperative that my leg remain at a 90-degree angle to my body; therefore, once I finished dinner, she and another nurse would assist me. Wonderful.

The old lady next to me, who hadn't eaten in two days, finished her dinner and asked the nurse for second helpings. Then she asked for an extra pillow and for the window to be cracked open. It was just the three of us in the room: the old lady, my mom, and me. It was quiet. Peaceful. We heard her perfectly when she took her last breath. My mom and I sat there in silence for a few beats waiting for an exhale, but it never came. Then my mom said, "I think she's dead."

It was the first time I had seen a dead body outside of a funeral home, and I couldn't stop staring. I'm convinced the old lady knew she was going. Ate her last meal? An extra pillow for comfort? The window open so her spirit could fly out? You bet I believe in that. My mom drew the curtains to give her privacy, and no doubt to shield me, and then she went to tell the nurses the lady in the room had passed away peacefully.

That's when all hell let loose. Nurses and doctors came barging into the room and immediately tried to resuscitate her. It's their job. And perhaps the old lady's wishes were to be resuscitated, but the calmness of her death turned into pure chaos. They wheeled my bed with me in it out into the hall while everyone rushed into the room. I sat there for a good hour. Once the shock of the situation subsided, I remembered something: *I have to pee!*

The nurse said everyone was busy and tossed me the bedpan. Ah, hells no. I hated using that thing in the privacy of my room — you think I'm using it in a public hallway?!?! You must be mad. I told my mom to start doing her stretches because I was going to need her muscles to lift me out of the bed and wheel me to the toilet.

What a friggin' fiasco. I told her a million times not to drop or lift my left leg.

"I got it!" she yelled at me. "You don't have to keep reminding me!"

I wiggled off the bed and into the wheelchair, my mom carefully holding my leg steady. We managed to get ourselves to the closest washroom: me wheeling and bringing my morphine with me because it was hooked up to my arm, and my mom walking backwards holding my leg. We manoeuvred quite well up to that point, and my mom wheeled me over the toilet — the wheelchair had a hole in the seat for this very purpose. I wiggled out of my pyjama shorts and finally let loose. What a relief to be peeing. My mom was still holding my leg, and I could see her making a funny face. Before I could ask what was wrong, she screamed, "You're peeing on my foot! You're not completely over the toilet!"

Boom, the woman dropped my leg. I screamed, she screamed, the nurses came running. Realizing she dropped my leg, my mom quickly picked it back up. But it didn't matter. The pain shocked me. I stiffened up, stopped peeing, and wouldn't speak to her.

The nurses helped me get settled into another room and checked my stitches to make sure everything was alright. I refused to talk to my mom, who was washing her shoe in the sink.

I begrudgingly asked the nurse for the bedpan.

"You serious?" she responded with a chuckle. "You still have to pee? You left quite the mess out there."

I didn't speak to her for the rest of the night either.

That time in the hospital was many years ago now, but I often think of that woman next to me. I remember her name too. For privacy's sake, I'm not sharing it. But I remember it well. Despite all the frenetic people in her room trying to bring her back, I hope she found peace.

As for my mother, she likes to remind me how much she loved those shoes. She kept wearing them after the incident, even though one of them — we know which one — started to squeak with every step.

By the time I was nineteen years old, I had already destroyed my body. Sprains, torn ligaments, fractures, reconstructive knee surgery, and a few knocks to the head as well. I continued to play sports for fun and I definitely watched sports all the time.

I love the smell of freshly cut grass and dirt. It just screams *soccer* to me. The squeaky sounds of gymnasiums as all different types of sneakers move back and forth on the polished courts is like music to my ears. And I love the smell of hockey rinks. They smell like black marker to me. My grandfather used to drive the Zamboni at a local hockey rink, and my grandmother and I would go and watch him. Fans were there for the hockey game, but I was there for the intermissions. Heck, even bowling alleys make me feel nostalgic. My grandparents and parents belonged to a bowling league, and I have vivid memories of being a kid sitting on top of the restaurant bar, watching my family bowl while the lady bartender kept an eye me. I would be eating a bag of salt 'n' vinegar chips and drinking a Coke. Cigarette smoke wafted through the air (it was the '80s) and mingled with the slight smell of menthol that came from the disinfectant they used on the rental shoes. Pins would get knocked over, and the reaction from the bowler afterwards told you if they bowled a strike or a spare, or if their ball took a ride down the gutter.

By the time I got to university, I had to make a decision about whether or not to keep playing sports. I wasn't the best athlete and my body was hurting; it couldn't keep up with my desire to play. It was time for a new chapter in my life. It was time to focus on my studies and my passion for broadcasting.

Little did I know, once I entered university, my two passions would eventually come together.

## CHAPTER 5

# THE ADJUDICATOR AWARD

Anyone who knows me knows I'm highly competitive.

I'll race you to the door. I'll test my aim against yours. Any game we play and any sport we play, I will always try to beat you. I don't care if you're my age or a kid — I will crush you.

But the first time I showed a real competitive edge wasn't through any sport. It was through music.

I started taking piano lessons when I was seven years old. I played right through my teenage years and even taught lessons for a while. That's when I discovered I would make a horrible teacher — seriously, my patience was severely tested.

I was always performing in concerts and I entered a lot of competitions. Second place meant nothing to me — I wanted first. And most times I got it. I'm not trying to flex; I'm just saying I have the medals to prove it!

I was pleased with my first places until one year, while getting ready for a competition I hadn't been in before, I heard about another award being handed out — the Adjudicator Award.

"What the heck is that?" I asked my instructor.

Peter was his name. A Russian man who played the piano exquisitely.

"Oh, that is a very special award. It's above first place," he responded.

*How can something be above first place? First is the best!* I was convinced.

"The Adjudicator Award is the award given by the judges. It means you are above all the rest. There is first, second, third, and then . . . there is the best."

I now had a new goal — win that judges' award. There was a woman from another music academy who taught a student who had won the Adjudicator Award the last few years. Peter wasn't so sure we could dethrone them. O ye of little faith. Peter clearly had zero clue how crazy I could become when I put my mind to something. I was getting that damn award.

I practised day and night for months. There were two pieces of music I had to perform, and I had to do so by memory. No sheets of music were permitted. The first had to be a classical song that was selected by the judges. We all had to perform the same one. The second was of my own choosing. I went with "You Needed Me" by the great Canadian artist Anne Murray.

The day of the competition arrived. Peter and I were standing in the hallway outside the room where the musical showdown was to happen, waiting to be introduced. The woman from the other school had multiple students competing that day, and she walked out of another room and was making her way down the hall towards us. She had a smirk on her face, and I heard her say to Peter, "Adjudicator, Adjudicator. I just got another Adjudicator."

Big mistake, lady. Big mistake. I was already motivated, but that put me over the top. There were about ten of us competing, but my eyes fell on the boy who was her student. Poor kid. He had no clue I was crushing him in my mind.

Competitions were held in front of a panel of judges and an audience of friends and family. The audience, not the judges, always made me nervous. But that day, I was so dialled in I didn't notice another living being except for the judges and that boy.

After we all performed, it was time to hand out the awards. Third place was announced, and then second place. Then it was time for the moment of truth. When first place was called, it was . . . the boy! The look of complete shock on his face was priceless. I saw him look over to his instructor, and she was equally stunned. I mean, the guy was a great pianist and all, but your gal is pretty damn good too!

I admit, I did have a teeny tiny moment where I thought, *Oh crap, what if my name isn't called at all?*

Naaaahhhhhhh, I won the Adjudicator Award!

It was an incredible feeling. I had a little more pep in my step as I walked out of that room and soaked up all the congratulations. But I was happiest when I saw Peter. I was thirteen years old, and at that stage of my life, I made everything about me; however, the win meant more to me because of him. He taught me how to play, he had prepared me for competitions and exams and concerts, and he believed in me.

At that moment, I learned that when you achieve something, the people who helped you achieve it are the ones who make the moment all the more sweet. I still feel that way today. After every big show — world championships and Olympics — I am so grateful to my crew behind the scenes who run a smooth operation so I can focus on my job on air.

But feeling warm and gushy isn't my only motivation when it comes to winning. Bragging rights are on the line as well, and I was so happy that Peter could now sing "Adjudicator, Adjudicator" in that woman's face!

## *CHAPTER 6*

# OK, I HAVE FAVOURITES

I often get asked, "What's your favourite sport?"

Quite a few people in this industry cover one sport for their entire career; others, like me, get to explore different worlds.

I've been very lucky and blessed to cover both professional and high performance sports. Ok, every sport and athlete I cover is considered *professional*, but I use that word to describe leagues. I use *high performance* to describe sports that are most known as Olympic sports.

My favourite sports are hockey and soccer; I pinch myself every day knowing I've been given the opportunity to host some of the biggest events for both of them.

But there is another sport that brings out the kid in me, the little girl who gets wide-eyed with amazement and turns into an adoring fan. That sport is track and field. From the first moment I ran around a track, I fell in love with the rush that comes from racing.

I remember exactly where I was when Donovan Bailey won gold in the 100m at the 1996 Atlanta Games — babysitting my cousin's puppy, Punkin.

I was in the stadium at the Rio 2016 Olympics when Usain Bolt was crowned the 200m champion.

There's this incredible photo of Brianne Theisen-Eaton being the last heptathlete standing after the final event in Rio 2016, en route to claiming bronze, that I'll never forget.

Summer of 2022, Donovan was my analyst for CBC's coverage of the World Athletics Championships, and the two of us were in the studio jumping up and down like crazed children when the Canadian men's 4x100m relay team crossed the finish line first. The men finally won world gold after twenty-five years.

I also remember the heartbreak I felt when Perdita Felicien hit the hurdle and went down at the 2004 Games in Athens. My heart sank when the Canadian men's relay team finished third in London in 2012 but were disqualified for stepping out of their lane.

And there have been heroic and courageous performances that continue to inspire generations.

American Jesse Owens at the 1936 Berlin Games captured four gold medals, and he did it right in front of Adolf Hitler.

Americans Tommie Smith and John Carlos, gold and bronze medalists respectively in the 200m, raised their black-glove covered fists during the anthem at the 1968 Olympics. The silver medalist from Australia, Peter Norman, wore an Olympic Project for Human Rights badge.

And there are so many examples of athletes fighting to cross the finish line despite an injury or exhaustion, determined to finish what they had started.

I've been a fan of athletics ever since I can remember, so when I was assigned to go to Budapest, Hungary, to cover the 2023 World Athletics Championships, I felt butterflies in my stomach for the first time in a very long time.

I had interviewed Andre De Grasse, Damian Warner, and Pierce LePage before, but watching them compete live and be in their element was amazing.

My mix zone area was right next to Jamaica's, and when the Jamaican sprinters stopped to talk to their TV people, I was in awe. I couldn't stop staring at three-time Olympic champion and ten-time world champ Shelly-Ann Fraser-Pryce when I first saw her. Honestly, I don't think I blinked.

Then, Marcell Jacobs, the first Italian man to be crowned Olympic champion in the 100m, which happened at Tokyo 2020, was suddenly right in front of me.

Dutch long-distance runner Sifan Hassan is tiny but mighty.

And then there was Noah Lyles, who captured three gold medals at those world championships and spent well over an hour making sure he stopped to chat with every reporter in the mix zone. A move greatly appreciated by me, as I was one of the reporters who was pretty far down the line.

Those world championships were great for Canadians, as four world titles were captured. Camryn Rogers and Ethan Katzberg took the titles in hammer throw, Pierce LePage in decathlon, and Marco Arop in the 800m.

There are so many more athletes I could name, but I think you get the drift — I love athletics.

I learned that at every World Athletics Championships, they hold a media race. I don't run anymore. My knees don't allow it. They balloon and cause me too much pain if I were to run. It's actually kinda sad because I'd give anything to sprint full throttle again with no pain.

But despite all that, I still signed up for the race. There was no way in hell I wasn't going to run on a world championship-calibre track. When I first started running as a kid, I dreamed of making the Canadian Olympic Team. I did eventually make it to the Olympics; I just took a different route — ha!

The race was the 800m distance. Couldn't they have made it the 400m? Holy geez, 800m is hard. You don't know whether to sprint or pace yourself, to breathe or cry, to stay upright or pass out. I made it across the finish line feeling relief and joy. What an experience!

I paid the price for my race. My knees swelled up and ached for about two weeks afterwards. Meh, it was a small fee; living out a childhood dream was absolutely priceless.

## CHAPTER 7

# MY DOGS KEEP ME SANE

I love animals more than humans. This is a fact. I've always found solace being around animals, and they truly amaze me.

When I was a little girl, my neighbour had a three-legged cat. I loved that cat as if she were my own. She wasn't fixed and had a few litters. One time, she was sitting under some bushes with her babies, and I poked my head in to have a look. The cat knew me, she knew I was a friend, but she still went into mama mode and gave me a warning smack across the forehead. It left a little cut. But even at a young age, I knew not to blame the animal. I got too close. I should've known better. I've also been bitten by a dog. It got me on the inside of my bicep. Ouch.

I remember my first-ever nightmare. I was no more than six years old, and I bolted upright in bed, tears in my eyes, breathing heavy. In my dream, I saw a little kitten. It was looking down at its paw, and as I approached, it showed me its paw, which was injured. The kitten had big eyes that looked sad, and it was pleading for my help, but there was nothing I could do. The sadness and fear of helplessness jolted me out of my sleep.

Although I love animals, I also have a healthy, respectful fear of wildlife. I keep my distance from wild animals because I don't want them becoming comfortable with human interaction. It will only hurt them in the end. The only time I'll interfere with nature is when I see an animal in distress.

One morning, I was going for a walk with my dog Pepper. A lovely, peaceful morning. Until the peace was disrupted by a clinking sound. Like glass tapping against something. That's when I noticed Pepé Le Pew. This poor skunk had its head trapped inside a glass jar, and it was struggling. It was losing air, and it was losing its life. I couldn't bear to watch. I tied Pepper to a tree farther away so she wouldn't get sprayed. The skunk was already stinky from the stress. I then found a long branch on the ground and tried to gently knock the jar off its head. Naturally, the skunk was scared and took a few steps towards me but collapsed. I was using a gentle singsong voice: "Come on, little skunky. Work with me. I'm trying to help you. Trying to save your life. Stay calm. Please don't spray me."

A gentleman across the street doing yardwork saw me and piped up, "Excuse me, miss, but that's not a cat you're trying to play with."

I couldn't help but laugh. The man was very sincere with his concern. He thought I had vision issues, and he didn't want me getting sprayed.

"No, sir. I'm aware it's a skunk. But it's suffocating to death!" I said.

I could see the wheels spinning in his head. He clearly had a love for animals as well, but, you know, no one wants to get skunked!

Finally, he caved.

"Here, give me that branch you've got."

He held out his hand, and I gave it to him. He had a much longer reach than I, so we were able to keep a safer distance. He was also a little rougher, but he did manage to knock the glass jar off the skunk's head.

Yeah! Success!

No sooner did the jar come flying off the skunk's head, the ungrateful little stinker took off and ran. No thank you or anything.

But I still felt great for the rest of the day knowing I saved a life . . . and still smelled like roses!

When I was around four years old, my parents were thinking of having another child. They asked me if I wanted a little brother or sister, and without hesitation, I told them I wanted a puppy. They asked a few more times and even got family members to pose the question, but my answer never changed: *I want a puppy.*

My parents began to worry that they would upset me if they had another kid and perhaps disrupt the family dynamics. I guess I was already giving off crazy vibes as a toddler! Ha! Or, as I prefer to describe things, I was already highly independent and self-sufficient and saw no need for sibling support.

Ok, maybe I was a little crazy and demanding.

I wouldn't let the puppy thing go with my parents. No brother arrived, no sister arrived, but neither did a cute little puppy. Finally, when I was sixteen, my parents gave in. For my birthday, they agreed to get me a dog. That's when my best friend entered my life — Lola.

When I first met her, she crawled into my lap and didn't leave. We took her home the very same day we met her. Lola was insane, but I loved her with all my heart. She got anxiety during rainy days, went crazy during thunderstorms and fireworks, ate my bath beads and candles, chewed gum and then spit it back out onto the carpet, ate my homework, and even peed on it.

But Lola was also a hero. One summer, my parents and I went on vacation, and my aunt watched her. Unfortunately, while watching Lola, my aunt had an emergency appendectomy. Lola stayed in bed with her and kept her company while she recovered. But one day, Lola went nuts. As a dog owner, you know what I mean when I say dogs have different barks for certain things. Another dog walking by, people walking by, a leaf blowing past the window; these are all non-threatening things that get a warning bark from the dog. Mail being delivered? That's more of a high alert bark. Still non-threatening, but now you know you have a package at the door. Someone is on your property, and they're not leaving? That's a code red bark. And that's the bark Lola was giving. My aunt was in a lot of pain in the bedroom upstairs, but she knew Lola's relentless barking meant something serious. She managed to get out of bed, go down the stairs, and just as she turned the corner to face the back sliding door, there was a man there, trying to break in. They had a slew of break-ins in the neighbourhood, and there was no doubt in my aunt's mind that this was the guy. The second he saw that someone was home, he ran. Who knows what would have happened if he got into the house, not knowing my aunt was there, and then seeing she wasn't in a good state. But seeing her through the window, he had no clue she was recovering from surgery, so he bolted. Lola saved the day. And then she proceeded to chew gum and spit it back into my aunt's purse . . . her Prada purse. It was reassuring to see that heroism didn't get to Lola's head, and she was still the same dog.

When I moved out of my parents' house and into a condo, Lola came with me.

I would sometimes take her to Leafs TV with me when I had a long day, and she would lie at my feet when I would go live to air with a show. One time, I made the mistake of leaving her outside the studio, and she didn't like that very much. For one segment during my *Leafs Today* show, if you listened closely, you could hear barking and scratching at the studio door.

In 2014, after eighteen years together, I knew I had to say goodbye to my ride or die. It destroyed me. Lola was my sweet sixteen birthday present and was with me throughout my pivotal years: high school, university, heartbreaks, celebrations, and my wedding day.

I was so emotionally drained during this time. I was preparing to host the 2014 FIFA World Cup, I was stressing over being out of work after the tournament was done, and now I was having to come to terms with life without her. I desperately wanted her to go peacefully on her own, but I couldn't watch her suffer anymore and made the dreaded appointment to say goodbye. I had two weeks to spend with her. I took time off work and didn't leave her side. She lay by me as I prepped my soccer notes for the World Cup. However, I forgot I had booked an appointment to donate blood during this time. I didn't want to cancel because I'm O-negative and that's a highly coveted blood type. So, I mustered up my strength and peeled myself away from Lola. "It's just for a few hours," I whispered to her. "I'll be back before you know it."

When I arrived at the clinic, they took my temperature, a standard procedure. They said I had a fever.

"What?" I said. "I'm not sick."

"No body aches, congestion, sore throat?" they asked.

"Nope. But I have been very stressed. In a few days, I'll be putting my dog down."

"Oh," the lady said sympathetically. "Try to calm down, and let's take your temperature again in ten minutes."

I did some breathing and managed to relax. When they came back, my temperature was normal.

But then we hit another hurdle. My blood wasn't flowing. The nurse tried everything. She tried other veins, she tried massaging my arm, she switched arms, but nothing. The blood wasn't coming out. It was strange. It was like my body had gone into lockdown. We finally had to give up. I wasn't giving blood that day. The nurse felt bad for me. She said immense stress can cause the body to do the things mine was doing. She gave me her condolences.

And then, on June 1, 2014, at the age of eighteen years, three months, and two weeks, Lola went to sleep forever in my arms.

I walked around aimlessly for weeks. The FIFA World Cup managed to distract me, but only for a bit.

I couldn't fathom getting another dog. Lola couldn't be replaced. I convinced myself that I wouldn't get another one. In fact, I was going to do things I was never able to do before. I was going to meet up with friends for drinks after work. I didn't have to rush home anymore to let Lola out so her little bladder wouldn't explode. I would book vacations last minute and not worry about having to find a dog sitter. My husband and I were going to live a life of freedom.

It sucked.

It lasted one year.

First, we got Pepper. She's half poodle, half King Charles Cavalier Spaniel. The most perfect dog. An angel. However, she's not a hero like Lola was. We once had a mouse in the house, and one night, it was rubbing itself all over our shag carpet. I managed to trap it in a box and release it outside. I returned to the bedroom where Pepper hadn't moved from the bed during the chaos and looked at her as if to say, *What the heck, man?* Her look back said, *I'm a dog, not a cat.* And she proceeded to curl up and go to sleep.

Pepper is so chill and wonderful that we decided to get another dog. Enter Ginger, the crazy one! She too is half poodle, but the other half is border collie, and her energy levels are through the roof. Not to mention, her athleticism is insane. I caught myself one afternoon googling all the competitions I could put her in and quickly realized I had the ability to become one of those crazy sports parents.

I can't imagine my life without them. We got Ginger in 2022, so it was just me and Pepper during the pandemic, literally. My husband was still with Toronto FC, and Canadian sports teams had to relocate to the

United States for months at a time because of travel restrictions. If it wasn't for Pepper, I would've felt totally alone. Instead, she made me laugh, she got me out on walks, and occasionally ate something that made her poo look weird and had me busy running to the vet.

My dogs keep me sane. And I don't pick sides by the way; I would own a cat if I weren't deathly allergic. My allergy started after our family cat, Toby, passed away. He was the absolute best. He let me put my baby bonnet on his head and burp him over my shoulder as if he were my baby. He was an outdoor cat and would leave me his version of presents: dead mice and sometimes dead birds. Yuck. He protected me fiercely and cuddled with me greatly. I was around seven years old when he passed, and that's when my cat allergy kicked in.

So no, I'm not just a dog person. I love cats too. Heck, I'd own a sanctuary farm for all kinds of animals if I could!

Be kind to animals. Love your pets like family, because they are.

Let wildlife be. Respect their space. Screw your stupid selfies that put them and you in harm's way.

As Mahatma Gandhi once said, "The greatness of a nation can be judged by the way its animals are treated."

## *CHAPTER 8*

# BECAUSE I'M A GIRL?

It bears repeating that when I was little, my parents never told me I couldn't do something because I was a girl. Because it's true, and because it perhaps explains why I react the way I do when I'm so obviously being singled out just for being a woman.

Sometimes, I'm oblivious to the reason behind the treatment because it just doesn't occur to me that my gender is the issue.

And it's not just because my parents used their words to break down gender stereotypes. It was their actions that spoke the loudest. My mom has always worked. She went back to work with the City of Toronto as an assistant to the councillors six months after I was born and retired when I was thirty-nine years old. I've only ever known my mother to have a career.

My father also hustled Monday through Friday and often worked Saturdays. And after all that work, they shared the household responsibilities. My dad was the one who would take me to my piano lessons, and my mom was the one who dropped me off at my dance lessons. If my dad happened to get home from work before my mom, he would cook dinner. If my dad was cooking, I knew that meant we were either eating pasta with beans (pasta e fagioli), pasta with peas (pasta e piselli), or BBQ.

When I was in elementary school, my mom made my lunch. When I was in high school, my dad started making it.

Side note: I was totally spoiled. I know.

We all cleaned the house together. We all did yardwork together.

My father never once told my mother he wouldn't do something around the house or take care of me if I was sick because that was the "woman's job." He did everything right alongside my mom. And my mother was always proud to have a purpose with her work. She worked in politics for many years.

So you see, I wasn't just told I could do things, I was shown that boys and girls are capable of doing the exact same things. Gender roles were extremely blurred in my household.

But sadly, outside of the home, I encountered many restrictions and criticisms because of gender bias.

Here are some stories.

I started volunteering at Rogers Cable York Region when I was nineteen and did so on and off until I was twenty-two. At that point, my volunteering became pretty consistent. I was in every week, sometimes multiple days a week. I was cutting my teeth doing just about everything: I was the restaurant reporter for a magazine show called *York Region Living*, where I got paid in food; I did stories for news, where I covered everything from market fairs to murders.

Being a restaurant reporter was a pretty fun gig. We filmed once a week and visited three restaurants on that day. The chefs made magnificent meals and always featured their most expensive dishes. The crew and I would eat at the first restaurant. The chefs never wanted the food to go to waste, and we were always happy to oblige with the clean-up. This meant we were stuffed by the time we visited restaurants two and three. Because the producer and cameraperson were getting paid and I was the intern, they would always let me take the leftovers home. But pretty soon, my "payment" was getting gobbled up by my dad. It didn't take him long to figure out which day of the week I worked on the show, and he knew that meant he was getting rack of lamb for dinner.

Occasionally, I went out on a sports story. My heart belonged to sports. I didn't accept my feelings at first. In the beginning, I studied broadcast journalism because I thought I was going to be an investigative journalist, a war correspondent giving a voice to the voiceless. Perhaps that desire came from my early days of watching *60 Minutes* alongside my parents. I was just a little girl and never fully grasped the moral of the stories being covered, but my goodness, that ticking clock absolutely fascinated me!

My college radio teacher encouraged me to pursue a career in sports. His name was Jeff Howatt, and he was also the program director at CHUM Radio. He had given us a weekly assignment: a two-minute radio hit that encompassed news, sports, traffic, and weather. We had to hand in a cassette at the end of every week, and he would sit and listen to it alongside you. One day, while going through my tape, he stopped it right after my sports update.

"Andi, I've listened to a handful of these radio hits by you, and one thing keeps standing out to me," he said.

"They're absolutely amazing and deserve an A-plus?" I said as I flashed a cheeky smile.

Howatt appreciated the effort and humoured me with an "of course!" But that wasn't the reason.

"What keeps jumping out to me is how your energy changes every time you start giving your sports update. You're livelier. You sound like you're having fun. Have you thought of focusing on sports journalism?"

I stared at him wide-eyed. What he said clicked; it was something I should have known all along. It was so obvious.

"I love sports. I've played them my whole life. But it never occurred to me to make a living out of covering sports," was all I could muster.

"So give it a go. See how you like it," he said.

That turned out to be life-changing advice.

I went to the volunteer coordinator at Rogers and told him I wanted to spend more time in the sports department. He found some opportunities for me, and I was having a blast. It was like I should've been doing this all along.

Then one day, something happened that made up my mind for good.

I was on my way to cover a lacrosse game. I was with a camera guy who was a diehard news junkie. He loved the thrill he got from covering breaking news. He listened to the police radio in the company minivan the same way I listened to the Backstreet Boys' *Millennium* album during my 1999 European vacation: constantly and intensely.

So, there we were, driving down the highway on our way to the game, and in the opposite lanes, we saw a car crash that had just happened. The car was on the shoulder of the highway, fire bursting from its engine, and people crawling out. The camera guy slammed on the brakes and pulled over alongside the guardrail separating the northbound and southbound lanes.

"We have to do something!" he said.

"Damn right we do! Those people need help." I cautiously opened my passenger door, making sure I didn't get smoked by a passing vehicle. Creating more work for the paramedics by having to peel my body off the asphalt wouldn't exactly be helping matters.

My camera guy went straight to the trunk of the van; I started to make my way over the guardrail.

He grabbed me by the collar and shouted, "What are you doing?"

"I'm going to help," I replied, giving him a look that said, *Isn't it obvious?*

"You can't," he said calmly. "You'll get in the way of my shot."

*Pardon?* That's when I realized what he had meant about having to do something. It was about getting the perfect shot for the news. Exclusive footage that other networks wouldn't have.

That's not my way of thinking, man. Not my world at all.

How do you not help people who clearly need it?

That's why I could never work for National Geographic; I'd love to, I love nature, and people closest to me would tell you I prefer the company of animals over humans. But I once heard a National Geographic journalist say their job is to document nature, not interfere with it.

*Are you crazy?* If I saw a baby elephant get turned around and separated from its herd . . . I'm going to try and help! No questions asked. No hesitation. I wouldn't last a day with National Geographic. And clearly, I wouldn't last in news reporting either.

That day changed everything for me. Shortly after, it just so happened that the sports host and producer at Rogers Cable announced he was leaving for Global Sports. Rob Leth was good to me. He was always willing to help me out, answer any questions I had. He even taught me a few linear editing tricks to make a one-camera shot at a sporting event look like it had been taken with five cameras. Take a baseball game as an example: Film the pitcher for a bit, then the batter, then the outfield. Get back to the shop and edit it together: pitch, hit, catch. Is it cheating? Maybe kinda sorta. But it's not like we were covering the Jays. We covered local teams as a bare-bones sports department and tried to make things look as polished as possible. Even using the word *department* makes me chuckle; it was a one-person band.

So, horrible car crash, Rob Leth leaving, me finally completing my post-secondary education — I'd spent four years at York University, where I majored in English and Mass Communications, and two years at Seneca College specializing in Broadcast Journalism — led to this moment of perfect timing. Rob encouraged me to apply for the sports host position. I approached the station manager, Lisa McClean-Stellick, and told her I really wanted the job and that I was a perfect fit. Lisa agreed; she too was a huge fan. She said she was meeting with the bigger bosses soon to discuss the next steps for sports. Besides being qualified, I had all the confidence in the world that I'd get the job by the mere fact that I was literally the only person other than Rob who covered sports for the station.

A few weeks went by, and I knew Lisa had her meeting, so I tracked her down.

"How did it go?" I asked.

She didn't look happy.

"I honestly don't know how to say this to you. I put your name forth, they like you, they know your work, but they're hesitating on giving you the job." She paused. I raised my eyebrows and gave her a look that said, *Go on.*

"They're hesitating because they're not quite sure how it would look having two women at the desk." She looked completely embarrassed for saying something that wasn't even her sentiment.

Silence. Incomprehension. Was she speaking another language?

I truly could not wrap my head around what she had just said. What in the world did gender have to do with it? Who cares if the news anchor is a woman and the sports anchor is a woman? After all, weren't there countless broadcasts that had all-male hosts? News, sports, weather, traffic, etc.

For the first time in my life, I was being told I couldn't do something because I was a girl.

I can only imagine how I looked to Lisa. Standing there frozen, brow furrowed, mouth slightly open, the hamster in my head working overtime to try to understand what I was being told. Before I could say anything that I would probably regret, Lisa came to life.

"Don't worry, this isn't over. I'm meeting with them again, and I'll let them know you're the best choice. This fight isn't over for me either." Phew, I had an ally.

And a very good one. She convinced the higher-ups that their concerns were ridiculous. I got the job. But it's still crazy to think I almost didn't because of a belief there's only room for one woman at the table.

## CHAPTER 9

# WAIT, THIS IS FOR THE LEAFS?

For two years, I was the sports host and producer with Rogers Cable York Region. Those two years were incredibly valuable. I learned how to host, report, write, do voice-overs, read highlights, and do my own shooting and editing. All that knowledge gave me a better understanding of not just my responsibilities but of the role others played in putting together a solid broadcast. I know what a cameraperson needs because I was a videographer. I know what editors need because I did my own editing. And I eventually learned what producers needed of me because, as my own producer, I realized how frustrating on-air talent can be!

But I was getting restless. It was time to move on. I had big aspirations.

The summer of 2006 was my ultimatum summer: If I didn't move on from Rogers Cable by August, I was going to give up on the industry.

My aunt, who owned a design firm, offered me a PR position with her company.

It was tempting, and I was young and impatient. And even though I was having a great time in my current position, knowing full well that I was one of a few from my graduating class who were working full time in the industry, I also knew that a broadcaster could get a reputation if they remained at a local station for too long.

But man, I was having fun.

During the winter, I hosted our live Junior A Hockey game of the week. Our location rotated between the Thornhill Thunderbirds, Aurora Tigers, and Newmarket Hurricanes.

While covering the Thunderbirds, I met former Toronto Maple Leafs defenceman Dmitri Mironov; his son Egor was on the team. I remember going up to Dmitri to introduce myself. He was kind and handed me what I thought was a business card; turns out it was his hockey card. He was giving them to everyone. Handing them out, just like that.

One night in 2004, I interviewed Jeff O'Neill. Everyone on the broadcast crew was freaking out. At the time, he was playing in the NHL for the Carolina Hurricanes. He was having his number retired by the Thunderbirds. A real NHLer was coming on our local Junior A Hockey broadcast.

I can't remember if I asked anything that made sense; I was so nervous, but Jeff was great. In just two years, I would be a proper NHL reporter, interviewing him as a member of the Toronto Maple Leafs. And a few years after that, we'd become co-workers and friends in the broadcast industry. Small world, as they say.

Jerome Dupont, 15th overall pick in the 1980 Draft by the Chicago Blackhawks, was the head coach of the Tigers. I remember him taking so much grief from the fans, and I never understood why. I've come to observe over the years that there is a fanbase who, as much as they idolize players who make it to the big show, harbour a lot of resentment towards that player. Envy? Most definitely. Especially if that fan was also a player but wasn't good enough to make it. Disappointment? I believe that too. A fan supports a player and then that player doesn't last in the pros — can't cut it — and the fan feels betrayed.

I'm no psychologist, so I'll stop playing one. But whatever the reason, there's this twisted glee certain fans feel when they remind someone they've fallen from grace.

So, whenever a chance presented itself to ridicule and berate a former NHLer, this type of fanbase would jump all over it.

After the first year of bouncing around between all three rinks, we struck a deal with the Newmarket Hurricanes to do a game of the week only with them.

The Ray Twinney Arena was an old and cold barn. So darn cold. Our makeshift studio was inside an unused dressing room. I would turn on all the showers and crank them too hot. The steam would warm our bones. But I never quite got the timing right of when to turn them off before the intermissions. My interviews with the players resembled a scene from *That '70s Show*; there was always this heavy haze around us. It looked like we were either up to no good or in a Stephen King novel, and the dead were about to rise behind us. However it looked, we clearly put on a good show because the arena was packed. Being on local TV raised the profile of the Hurricanes, and all the kids wanted to be where the action was. Many years later, I spoke with Connor McDavid's mom, Kelly, and she said Connor watched those broadcasts, and because of that, he wanted to be at every Newmarket Hurricanes home game. I tell myself I played a small role, perhaps tiny, teeny tiny, in igniting McDavid's passion for the sport. Hey, we all can dream.

Funny how exposure works. I was told the Tigers and Thunderbirds didn't want their games on TV anymore because they felt more people would stay at home and watch instead of buying tickets to the game. Hadn't they heard of Rocky Wirtz and the Chicago Blackhawks?

The former owner of the original six franchise decided not to televise home games because he thought it was unfair to season ticket holders. The TV blackout lasted for twelve seasons, and during that time, attendance suffered. As they say: Out of sight, out of mind.

By 2006, I wanted so badly to move on. I knew I was ready. I had enough material to create a demo tape on good old-fashioned VHS tapes. On the label, I even put this cute image of a woman holding a microphone. As cheesy as this was, I prefer to think I was using "emojis" before they were a thing!

I sent clunky tapes everywhere.

I interviewed at the Score. They were hiring a voice-over person to do the highlights. They said I was overqualified for the job. I was flattered but also disheartened. It would've been cool to work at that network. After all, on my desk at Rogers was a little TV that I tuned in to the Score every afternoon, watching Caroline Frolic.

I interviewed at Sportsnet. I was supposed to do reads at the desk by myself, but to my surprise, and even that of Sportsnet Hockey's senior producer at the time, Jeff MacDonald, Darren Dreger joined me on set. He treated it like a real broadcast. I was so nervous. Dregs doesn't present as a warm and cuddly dude. Years later, we would become co-workers at TSN, and I would come to know him as a funny and great guy, but that wasn't the case in 2006. He scared the shit out of me.

I didn't get the job. I was underqualified.

Jeff likes to blame Dregs and says he's the one who said I wasn't ready. Jokes aside, whoever said it, they were right. The diamond still needed polishing.

But I was getting antsy. Too good for one job and not good enough for another. I was feeling stuck.

It was the middle of August, and I was covering a charity golf tournament with a lot of Toronto Maple Leafs players in it. A camera guy from Rogers Cable, Armando Cavalheiro, had recently made the move to Leafs TV and was covering the event. Half joking and half most definitely not, I told him to keep me posted on any job openings. He promised he would.

A few weeks later, he kept his promise.

I was working out at the gym. This was before we had our cellphones attached to our hips. The only thing in my hand was my iPod.

As I was sweating away, I suddenly heard my name being called over the gym speaker system. "Andria Petrillo, please come to the trainer's office. Andria Petrillo. Trainer's office." I turned down my Eurobeats, and I could see into the offices. I motioned "me?" and the employee nodded. I walked over, and she said, "You have a phone call. It's your mother."

Holy shit. Ok. It's amazing the number of thoughts that go through your head in two seconds, and they aren't good.

It was instant relief when I heard her voice, and she wasn't crying. But she was a little excited. "Andi, Armando called and left a message. It sounds like they're hiring at his new place. Something about auditions. But he said you have to act fast!"

"Uh, ok," was all I could say. It was 8 p.m. I didn't know what I was supposed to do at that moment with the news she had just given me. I was just happy there wasn't an emergency at home and slightly embarrassed that my mommy had me paged at the local gym. But I know why she couldn't wait the extra thirty minutes for me to get home: She knew how badly I wanted to elevate my career. She knew this phone call from Armando could potentially change everything. I decided to call Armando back the following morning. The prospect of an audition somewhere had me buzzing with excitement. You've never seen anyone crush a StairMaster the way I did after that phone call!

When I got home, I got my clunky VHS tape with accompanying resume ready. There was no time to mail it; I had to hand-deliver it the next day. We lived in Maple, Ontario, a suburb about a forty-five-minute drive from the Leafs TV studios in the east end of Toronto. But with traffic, it took me over an hour to get there — there is always traffic in Toronto.

I was told to ask for Dean Bender. He wasn't there. Crap. A guy by the name of Chris Clarke took my tape and promised to get it to Dean. One hour and twenty minutes for a one-minute drop off. I turned around and drove home. Another hour on the road.

The next day, I followed up with Dean. I got him on the phone, and my heart sank when he said he never received my demo. I was going to kill that Clarke guy.

Dean said he'd look for it and call me back.

About an hour later, he called back and said, "Good news, I found your tape. Bad news, we already filled the position."

I was at a loss for words.

"I'm just kidding!" he said gleefully into the phone. He got a kick out of my mute reaction.

"Clarke still had it, but I got it and watched it. I would love for you to come in for an audition."

Aaaaaahhhhhhh! That's how I felt inside. But I very calmly said, "Wonderful! Tell me when."

I would come to learn that Dean was a bit of a jokester. He had a really good sense of humour. And he also gave me some great advice, but at the time, I didn't quite grasp the importance of his message. He told me, "I've seen a lot of good women leave this industry because of what people say about them. People will make assumptions, they will gossip, and sometimes they will outright lie about how you're conducting yourself. Don't ever let those people win."

When it came to the audition, there was a bit of misinformation on Armando's part. He believed they were hiring a new Toronto Marlies reporter. The Leafs' AHL affiliate team. So, I spent all night brushing up on my Marlies knowledge.

My audition was with John Bartlett. Made sense; he was the Marlies' play-by-play voice. But all he did was ask me about the Leafs. Huh? Ok, that's fine. I follow the Leafs, I love the Leafs, I know everything about the Leafs.

Once the audition was done, I interviewed with Dean and another gentleman, Frank Hayward. They kept talking about the Leafs too. They said they had to speak to John Ferguson Jr., then the general manager of the Leafs, about a woman travelling with the team. Finally, after about an hour, I had to ask what the heck I was actually auditioning for. But of course, I played it cool.

"Gentlemen, just to confirm (because I had no friggin' clue) this is for the Leafs reporter job, correct?" I was trying to sound confident and nonchalant, not like a complete amateur who thought she was there for the Marlies gig. I was now having an internal meltdown because it was becoming more and more evident that I was on the brink of landing an NHL job.

They confirmed the job was for the big show. My nostrils were flaring uncontrollably.

They asked if I had any questions for them. I sheepishly squeaked, "What does the position pay?"

It was double what I was currently making. Oh Lord, catch me when I fall.

I kept a calm exterior and stiffly slow-walked to my car. Once inside, I released all my energy. I called my mom and blew her eardrums out when I screamed, "It's for the Leafs! The job is for the N-H-L!"

I think it worked to my benefit not knowing the actual position they were hiring for because maybe my nerves would've gotten in the way. Maybe I would've toe-punted the audition.

I clearly impressed them, because I was barely home a few hours after the audition when Dean called and offered me a two-year contract. That poor telephone receiver was covered in saliva with how quickly I spit out "YES."

My parents, while happy for me, were hesitant. Coming from nothing, it meant everything to them for me to have the opposite life. And that meant finding a secure job with a good salary, benefits, vacation and sick days pay, and a nice pension. They wanted stability for me, and freelance work is anything but. The two years I was at Rogers Cable York Region were the only two years of my life that I was a salaried worker; I've been a freelancer since 2006. Working and performing for my next contract, just like an athlete.

My mom weighed the pros and cons with me, and we both knew the risks were worth the reward.

I felt both relief and satisfaction. In my heart, I knew I was meant to be on this path, but with the recent rejection and my ultimatum deadline looming, I was beginning to wonder, Was my gut instinct wrong?

To know that my vision of who I was meant to be was right all along felt vindicating. There was no way I was going to look back.

Covering the Leafs was a dream come true. My first big interview was with Tie Domi — he had just announced his retirement. It was too bad that I wouldn't get to see him play, but here he was, standing right next to me!

When I first walked into the Leafs dressing room, I took a few seconds to soak it all in. There was Darcy Tucker. Mats Sundin was bigger than I thought. And there were Tomas Kaberle and Bryan McCabe, the great defensive pair for the team. My eyes were taking in the room in disbelief.

It became apparent early on that I was going to have to earn the players' respect. After all, in the first year I travelled with the team, I was privy to player injuries that weren't made public. I would see them walking up and down the airplane aisle with ice packs.

Mats Sundin, a true captain, kept his eye on me. In the beginning, I would say hi — no response. I'd smile and wave — nothing. There was definitely no preferential treatment in the media scrums either. A *scrum* is when the reporters form a semicircle around the subject, along with their camera operators, and start blurting out questions.

During road trips, the players would get on the plane first, followed by the travelling media — there were only about nine of us. I never understood that system because we always sat at the back of the plane, and we would have to fight our way through the players who were still trying to get settled into their seats. On this one road trip, the aisle was clear, and it was an easy path for me to get to my seat. But not so fast. Mats decided to stand up at that moment and grab something from his bag in the overhead compartment. Or so I thought.

"Excuse me, Mats. Can I get through?"

No response. He just kept rummaging.

I realized pretty quickly that he was holding me up because he could. I wasn't offended. He was the captain, and this was his team, and he made sure everyone knew it.

When he was done doing nothing with his bag, he sat down and looked at me. I smiled at him, got no response, and made my way to my seat.

Shortly after that, a few months into the season, Mats accepted me. We were in New York for a game against the Rangers. I ran into him in the hotel lobby. I did my customary wave and . . . he smiled back!

"Andi, where are you going?" Was Mats talking to me? Holy shit.

"Just meeting the crew for dinner," I told him.

"Ok, have a great dinner." And with that, he walked away.

I took that exchange as a major win.

I think Mats was one of the best captains. Many nights, I stood outside the dressing room door preparing for my intermission interview, and I would hear him talking to the team. He was very vocal and very motivational. Some of his pep talks had *me* wanting to run through a wall!

After I had earned Sundin's trust, he was way more chill around me and actually cracked some jokes. (He's pretty funny.) And when he came to town as a member of the Vancouver Canucks, I was one of the media members he gave a hug.

As for the rest of the team, I knew I had become accepted by them when my hotel key went missing.

The players loved to annoy one another by stealing their room keys.

Many road hotels had a table set up in the lobby upon our arrival with our room keys on it. To spare themselves from having to check in over twenty people at once and to prevent the players from having to wait to get in their rooms, the hotels would have us already checked in. All we had to do was walk up to the table, find the envelope with our name on it, grab it, and go. But some guys would run in ahead of everyone else and take keys and throw them away, forcing their teammates to stand in line at the concierge to check in. A small thing, an annoying thing, and something that always got a chuckle. Every hotel we arrived at, we always waited to see which guys had their keys stolen.

One road trip, my key was gone. All I wanted to do was go straight to my room and take a nice shower before dinner, but now I had to go stand in line and do the check-in process while everyone else went to their room. Sure, I was a little miffed. But I stood in line with a smile on my face the whole time.

As the season went on, the players and travelling media developed a great rapport. After all, you're seeing each other more than you're seeing your family during the season. We were so comfortable that we had zero issues chirping each other. And boy, did we media do that after one game in Montreal. It was March 17, 2007, and the Leafs had a game in Montreal during the St. Patrick's Day celebrations. Jeff O'Neill arrived at the rink in an all-green suit. Head coach Paul Maurice told the players that if they pulled off the win, he would delay our flight home until the next day so we could partake in the city's festivities.

Defenceman Pavel Kubina tied the game up 2–2 in the third period. No goals in overtime, so it went to the shootout. The Leafs ended up losing, but we thought for sure Maurice would still postpone the flight, given how close the game was. Nope, we boarded that night and went home. Bonsie, Ralphy, Beyak, and I slowly made our way down the plane aisle shaking our heads at the guys. We could've had a night!

I loved my travelling crew of producer Mark Askin, Joe Bowen (Bonsie), Harry Neale, Dennis Beyak, Jim Ralph (Ralphy), and Paul Hendrick (Henny). Many nights on the road I would sit between Bonsie and Ralphy when they were doing radio and get my own live and in-person call of the game.

Ralphy was always ready to crack a joke.

Henny was always ready to drop a cheesy pun.

Beyak loved his desserts after dinner and would be the first person in the gym the next day.

Mark is one of the most prepared producers I've ever worked with and a walking encyclopedia of hockey knowledge. He will never leave you out to dry.

Bonsie never hesitated to give me advice when I needed it.

And then there was poor Harry Neale. I say *poor* because he had to deal with me frequently forgetting my hotel room number. Based on our last names, our rooms were often next to each other. When you're on the road for forty-one games, you tend to forget which room you're in. More nights than not, I would try my room key on his door and keep jiggling the handle, wondering why it wasn't working. And then I would hear his voice from the other side: "You got the wrong fucking room again, Petrillo!"

The Leafs came so close to making the playoffs that year. It would've been their first time back in the post-season since before the lockout.

It literally came down to the final game of the season, and the Leafs needed outside help. The hockey gods couldn't have scripted a better final game. It was between two great foes: the Leafs and the Habs. Both teams desperately needed a win to keep their playoff hopes alive. And the game did not disappoint. It was at the Air Canada Centre, and the place was packed with both sets of fans. It was an absolute barnburner; six goals were scored in the second period alone!

For the last five minutes of the game, I was outside the Leafs' dressing room getting ready for my postgame interview. I watched the rest of the game on the monitor just outside the room. The Leafs had a 6–5 lead, and as the clock ticked down, the place rumbled. And I mean rumbled. I was in an area of the arena below the seats, with the exception of the platinum section. The crowd roared, stomped their feet, and pounded the backs of the seats in front of them. The dressing room security and I looked up at the ceiling, thinking for sure it was going to come down on our heads. Thankfully, it didn't. What an incredible night. The Leafs did what they had to do to stay alive and, in the process, eliminated their biggest rival. Now they had to sit and wait for the result of one particular game that would decide their fate: the New Jersey Devils vs. the New York Islanders. The Leafs needed the Devils to beat the Islanders in regulation. But guess who the Devils decided not to dress that night? One of the best goalies ever: Martin Brodeur. The game went to a shootout, the Islanders got the one point they needed to pass the Leafs in the standings . . . and just like that, my first year working in the NHL was over. No playoffs. What a bummer. But what a thrilling ride as well. I couldn't wait for the offseason to end so I could do it all over again.

## CHAPTER 10

# ADVICE THAT FUELLED ME

When I was still working at Rogers Cable York Region and desperate to move on to a bigger network, I attended a gala with my aunt Anna at Casa Loma in Toronto. It was a charity event, so there were live auctions and silent auctions taking place.

As I was perusing the items up for bid in the silent auction, one caught my eye: lunch with CTV News anchor Lloyd Robertson.

I wasn't in any financial situation to place a bid. My aunt noticed I was lingering at this item, so she came over to take a peek. When she saw what I was looking at, she immediately signed her name.

"Zi'Anna, you don't have to do that!" (*Zia* means "aunt" in Italian.)

"I know I don't have to; I want to." She loves saying that.

"Ok, but if it gets out of hand, I don't want you spending a crazy amount of money."

"Don't worry, it won't get crazy, and no one will outbid me." She smiled devilishly.

We stood there waiting for the auction to close.

A couple came along and wrote down a bid for the lunch. Before they could even put the pen down, my aunt took it and outbid them. She then turned to them and said, "It doesn't matter what you bid; I will go higher. You're not getting this lunch. My niece is an aspiring journalist, and I'm getting this for her no matter what. You might as well just walk away now."

She wasn't nasty when she said it, but I wouldn't say my aunt was messing around either. The couple got the message loud and clear and graciously bowed out of the bidding.

The auction finally closed, and we won a lunch for two with Lloyd Robertson! Of course I brought my aunt with me.

The lunch was held at a fancy French restaurant called Auberge du Pommier.

It was very lovely, and Mr. Robertson was a gentleman.

When he asked what I wanted to do in the media industry, I told him I wanted to focus on sports. Here was his advice: "It's great to have a passion for something. Clearly, yours is sports. But just be aware of this — it's a very niche group in the industry. It's small, and it's hard to get your foot in the door. Don't just limit yourself to sports. News offers way more opportunities. Be more open-minded to other things."

I already know some of you are thinking this was horrible advice. Especially since you're hearing this story after I did make it as a sportscaster. Plus, why would someone discourage someone else from chasing their dreams? But that's not what he was doing, and even in that moment, I completely understood what he was saying. I appreciated his honesty. He was telling me the truth about an area in the broadcasting world that can be very cliquey and difficult to crack. I wasn't offended by what he said because he wasn't trying to discourage me. Discouraging and pointing out difficulties are two different things. Mr. Robertson never said, "You're not going to make it." He simply said, "Take into account the challenges you will face."

Plus, he wasn't wrong about news. In news, you can branch off into so many things: crime reporter, political reporter, entertainment reporter, features, documentaries, etc. And there was a part of me that took what he said as a challenge. I was going to prove that I could turn my passion into a reality.

I'm a believer that you need someone in your life who's going to push you and question whether or not you really want something. A devil's advocate. My mother is that person for me. Sometimes it drives me crazy when she asks, "Are you sure?" "Did you think about this?" "Did you consider that?"

If I still wanted something badly after I'd thought about all the things my mother made me ponder, then I knew my feelings were real and I would work for it with all my might.

On that day inside Auberge du Pommier, Lloyd Robertson was my devil's advocate. His advice fuelled me, and I am grateful for that.

## CHAPTER 11

# MICHAEL LANDSBERG SAVED ME

Michael Landsberg saved me from making a decision that could've haunted my career.

I first met Michael while I was working at Rogers Cable. I was twenty-five years old.

At the time, I was hosting the Junior A Hockey game of the week. A gentleman by the name of Kevin Huhn reached out to me and said he'd love to be a part of the coverage. He had written a book called *Hockey-ology: The Ultimate Guide to Fun and Success for Minor Hockey*. We met for coffee, and I liked him instantly. Kevin had a great knowledge of the game and was very personable. I decided to make him a staple during the first intermission of our Thursday nights.

We had a blast together. We bantered about the game, players, tactics, and any big stories surrounding the world of hockey. I mean, we weren't giving Coach's Corner a run for its money or anything, but I thought we made a great team.

At that time, Kevin had made a few appearances on TSN's *Off the Record* hosted by Michael Landsberg. It was a very popular thirty-minute round-table sports talk program that featured current pro athletes, as well as popular figures like musicians, actors, and wrestlers. When Kevin was asked again to be a guest, he took the opportunity to mention to the show producer that he was working with an up-and-coming sports host he thought would be a good guest for *OTR*. Michael was intrigued and gave the ok. To say I was nervous would be an understatement. I was beside myself with both excitement and fear. I loved *Off the Record* and watched it all the time. I told everyone and anyone who crossed my path that I was going to be on the show. This was a big deal — I mean, I booked an appointment at my hair salon for a blowout, and I usually only do that for family weddings!

Kevin and I arrived at the TSN studio together. The other two guests on the show that day were two former NHLers: Ric Nattress and Bob McGill. Bob, known as "Big Daddy," would later become my co-worker at Leafs TV.

I was so nervous, and Michael was so calm. He assured me that he wouldn't hang me out to dry, he wanted everyone to look good, and he would make sure my talk time was respected. In fact, the entire panel put my nerves at ease. *OTR* was a show known for Michael and guests going at each other, in a playful way, of course, but that's intimidating as all hell to a newbie who still lacked confidence.

Once the taping of the show started, I felt right at home. Ric, Big Daddy, and Kevin had all been on the show before and knew what to do. Michael was such a pro and made sure I didn't feel lost. I was floating on cloud nine after the show. Michael asked me to be a guest again. We chatted briefly after that first taping, and I told him how my dream was to join the big sports networks. He said to bring a demo tape the next time I was in, and he would critique it for me.

I hustled to get something put together. Demo tapes are always tricky because you have to ask an editor you trust not to tell anyone that you're looking for another job. And you sometimes have to ask other people for help finding footage to include in your demo, and they always get nosy and ask, "What for?" and you have to say something like your mom really wants to watch it again or some crap like that. Nowadays, it's so much easier to grab clips of your work off YouTube and send them over to an executive producer. Regardless, I put something together. Michael told me to include all my skills: hosting, reporting, interviewing, and reading highlights. I think it came out to just under seven minutes. In the world of TV, that might as well be a mini documentary!

When I brought it to Michael, he said the same thing: "You have to shorten this. No more than three minutes. Plus, a person watching this will know in thirty seconds if they want to keep watching. So, make sure your intro is engaging."

That wasn't the only advice he gave me that day. It was the second show I did on *OTR*, and a professional athlete was also on the panel. Afterwards, as I was sitting with Michael going over my demo, the athlete sent a friend over to ask for my number. Michael looked at me for my response.

"Thank you, but no," I said. As simple as that.

As soon as the friend left, Michael turned to me and said, "I would never tell you what to do. You're in charge of your own life. But I'm happy you gave that answer. You have your career to think about. And throughout your career, you're going to have a lot of athletes ask you out — and they're not exactly looking to marry you. Go with your gut."

It was great advice. And he was so matter-of-fact about it. No beating around the bush. He basically said I could do whatever I wanted to do but also made me understand that these were things I was going to have to navigate in this industry and to not be afraid to stand my ground.

A few years into my career with Leafs TV, when I was first learning how to deal with horrible people on social media, he also told me to learn to be "un-insultable."

"How the heck do I do that, Michael?" I asked.

"You'll learn," he said. "But you'll have to work at it."

As wonderful and as helpful as all his advice so far had been, it was another piece that saved me big-time.

At that time, I was in my twenties, fresh out of school, and broke. I was very lucky that my parents let me live with them rent-free and did the grocery shopping and all the other things most Italian kids take for granted, but I still needed to make my own money.

While working at Rogers Cable, I befriended a guy who ran a little production company. In the beginning, he would throw some voice-over work my way, a few hundred dollars here and there. I was squirrelling away all my pennies.

One day, he asked if I wanted to be in a commercial; he said the pay was two thousand dollars. That was huge for me! I had never received that kind of money in one lump sum before.

I agreed in principle and went to his studio to meet the man I'd be doing the commercial with. And it was . . . Dr. Ho! For those of you who aren't familiar with Dr. Michael Ho, he's a Doctor of Chiropractic and Acupuncture who has invented devices to help with pain relief. It's these very devices he sells through infomercials, and he was looking for new faces to help him sell his latest products.

Let me preface this by saying Dr. Ho was a lovely man. Full of energy and quite jovial. What you see in his infomercials is what you get. To sweeten the deal, I was told I would also get one of Dr. Ho's pain reliever products on top of the money. I was stoked. I called Michael after the meeting and told him about the gig I had just landed.

"Andi, this isn't a commercial, it's an *infomercial*. And there's a difference. The latter can live on for years. I have a feeling you're going to have a great career. Can you imagine if one day you're hosting the Stanley Cup Final and then this Dr. Ho infomercial airs? Do you want to be known as the 'Ho Girl'?"

I hadn't thought of it like that. Why would I? I knew nothing about this business and what could or couldn't come back to haunt me. I didn't understand how contracts worked and how long someone could own the rights to my image. But I pushed back a little.

"C'mon, Michael. It can't be that bad. And it's not like I'm shooting porn, it's selling a pain reliever product! And plus," I admitted sheepishly, "it's good money. I've never made that much before."

Michael wasn't moved. "You'll make much more in a successful career, trust me. But if you want to take the risk, it's yours to take. But I'm telling you, those infomercials have no expiration date. They can air for many, many years, and you won't get any royalties."

What a buzz kill. I already had plans for that money. But he was right. I didn't want anything to jeopardize my career. Even if it seemed harmless, I couldn't take the chance.

I called the guy who was producing the infomercial and told him I was out. He wasn't happy. He told me he wasn't going to give me any more work. But I stood my ground.

And you know what? To this day, I still see those Dr. Ho infomercials. Michael was right.

## CHAPTER 12

# JEAN SKIRT AND PURPLE NAIL POLISH

When I think back on the first press conference I attended, I can't help but shake my head and chuckle. That doesn't mean I'll let the camera guy assigned to me off the hook for staring down his nose at me: Don't judge a book by its cover. After all, another saying is true: I didn't know what I didn't know.

I was still volunteering at Rogers Cable, soaking up all the experience I could. I received a call from a producer asking if I could attend a "presser" at a local school. I said yes before asking what it was for. I had never been to a press conference before, and I wanted to know what it was like. I wanted to know when to shout out a question, and I wanted to know what it was like to be in a scrum.

I was told it was for Liberal politician Dalton McGuinty. It was around 2002 or 2003, when he was running for Premier of Ontario, and he was making the rounds. I was in my early twenties and had zero understanding of what attire was appropriate for what occasion.

When I arrived at the school, I walked into a room with people dressed professionally. I had wild bleach blonde hair, purple nail polish, rings on every finger, a jean skirt with frayed thread on the bottom (on purpose), knee-high black velvet boots, and a cute pink sweater with tassels. I thought I looked great. Everyone else thought I was one of the high school students who were studying after school. And that included my camera guy. We had never met before, and he did not hold back his disgust. He made it known to me that he was perfectly capable of doing on-air reporting as well and that I didn't need to be there. In fact, he told me he didn't know why I was there. Then he used the word *pontificate* when describing McGuinty's speech, assuming I wouldn't know what it meant. I could see he was pleased with himself. I looked at him and said, "How ironic."

That caught him off guard and made him even more miffed with me.

It was no skin off my back. I experienced a presser and a scrum and learned just how nervous they made me. They can be intimidating because you want to ask an intelligent question, or at least one that will garner a good answer.

I also learned that I needed to go shopping for some professional clothes. But I still wear purple nail polish!

To Mr. McGuinty's credit, he answered all my questions with the same zest as he did everyone else's.

## CHAPTER 13

# DOUBLE STANDARD

Let's play a little game.

You see a male reporter. He's in the dressing room, sitting next to a player having a private conversation. What do you think they're talking about?

Now you see a female reporter. She and a player are sitting together, just the two of them, talking. What do you think they're discussing?

If you thought the same thing for both the male and female reporter, good for you. You're an evolved human being.

Sadly, so many others, including fellow reporters, have double-standard thoughts.

Many still assume that if a male reporter and player are in a corner talking amongst themselves, it must be because the male reporter is getting a scoop. Some inside knowledge. Or the reporter and the player are friends, just shooting the breeze.

But a woman? Sheesh, she must be flirting. The player must be making a move on her. Maybe they're already sleeping together?

Ugh, infuriating.

Let me take you back to the 2011–12 NHL season. Nothing special about it from a Leafs performance perspective. But I'll never forget an exchange I had at practice one day.

Luke Schenn was on the team. Great guy. He was an absolute pleasure to deal with; all the media thought so. He was kind to everyone and always willing to give an interview. Most players can't take their gear off fast enough after practice to avoid the media. Luke was usually still on the ice after the room was opened to reporters, so he always walked into a full dressing room. And he was great about it. He made the time to talk about anything and everything with anyone who would chat with him. Bob McGill, Paul Hendrick, and I would more times than not make our way to his stall after our obligatory interviews and talk to Luke about the team, life, best restaurants in the city, you name it. Sometimes, I would talk to him on my own. Luke treated us like we were co-workers, not intruders. What a breath of fresh air.

March 16, 2012, was the day my husband proposed to me. We had gone to Montreal for the weekend. We took in a Leafs vs. Habs game and a Major League Soccer match. CF Montreal had just entered the league, and they were kicking off against my husband's former team, Chicago Fire. Hockey, soccer, and a diamond ring. I'd say it was a pretty sweet weekend!

The next Leafs home game was March 20, and I was running around doing a bunch of interviews. A scrum started in the Leafs dressing room, and I dashed inside, a little late. Luke was sitting in his stall and yelled out as I ran past, "Hey! What's that on your finger? That wasn't there last week!"

I gave a quick, embarrassed smile and nudged my way into the scrum. When it was done, I went straight to Luke to show him the ring. He offered up his congratulations and asked how my husband proposed. It was nice of him to notice; it was nice of him to care enough to ask about it. But he did that with everyone. He was the social butterfly in the room.

A few days later, I was standing at the boards watching a Leafs practice. A reporter who hadn't covered the Leafs beat in a while came over to say hello.

I knew her well, so there was no need for small chat; she got right to the chase. "Some of the guys are saying you and Luke are sleeping together." She nodded towards the media room overlooking the ice.

"What the fuck? Are you serious?" I said.

"They said you and Luke talk to each other a lot, so they're assuming you must be hooking up. I wanted to come straight to you and let you know what they're saying."

All I could do was laugh in disbelief. I felt so embarrassed. Not because of anything I had done. I felt embarrassed for those men who had such an ass-backwards way of thinking. I was embarrassed for Luke, who was just being a decent human being but fell victim to a double standard. McGill and Hendrick also talked with him a lot, on their own, but no rumours started about them. But me? Cue the gossipers. How pathetic. I also felt embarrassed because, every day I showed up to work, I would give these guys a cheerful hello only to find out what they really thought of me.

I remembered Dean Bender's words all those years ago: *I've seen a lot of good women leave this industry because of what people say about them. People will make assumptions, they will gossip, and sometimes they will outright lie about how you're conducting yourself. Don't ever let those people win.*

I stood there stewing and then finally said to her, "Tell my fellow journalists that I'm sleeping with half the team and I'm going after their wives next."

These words were followed by the most dramatic eye roll possible and an angry huff.

Unfortunately, they got to me. I started to become more aware of people staring at me when I was talking to a player alone. I would cut conversations short if I felt people were noticing me sitting alone with an athlete. I became very guarded. Thankfully, that period of paranoia didn't last long because I came to my senses. I wasn't going to let gossipers win. Plus, in order for me to do my job properly, I had to have private conversations with athletes; that's how I would get them to trust me and give me certain information I needed to do my job. After all, that's what the male journalists were doing.

Now that I'm older and I've been in this industry for a long time, no one seems to bat an eye when I'm having a private conversation with a male athlete. Or maybe they are, and I just don't give a shit? Whatever the case, I'm going about my business, loving life, not giving a care in the world about gossip.

So how about we play that game again? Have I succeeded in changing your thoughts when you see a male reporter versus a female reporter having a one-on-one chat with a player? I hope so. Because this is part of how we eliminate gender bias in the sports profession.

## CHAPTER 14

# ONE DAY IN HAITI

I didn't think I was going to make it to my thirtieth birthday.

The month before my special day, I went on two eye-opening journeys — two very dangerous journeys.

First up, Haiti. Maple Leaf Sports and Entertainment, under the leadership of COO Tom Anselmi, had procured a ton of supplies for Haitians whose lives were upended by the devastating earthquake that struck in January 2010.

Tom had been informed that if he wanted the supplies to get into the hands of the people who needed them, MLSE would have to be on the ground to personally distribute them.

You see, as wonderful as it was to watch the world come together to help — celebrities holding concerts to raise money and people donating everyday essentials — the logistics on the ground in Haiti were complicated. All these donations were being shipped to Haiti, but once there, no one could determine where they should go. We were told it wasn't the military's job to decide who got what goods; they would be accused of playing favourites, so they had to wait for instructions. That meant essentials — diapers, baby formula, toiletries, clothes, canned food, you name it — all sat in shipping containers on the airport tarmac in Haiti guarded by armed military.

So Tom arranged for delivery trucks to meet us once we landed; one would take us to an orphanage and the other to a makeshift hospital.

I tagged along with a camera operator to document the day. But we were definitely expected to also help out!

It all started off well and good. The plane was jammed with so many things, it made us feel good knowing we were playing some small part in helping people in need. Once we landed, my heart sank. I saw all the shipping containers and learned the truth about how all these much-needed donations were not getting to the people. I found out that the military needed to be on guard 24/7 because people were breaking through airport barriers to steal things and sell them on the black market. The Haitian people were becoming so desperate that they were turning on one another, and it had become hostile territory.

But my spirits were quickly lifted by a little visitor. A boy, maybe six years old, who had been orphaned by the earthquake, came to say hello. He was with one of the charity groups there to greet us. A precious child with a massive smile. He had been through so much heartache and was still finding a way to be happy. He was over the moon when we invited him onto the airplane. He had never been on one before.

I was seriously trying to figure out how I could sneak him back home with me.

We loaded the trucks, and I got on the one bound for the orphanage. Among the many supplies we were bringing were boxes of Raptors and Leafs T-shirts. Clothes for the children.

The drive to our destination left me speechless. Tent city after tent city. Our driver said new ones were popping up daily, while the mansions on the hills continued to be rebuilt.

"Hmmm," I said quietly.

"Hmmm indeed," he responded.

We drove the rest of the way in silence. I watched as women washed their clothes in muddy water while children bathed beside them.

We had military escorts with us.

When we pulled up to the orphanage, the workers were overjoyed. They had just handed out the last of their baby formula to a father whose wife had died in the earthquake, and they were desperate for more.

I stood there for a while taking everything in. I was dumbstruck with sadness. I was trying to figure out how I could take all these children home. Surely, they could fit on the plane? No, Petrillo, not realistic. Ok, I'll convince Tom we have to come back with more food, more clothes. Probably not going to happen either. It wasn't easy planning a trip like this.

Then I cursed Mother Nature. I tried to summon all my witchy power to turn back time and stop the earthquake from happening.

*Ugh, Andi, you watch too many vampire and witch shows, gotta stop.*

I didn't realize during my pondering that two guys had gotten close to me. I had my phone and my camera guy's phone hooked onto my jeans, plus the microphone. One guy was eyeing these goods. My guard immediately went up, and I squared up to them. "Can I help you?"

"We just wanted to come and say hi. Where are you staying?" one of them said.

"I'm not staying. I flew in for the day and leave tonight."

"Oh, that's too bad. You can stay with one of us. Haiti is very beautiful."

One guy started walking a little closer to me.

"What do you want?" I said, loud enough for the military escorts supervising the unloading of the truck to hear. My camera guy heard too.

"Ok, ok, no need to get loud. We were just trying to be friendly."

They left pretty quickly once help arrived.

During this encounter, one of the nurses overheard me say I was leaving that night. She cornered me after the two guys left and begged me to take her on the plane with me. She said spirits were talking to her, telling her another earthquake was coming, and she needed to get out.

The military escorts gently guided her away. She kept going on about prophecies and the end of days and how she needed to escape.

It was excruciating to watch. Other nurses said she wasn't the same after the disaster.

Would I be the same way if I were in her shoes? I shivered at the thought.

It was finally time to start handing out some T-shirts. The kids were happy. Their smiles wiped away all the tension from the previous two encounters. They squealed with delight when they received their Raptors-red and Leafs-blue shirts. And then the squeals turned into screams.

I was on my knees, crouched over the box, little kiddies all around me, handing out the gear. A lot of kids were leaning on me, no big deal because they were so small, but then I felt a push, and I was being crushed from behind. A couple of large men stormed in, grabbed the box another volunteer had, and were making their way towards me when the soldiers stepped in and chased them off. The poor kids had been pushed and trampled on by these men.

The kids ran off, terrified. I was still on my knees, frozen in disbelief. I wanted to grab them and hold them close. Let them know everything would be alright. But would it? The Haitian people were becoming more aggressive with theft. In fact, it was a surprise even to the military that we were attacked at the orphanage. They had sent the majority of their escorts with the people who went to the hospital because those were the supplies most likely to get stolen and sold on the black market.

I was relieved when we made it back to the airport.

That trip left me confused. I had started the day feeling good about myself because I was helping people in need. But I ended the day feeling useless. Did I help anyone? Did I actually make a difference? For the first time in my life, I was exposed to the harshness of human behaviour in times of desperation. It's easy to judge. But would I act the same way? Especially if I was seeing all the new mansions being built on the hilltops while I went without food?

Humans: I'm still trying to figure us out.

## CHAPTER 15

# THE DAY I LOST A STANLEY CUP RING

"I lost the Stanley Cup ring. It's somewhere in the desert, never to be found again. I'm a dead woman."

That's all I kept saying to myself as I frantically looked for the 1989 Calgary Flames Stanley Cup–winning ring. It belonged to Colin Patterson. We were in Afghanistan together, along with other NHL alumni, on a mission to showcase the Stanley Cup and cheer up the troops. We spent a week at the main base, Kandahar Airfield. The trip was organized by MLSE. In particular, COO Tom Anselmi. He was good at showing support for our troops. He is also just plain good. I went to Haiti because of him, I went to Afghanistan because of him, and all because he's always trying to do right by people.

But the desert is a nasty place. So hot, steaming hot, and sand everywhere. I got what was called KAF-hack. I lost my voice because of all the damn sand I was inhaling.

For the first few days, the only noise I could make was a squeak. I'd try to talk, and instead, I would squeak out sand. Cough — sand. Sneeze — sand. Fart — sand. Those little grains were everywhere and in everything.

One day, we were touring the base. Colin brought his ring to show the troops. I asked if I could look at it. He was very generous with it. In fact, most hockey players are. One time on my radio show, *Leafs Lunch*, Bryan Trottier was a guest, and he pulled out a little bag that was holding all seven of his Cup rings. I guess when you have that many championship rings, you need a bag! I kept staring at the rings, and he could see I was really enamoured by them. So he said, "Feel free to wear them."

"You sure?" I had asked.

"Of course," he responded. "What's the point of having these rings if I can't see the joy they bring to people when they put them on?!"

Colin was the same way. Except his hands were exceptionally larger than mine. The ring fit around two of my fingers. Even so, it was still loose. I made a conscious effort to squeeze my fingers together the whole day in order to keep the ring safely on my hand. My right hand looked like a mitten.

The day got away from us because we took our time visiting and spending time with as many troops as possible on the base, but we were on a tight schedule. I blame Lanny McDonald. I say that, of course, in jest. But man, what a personality — everyone loved him. Especially the snipers. Those dudes didn't say a word. Stoic, quiet, and very intimidating. But Lanny came along, and their faces lit up with the biggest smiles. Pfft, I worked my charm and got nothing. Lanny twitched that famous moustache, and the snipers fell for it hook, line, and sinker!

But when we got back to our barracks, we had to hustle. The NHL alumni guys were scheduled to play a ball hockey game against the troops. Daren Millard and I were doing live commentating for the games. Once the tournament was over, a rock concert would be put on for the troops by the band Default. We had a tight schedule, and we were behind.

I dumped my bags and camera equipment on the floor and dashed into the washroom to freshen up, then into my room to change. Dash, dash, dash. *Ok, phew. I'm ready. Breathe.*

Just as I was catching my breath, Colin walked past my room on his way to getting ready. "Hey Andi, when we hop back onto the bus, I'm gonna need the ring back."

My world stopped moving. I also stopped breathing. My body started tingling, and not in a good way. It felt like I was suspended in the air, and I started to sweat. I didn't have to look down at my hand to know the ring wasn't there. I didn't feel its weight anymore. But when did I stop feeling its weight? When did it come off? *Oh God, I'm going to be sick.* I kept picturing this beautiful ring somewhere in the desert. Sand, so much of that damn sand. I envisioned the Stanley Cup ring on the ground with sand blowing all around it and eventually covering up the iconic flaming C logo forever . . . never to be found again.

"I lost the Stanley Cup ring. It's somewhere in the desert, never to be found again. I'm a dead woman." Those words kept ringing in my head, but I finally gave it a shake.

It felt like I had been frozen on the spot in my room forever. But after watching Colin walk the rest of the way down the hall, I quickly sprang into action. I did some heavy-duty praying as I retraced my steps. My hope, my only hope, was that I had lost it somewhere in the barracks.

Under the bed, nope. On the bed, nope. In the shower, nope. Sink, nope. Toilet, dear God, please no, nope. Right outside, by the bus, on the bus, nope nope nope. I was feeling dejected and started practising my apology. But where to even begin? And that's when I saw a spot I missed. I hadn't checked the pile of camera equipment that I had quickly dumped on the floor when we first returned to our rooms. I approached it slowly. This was my last hope of finding the precious ring before offering myself up to be tarred and feathered.

I peered down, and there it was. Just chilling. Not a care in the world; nestled nicely between a sweater and leather camera bag. Absolute chaos was ensuing all around it, and it was just patiently lying there waiting to be found. It had fallen off when I tossed everything down onto the ground in a mad rush to get ready.

For the first time in . . . thirty seconds? Ten minutes? Five hours? I could feel my breathing again.

I calmly picked up the ring, stepped into the hall, made my way onto the bus, and handed the Stanley Cup ring back to its owner.

"Here you go, thanks for letting me wear it," I said with extreme nonchalance. I gave no indication that just minutes earlier I was on the verge of a nervous breakdown.

"Anytime. And thanks for keeping it safe," Colin answered.

If he ever reads this book, Colin Patterson will be learning for the first time that I thought I had lost his ring to the deserts of Afghanistan forever.

That trip to Afghanistan was eye-opening and fulfilling. There were so many brave men and women putting their lives on the line to defend our freedoms, and we were able to bring a little taste of home to them. Many of them were hockey fans, and they were thrilled to take their picture with the Stanley Cup. If we were able to take their minds off the war for just a little while, then the trip was worth it. But we were still in a war zone, and we were lucky nothing bad happened while we were there. We heard that a week after we left, the very spot where the Stanley Cup had been on display for all the troops to see was hit by a bomb. I shudder every time I think of what could have happened if that bomb had hit just a few days earlier. Life or death can sometimes be boiled down to timing; it can also come down to the decisions we make. For so long, I thought I wanted to be a war correspondent. My love for sports and the suggestion to pursue a career in sportscasting by my college radio professor had put me on my current path. However, I can't help but think what could have been. Our trip to Afghanistan included a visit to the memorial site that honoured all the Canadians who perished in the war. A ceremony was held for Mr. John Babcock, the last known Canadian veteran of World War I, who had passed away just a few weeks earlier at the age of 109. All those in attendance signed a book. When I wrote my name down, I said a little prayer of thanks to Mr. Babcock and then made my way through all the memorial plaques. Too many lives gone way too soon. And then I stopped in my tracks. Frozen, wide-eyed, heart pounding, I stood staring at the plaque that bore the name Michelle Lang. The first and only Canadian journalist to be killed in Afghanistan. She and four soldiers were killed after being hit by a roadside bomb. Could that have been me if I'd continued on my path to becoming a war correspondent? I couldn't stop staring at her image. I said a little prayer for her as well and thanked her for her service.

Brian Burke cuts an intimidating figure. But in Afghanistan, I saw his soft side.

I had known Burkie for a few years at that point. He took over as general manager of the Leafs in 2008 and the trip was in 2010. He was always kind. Whenever I needed an interview, he made it happen. When I needed information, he would get it to me.

One year, on Family Day, the Leafs held an open practice. Part of the festivities included me doing a sit-down interview with Burkie at centre ice. I brought my parents to work with me. Funny how the tables turned on that one.

When I told him my parents were there, he sought them out after the interview and sang my praises to them. He didn't have to do that. But he wanted them to know how hard I worked, and he knew it would make them proud.

We left for Afghanistan in March of 2010. Brian's son, Brendan, had passed away in a car accident in February of that year. I didn't think Brian would be on the trip. Everyone knew he was in mourning, and we all completely understood if he cancelled. But on the morning we left, there he was.

On one of our flights (it took many to get to a war zone!), we sat next to each other and I asked him why he was still making this journey. Didn't he need more time to heal?

"How can I let these brave men and women down?" he responded. "They were told I was coming. I can't disappoint them."

"Yeah, but Brian, I think people would understand. You lost your son."

I was crushed for him. No matter how hard I tried, I knew I would never be able to know what he was going through.

We sat in silence for a while. To change the subject and lighten the mood, I laid out some of the gossip magazines I had brought on the trip. We immersed ourselves in the fashion and drama of the lives of celebrities. It was a nice distraction.

The journey to Afghanistan was crazy. We first had to fly to Dubai, where there was a military base. We flew there in the prime minister's old plane. It was a comfortable ride, but the flight from Dubai to Afghanistan, not so much. We had to hop on a cargo plane. We were jammed up against each other. I was squished from both sides and bumping kneecaps with the person in front of me.

When we were getting close to Kandahar Airfield, we had to put on helmets and protective vests. And then they turned the lights off on the plane. It was pitch black. Total and complete darkness. The only thing I could see were the glowing hands on Ryan VandenBussche's watch. Ryan is a former player who laced up over the years for the New York Rangers, Chicago Blackhawks, and Pittsburgh Penguins.

When I asked why we had to kill the lights and wear all this gear, I was told it was because we were landing at night and didn't want to risk being seen by the enemy and getting shot down.

Yikes, that was not the answer I was expecting!

I slowly took my helmet off and slid it under my butt.

"Why did you do that?" asked Ryan.

"Because I'm thinking if they're going to shoot at us, they're most likely going to do it from below, so I'm going to protect my ass!"

Burkie likes to call me a superstar. But in Afghanistan he was the true star. He was so great with everyone.

Even when I took the microphone before one of the ball hockey games and introduced him teasingly as the GM of an Olympic team that was second best, he took it on the chin and played along. Canada had just defeated the United States in men's hockey at the Vancouver 2010 Olympics, and they did so in overtime; the golden goal by Sidney Crosby.

There was a Tim Hortons on base, and one morning, he woke up early to make sure he was the first one there when it opened and then stood at the front of the line paying for all the soldiers' breakfast. I have no clue what he spent that morning, but he was there for a very long time.

Breakfast, lunch, and dinner we sat with a different group of soldiers. They were all excited to meet Burkie. But he always encouraged them to tell their stories. Listening to their sacrifices, hearing the things they had witnessed, it was all very sobering.

We sat with soldiers who had been injured, some who'd lost limbs, but just meeting hockey people cheered them up.

One day, we walked into a room that had TVs and satellite feeds. On one of the screens was a live mission — we were seeing soldiers in action scanning a village for terrorists. I couldn't believe my eyes.

"Is this happening right now? Could those soldiers actually die right now?" I asked in complete disbelief.

Someone answered that every mission is dangerous, but that's what those people in the room were for; they were the eyes in the sky, and they provided communication and any information the soldiers needed to keep them safe.

I was scared to breathe. I didn't want to be any kind of distraction during such a critical moment.

Another day, we were taken to the makeshift hospital on base. We came across two little Afghan boys who had stepped on IEDs — improvised explosive devices — and the doctors had saved them. While touring the hospital, I noticed a door with a lot of locks on it. There was a tiny window that I needed a step stool to reach. I propped myself up and peered in. I saw three men sitting in the room. One looked up, and we made eye contact. I got a horrible feeling. Without peeling my eyes away, I asked the doctor, "Who are these people?"

"They're Taliban," he responded.

"Why are they here?" I was still in a staring contest with one of the men.

"Because they suffered injuries, and we took an oath to help everyone in need. Once they heal, we'll hand them over to the authorities."

I thought I knew what hatred was. I thought I had experienced it at some point in my life. I'd had a boyfriend who had cheated on me, and there was this group of girls in high school who'd annoyed me. But I hadn't truly felt hatred until that moment. I hated those men — no, *monsters* — with my entire being. It was visceral.

It devastates me to my core what has happened to women since the Taliban has once again taken over Afghanistan.

Women are hated for simply being women. How despicable.

It wasn't all serious in Afghanistan. One morning, I definitely had a brain fart moment. Burkie caught me in an embarrassing, yet hilarious, situation. I never really adjusted to the nine-hour time change; plus, it's not exactly easy to get a good night's sleep in a war zone when you can hear fighter jets taking off in what felt like every fifteen minutes.

So, one morning, I decided to just get up instead of fight the pillow and start my day with a shower. You know, to wash off all the sand that gets *everywhere*.

It was around four in the morning. The building we were staying in was very bare bones. Toilets and sinks were in the same building as the beds, but the showers were in a separate portable.

In my pyjamas — yes, I brought pj's to Afghanistan — and two towels in hand, I shuffled outside, down a flight of stairs, and crossed a little dirt road to the showers. The sign in the showers read, "3 mins showers. Don't waste hot water." Um, yeah, it takes three minutes alone to shampoo my hair. I swear I tried my hardest to be quick, but I know I wasn't. While I was towelling off, a soldier came in to take her shower. She immediately was hit by the steam I had created. Oops. I was truly embarrassed. I was also equally impressed by how quickly she disrobed, showered, dressed, and left — I was still putting cream on my legs!

Time to leave the showers. Uh-oh. I forgot to bring clean clothes to put on. I didn't want to put my pj's back on, which would have been the wise thing to do, but I was still jet-lagged. I was so tired, and sand had infiltrated my brain. I thought to myself, *No biggy, it's like five in the morning. No one is up yet. I'll just sprint across the little road wearing just my towel and hustle up the steps. Easy peasy.*

Except, it wasn't.

The second I opened the door, a jeep with a handful of male soldiers drove by. They were so stunned to see a woman in only a towel wrapped around her body and one wrapped around her hair, that they all turned to look . . . including the driver, who proceeded to drive right towards a building. He swerved in time and avoided a crash. Just as they drove away, slowly, I might add, I heard a voice.

"What the fuck are you doing, Petrillo? Where the hell are your clothes?"

Of course, it was Burkie. He was also messed up by the time change and couldn't sleep, so he was just chilling outside.

"I didn't think anyone would be up this early!" I yelled defensively.

"It's a goddamn war zone. It's a 24/7 operation. There's no nine to five bullshit here."

"Argh! Leave me alone! I screwed up!"

Burkie was reprimanding me the whole time I ran up the stairs and back into my room, but he was doing it with a smirk. We both found the situation extremely funny.

I made it back inside without putting any other soldiers in danger.

In 2023, Brian became the executive director of the Professional Women's Hockey League Players Association. As the host of PWHL games on CBC Sports, I've had to call him up from time to time for information. And to this day, Burkie answers and Burkie delivers.

## CHAPTER 16

# IT ALL STARTS WITH A CAT

I'm the fictitious president and proud member of the non-existent Goalie-Huggers Group.

And it all started with Felix Potvin.

It was during the 1992–93 NHL season. I was an impressionable twelve-year-old kid who loved playing rollerblade hockey on the streets. When Potvin started playing for the Leafs that year, I don't know what it was, but I became mesmerized.

The long run into the playoffs definitely helped. I loved that his nickname was "The Cat." When I was a kid, I had a fascination with panthers. In fact, I went through a very nerdy stage where I would write letters to my friends and sign-off as *The Panther.* At the time, I thought I was so cool. But now, as I share that story, I'm cringing.

But thanks to Potvin, I wanted to play goalie after so many years of complaining about being made to because I was the youngest kid on the street. Being in net gave me the chance to flash my glove just like him.

"You see," I would tell my friends, "I have the same reflexes as Felix the Cat!"

My friends were quickly annoyed by me yelling "Like the Cat!" every time I made a save . . . even the really easy ones.

When I was in grade 8 getting ready for my Catholic Confirmation, it was customary to choose a confirmation name. Usually, the name of a saint is chosen to help guide you in your faith. I chose the name Felix. Now, in my defence, there are many Saint Felixes out there. But when my teacher asked me to elaborate on which Felix I meant, I wrote "Potvin." Busted. When I tried to defend my choice by saying he played like a saviour in the playoffs, it didn't exactly help my cause. There was no way the church was going to accept a hockey goalie as my confirmation name. Instead, I chose Joan of Arc. You know, the woman who transcended gender roles and was a bad-ass military leader while still a teenager? She was burned at the stake. One of the accusations made against her? She wore men's clothing. How *blasphemous*. But I digress. Back to Felix.

Never in a million years did I think I would one day meet the guy. And Felix wasn't just an athlete I looked up to. He was the athlete who took my fandom to another level. I didn't just watch the games to see if the Leafs won or lost. I started to care about save percentages. I paid attention to strengths and weaknesses. I tracked special teams.

No no no, Felix Potvin wasn't just an athlete to me, he was the gateway to what I eventually became: a sportscaster.

I started to see and think about the game more critically because of my interest in his performances.

And then . . . I met the man.

It was the 2006–07 season. My first year covering the Leafs for Leafs TV. Members of the 1993 Leafs team were being honoured before a game, and one of the security personnel, a lovely woman named Celeste, knew I was a huge Potvin fan. When my pregame duties were over and the game was about to start, she approached me and asked, "Wanna meet Potvin?"

I thought she was joking. She said she was in charge of watching the private box the 1993 alumni were in, and she'd be happy to take me there to meet my idol. I said yes, but the whole time I was following her from outside the Leafs dressing room all the way up to the box, I was in a trance. Was I really going to meet Felix Potvin?

I was so stunned about getting to meet him that I totally forgot about the three pieces of gum in my mouth. You see, there was a time when two of Joe Bowen's sons, Sean and Derek, were equipment guys with the Leafs, and before taking to the ice for a game, they would roll up a gum "sandwich" for some of the players: a strip of Juicy Fruit wedged between two strips of Big Red. Half of the Leafs players would start a game with one cheek looking like a squirrel stowing away some nuts. I'm willing to bet they had the best breath of any team in the league.

Once all the players got their pieces, Sean and Derek would toss me one as well. As you can imagine, fresh pieces of gum in your mouth make for a lot of saliva. And this saliva was building up as I was making my way to meet Felix Potvin.

When we got to the alumni box, Celeste grabbed me by the hand to lead me in. But I didn't need any guidance; I spotted him right away.

Celeste called Felix over and said, "This is Andi Petrillo. She's a reporter for Leafs TV and covers the team all year long."

He stretched out his hand to shake mine. I did the same.

"Nice to meet you, Andi."

"Nice to meet you too." And then it happened. The embarrassing moment we all dread when meeting someone we want to impress. I spat all over his hand as we were shaking. Dear Lord, I wanted to die. Felix made a funny face. It was for a fraction of a second, but I saw it, and it added to my humiliation. I knew that he knew that he had just gotten spat on. I took a huge gulp of saliva, moved the gum sandwich to one side of my mouth (how professional), and attempted to have a conversation.

"I've been a huge fan of yours for forever. This is really special to be able to meet you."

"So, what do you do for Leafs TV?" he asked.

"Mostly rinkside reporting for all the games — home and away. Pretty cool to travel on the charter. And I host some shows too."

"Wow, you do all that and travel with the team? They never allowed women to do that when I was playing. Good for you."

And then I stood there and just stared at him.

Not creepy at all.

I honestly didn't know what to say. I'm never at a loss for words, but I just stood there. He politely excused himself.

I was so thankful to Celeste. She told me to go back and ask for a photo, but I was way too embarrassed.

It's ok though. A few years later, in 2009, he was a guest on the pre-game show I was hosting on Leafs TV. This time, I was way cooler, and I finally got my photo.

During the pandemic, I also had him as a guest on my TSN 1050 radio show, *Leafs Lunch*. I threw it out there that I had a co-host position open and asked if he'd be interested. He laughed and said no. Hey, I tried.

I have a painting of Potvin in my home office. When I do shows at home, you can see it in the background. Artist David Arrigo, who does a lot of cool art in the sports realm, made it for me in 2009, on the night Potvin was on the set of Leafs TV. I was hoping to get it signed, but Potvin had been whisked away. That's ok, I love that art piece just the same.

Potvin was the first goalie of many I adore. The ultimate one being my husband, of course, Jon Conway. But I also greatly admired the career of Italian international goalkeeper Gianluigi Buffon. Back in 2015, my husband was the goalkeeper coach with Toronto FC, and the club had just signed Sebastian Giovinco from Juventus; that's where Buffon played. Naturally, when I met Giovinco, all I could do was ask him about Buffon. Clearly, the language barrier caused Seba to misunderstand my enthusiasm, because at one point during our conversation, he said, "But why are you asking about Buffon? You have a goalie, yes?" and he pointed at Jon.

"Ohhhh, no, no, no. Seba, I'm just a fan. I'm not looking for a new husband!" I explained.

I also fell in love with Canadian goalkeeper Erin McLeod. Her Canadian flag–style mohawk in 2002 during the FIFA U-19 World Championships was just so friggin' cool.

For the inaugural Professional Women's Hockey League draft, which was held on September 18, 2023, Shannon Szabados was one of my analysts. After watching her represent Canada for years, I was fangirling the entire time she was sitting next to me.

Pick any goalie in any sport, and I'll find a way to defend them.

During the 2014 FIFA World Cup, we had just finished covering a game that Mexico was in. I don't remember the opponent, I just remember their goalkeeper, Guillermo Ochoa, standing on his head. For the postgame show, we had to come up with who we thought was the player of the game. Nigel Reed, one of the analysts on my panel, said there was no way we could choose a goalkeeper, that the recognition was typically reserved for a field player. I don't even remember who he was arguing for because I was so adamant about my choice. I won.

Sportscaster Gord Miller loves to joke that a goalie can do no wrong in my eyes. If a goal is scored, it's because their teammates did something wrong.

During Frederik Andersen's time with the Leafs, I defended him constantly. Gord would say, "Andi, there could be a dead body on the ground and Freddy would be standing over it with a smoking gun in his hand and you'd still say he didn't do it."

I dated a guy who was a huge Chicago Blackhawks fan and loved Eddie Belfour. As a gift, I had a replica Belfour goalie mask made. I waited for Belfour after a game when he was in town with the Florida Panthers and asked him to sign it. He was impressed by the mask and was very gracious. When I broke up with the guy, I seriously thought about asking for the mask back. I didn't, that wouldn't have been right. But man, that's the one gift I regret giving.

Yup. Like I said: I'm the fictitious president and proud member of the non-existent Goalie-Huggers Group.

And it all started with The Cat.

## CHAPTER 17

# DON'T GET BLOOD ON MY BLOUSE

"Whatever you do, don't get blood on my blouse. I still have a postgame show to do."

Not exactly a sentence you'd think you'd say at work. But one night, I did.

It was 2007, and I was a year into my Leafs TV job and couldn't be happier. It would've taken a kidnapping to keep me from showing up to work because I loved every second of being at the rink doing interviews, hosting *Leafs Today*, and travelling to games. If I had a cold? I'd just eat an orange and get to work. Fever? Drink some chamomile tea and get to work. Nauseous? Chew on some ginger and get to work.

I. Loved. My. Job.

But a few months into the 2007–08 season, I was in a lot of pain.

The right side of my jaw alternated between extreme pain and numbness. Sleeping hurt, being awake hurt, and talking definitely hurt.

Like most stubborn people, I completely ignored it. *Perhaps it will just go away on its own?*

A few months into the season, the Bruins were in town. I was friends with their sideline reporter, Rob Simpson, and we decided to grab dinner the night before the game. I was not in good shape. My lower right gums were so swollen that it hurt to move my lips. Talking was a struggle, and there was a strange liquid in my mouth. I know, disgusting. I was grossing myself out.

In fairness, I did finally go to my dentist, and they chalked up my pain to teeth grinding at night. I knew that wasn't right. I knew I should've gotten a second opinion, but perhaps I was afraid of the news. I didn't want to interrupt my life, which was going so well.

So, I met Rob at the Park Hyatt Rooftop restaurant and suffered through my meal. Barely ate a thing. I knew I was in really bad shape when Slash . . . yes, that Slash . . . walked into the restaurant, and I had no energy to get up and say hi. I would've loved a photo. The guitarist from Guns N' Roses, who I had a crush on growing up, was standing right in front of me and I did . . . nothing. Instead, I was praying my jaw would fall off and take the pain with it.

I had to cut dinner short with Rob; I said goodbye and spent the night in my condo with an ice pack on my face. I didn't want to call my dentist; they proved to be useless. So, I looked up another dentist and left a message at three in the morning.

I finally fell asleep and was awakened by a call at 9 a.m. It was the new dentist. The receptionist, whose name was Karen, immediately went into mother mode and told me to come right away to see the dentist. When I got there, she said, "Anyone who leaves a message at 3 a.m. sounding the way you did deserves the first appointment of the day!"

Karen still looks after me to this day.

This dentist knew something was wrong and that it wasn't a case of grinding my teeth. Right away, he sent me to a specialist who had an x-ray machine for panoramic radiography.

The x-ray showed a growth.

"It could be benign, it could be cancer," the specialist said.

I wasn't comprehending. "So, what does that mean? Because I'm very busy. I'm not sure I can schedule in more doctors' appointments."

I don't know if I gave that stupid response because I was in shock or denial.

He looked at me in complete disbelief. "This is your health we're talking about here. You find the time."

I sat there like a petulant child.

An appointment was made with an oral surgeon for November 27, 2007, the morning of a Leafs game. They were hosting the Habs.

The surgeon called me into his office and didn't mince words. "I looked at your x-rays. It doesn't look good. I estimate this tumour has been growing for about five years and it's starting to wrap itself around your nerves. We have to operate immediately. You should know, there is a risk of paralysis with these types of surgeries. But rest assured, I'm one of the best."

My first thought was, *This guy's cocky.*

My second thought was, *What. The. F*%k.*

Cue another stupid response by me: "Oh no, sorry doctor, but we can't operate today. I have a hockey game to work tonight. It's always a good night when the Habs are in town, and I have to be there. Not to mention, my career is all about talking on TV. Paralysis is out of the question."

As if I had a say.

Eyebrows raised, he said, "You work in hockey? I've done a lot of work with hockey players. And you should also know that when I told a hockey player he needed work done, he knew I was being serious. You've heard of Patrick Roy, right?"

*Umm, yeah, doc.*

"Do you remember his famous back and forth with Jeremy Roenick during the playoffs because Roy missed a game? Well, that was because he needed to have his wisdom teeth removed. They were causing him problems. I'm the one who removed them."

It makes no sense, but the fact that he operated on one of the greatest goalies ever put me at ease. And if Roy was willing to miss a playoff game, I guess I could miss a November game because of a possible malignant tumour. Same same, right?

I went into surgery thirty minutes later. The surgeon was able to remove 90 percent of the tumour. The remaining 10 percent was too close to my nerves and he didn't want to risk any damage. He said that sometimes when the majority of a tumour is removed, the other parts will detach themselves from the nerves, and at that point the rest can be removed.

Since I had zero expectation of going into surgery that morning, I had phone calls to make. First, I called work. With a mouth full of gauze and the numbing agent still in full effect, I told them what had happened.

The second call was to my mother. Like a typical Italian woman, she started yelling at me.

"How could you not tell me?"

"It happen' tho fat, Mum."

"I can barely understand you!!!"

"I gaw stuh in my mowf."

"Are you ok to drive home?" — expletives in Italian — "I can't believe this. How could this happen? I would've been there. I'm leaving work. I'll be at your place soon. Unless you need me to pick you up?"

All I could do was laugh. My mother was talking a mile a minute, having a freak out, and I was still in shock over how quickly my day had changed. The good news was that the surgeon said he believed the tumour to be benign. Tests were being done to be 100 percent certain.

"What's so funny? This isn't funny." My mother was still having a meltdown.

"Ok mah, see you sooooon."

I missed a couple of work days because my face was more swollen than Eddie Murphy's character Professor Klump.

The surgeon called me with great news: The tumour was benign, phew.

I also avoided any kind of paralysis: double phew.

It's crazy, because when I look back on those years before discovering the tumour, the right side of my jaw was definitely bigger than the left. I just thought my face was lopsided. In fact, someone said something nasty about me on one of those chat sites about how I looked like Quagmire from *Family Guy*.

*Well guess what, nasty human? It turned out I had a tumour growing. Be a better person!*

But I wasn't out of the woods yet. The tumour had damaged one of my back molars and the tooth cracked in half. Holy geez, just when I thought the pain was over, it wasn't.

The tooth cracked the night before a game, and I couldn't get an appointment with my dentist. So, I did what any masochist would do . . . I went to work. The tooth cracked into more pieces during the pregame show. These pieces needed to be yanked. One of my analysts, former NHLer Mark Osborne, suggested I go see the Leafs dentist for help.

Never in a million years would I think to bother any of the medical staff for the Leafs, but I was desperate for relief. I estimate I was living with extreme pain in my jaw for about three months.

I waited for the first period to start then hesitantly knocked on the door of the dressing room I knew belonged to the doctors. I told them my situation, and the dentist, Dr. Charles Goldberg, completely understood. But he had conditions. "Andi," he said, "I'm here for the Leafs. If anything happens to a player, I have to immediately go to them. So, if we want to work quickly, it means I can't give you any numbing. And if a player comes in, you have to give up the chair for them."

There was a TV in the room showing the game. I laid back in the dental chair and said, "Whatever you do, don't get blood on my blouse. I still have a postgame show to do."

And then I watched the game and prayed no player took a puck or stick to the mouth.

Dr. Goldberg worked as quickly as he could, and I definitely broke out in a sweat from the pain. But once it was over, I was given temporary relief until I could see my dentist. I was able to watch the rest of the game comfortably and then get through my postgame show . . . with no blood on my shirt.

Fast-forward to 2014. I was hosting the men's FIFA World Cup. It was my first time hosting this prestigious tournament, and without a doubt, I was nervous. In fact, there were days where my tongue felt too big for my mouth, and I just chalked it up to nerves. But a little voice inside my head told me to get things checked out once the tournament was over. And what do you know? The damn tumour was back. This time it was growing inwards and touching my tongue. Once again, my oral surgeon explained the risks: If he nicked my tongue, I could have a permanent lisp. Once again, he did a brilliant job, and the surgery was a success.

Sometimes I wonder how I got through that summer of 2014: I was out of a job, I had just lost my dog, and the tumour returned.

Thank goodness for my incredible family and friends.

It's still so crazy to think I've had two minor surgeries on my jaw that could have gone terribly wrong. The first surgery, there was the risk of paralysis on one side of my face. The second surgery, my speech could have been altered forever. Both worst-case scenarios that could have ruined my career.

I feel blessed every day going to work and getting to do what I do. Especially knowing how quickly it can all be taken away.

## *CHAPTER 18*

# A FRIEND LOST

The last words I spoke to Wade Belak haunted me for years.

Wade and I became instant friends. I think we got along so quickly because we both felt like fish out of water during the 2006–07 season.

That was the year I started working in the NHL. A dream come true.

It also marked the start of transition for the "goons" in the game of hockey. The NHL had been shifting away from guys who strictly fought. The league still wanted tough guys, but they had to score too. More power forwards, speedy players, and all around top-notch skilled guys were coveted. Staged fights and scary enforcers were being criticized at every chance.

Wade was trying to figure out if he still belonged.

I was trying to figure out if I fit in at all.

It was early into my NHL job, and we were on a road trip in Philadelphia. Morning skate had finished, and I had just wrapped up all my interviews. I was sitting cross-legged on the floor, alone in a hallway, going through tape and writing down time codes and brief recaps of what the interviews entailed to send back to my producers at Leafs TV for the show later that night. The Flyers players had already left and so had the Leafs; the arena was quiet except for a few equipment guys getting things ready for that night's game. I suddenly heard the slow tapping of someone's shoes on the ground as they made their way towards me. I looked up and saw then head coach of the Toronto Maple Leafs, Paul Maurice. Paul knew I was trying to fit in. He knew I was working extra hard to prove I belonged. He looked down at me and said, "I know what it's like to be the new young kid on the block who's trying to gain everyone's respect. When I was named head coach of the Carolina Hurricanes in 1995, I was only twenty-eight. A lot of people doubted me, but I believed in myself. Believe in yourself, and you'll be just fine."

I needed to hear those words at that exact moment.

When the Florida Panthers won the Stanley Cup in 2024 with Paul Maurice as their head coach, I had a huge grin on my face watching him hoist Lord Stanley's mug. He finally did it.

My location for the Leafs TV pregame shows during games, whether on the road or at home, was just outside the Leafs dressing room. We timed some of my hits to coincide with the players walking out for warm-up and coming off. Without fail, Nik Antropov and Pavel Kubina would tap my ankles with their sticks while I was doing a live hit. They thought it was hilarious; I thought I would need crutches. My last hit before puck drop was to read out the starting lineup and healthy scratches. Many nights, Wade Belak was on the latter list. After the team took to the ice for the game, he would pop his head out, grab my microphone, and read the lineup and scratches live on air. He would always act shocked when he read his name. It got a great chuckle from everyone. He knew how to poke fun at himself. But I knew he was struggling.

We were on a road trip in Florida. It was the day before the game, and I saw him in the hotel lobby. He was really sombre. I asked what was wrong. He said he was trying to get into the right head space for the next day. Paul Maurice was putting him in the lineup.

Wade was playing because Bryan Allen was playing. He was the tough guy for the Florida Panthers.

Maurice wasn't dressing Wade to score goals or block shots; he was putting him in . . . just in case.

I always loved the tough guy. Still do. They're a special human who puts their health and sanity on the line every time they're in a game. They do it for their teammates, for the fans, for the crest. I know we've come a long way in understanding the consequences of that kind of role, and I know now not to glorify it. But I'll never belittle the role; I'll never look down on any of the guys who filled those shoes. They're damn warriors. And they're damn loyal.

Wade was psyching himself up for a fight he knew he couldn't back down from. It occupied his thoughts all day, night, and next morning. How exhausting for him.

Wade and Allen did drop the gloves. Over the sound system, they started playing LL Cool J's "Mama Said Knock You Out." It wasn't a lively bout, no crazy haymakers. But Allen snuck in a punch near the end and got Wade right on the nose.

After the game his eyes were almost swollen shut, and he had a splitting headache.

Leafs won 3–2. Next stop on the road trip was Pittsburgh.

We spent the extra night in South Florida. Everyone was going out to enjoy Miami. I saw Wade in the hotel lobby as I was leaving with some other media folks. He was watching all his teammates head out for a night on the town, but he was going straight to his room; he was spending the night in the dark with an ice pack on his face.

Wade walked to the beat of his own drum.

He didn't care what people thought of him.

You see, the world of sports can be very childish, a lot like high school. Image and perception are everything.

The guys on the team were great. I was fortunate to be travelling with a good group. But they were also hypersensitive about their fellow teammates' opinions. If anyone spent what was considered too much time with a female reporter, they would be teased to no end. It was no different than how the male reporters saw things: If a female reporter was seen talking too much to a player, something intimate must be going on.

As you can guess, this made things, and sadly, in some cases, it still does make things, difficult for a woman to do her job if everyone was scared to talk to her for too long!

Wade didn't care for this foolish behaviour.

This one time in Montreal, the group of media members I was with wanted to make it a late night. I threw in the towel, bid everyone goodnight, and made my way back to the hotel. I was walking back, by myself, on a cold, dark night. Wade was coming from the hotel to meet up with some teammates. When he saw that I was alone, he did a 180 to walk me back to the hotel. I told him not to worry. Plus, what would the guys think if they saw us?

He dropped a couple of swear words and said, "Who cares what they think? If a guy had a chance to walk my daughter home and keep her safe, and he didn't because he was afraid of what his friends would say, and something did actually happen to her, I would kill him."

I chuckled because I knew he was telling the truth. He loved his daughters. And he was a gentleman. He wouldn't be able to live with himself if something did in fact happen to me and he could've prevented it.

Another time, we landed from a road trip in the wee hours of the morning. A blizzard had come through Toronto. Our cars were covered in a foot of snow. Everyone was tired and cold. Just as I was getting ready to start cleaning off my car, I saw that half of it was already done. Wade had come straight to my car to help. I could see some of the other guys looking over through the side of their eyes. They could judge all they want — Wade didn't care.

He was traded from the Leafs to the Panthers in 2008, and we didn't see each other much after that, but we kept in touch.

When Wade retired in 2011, I put him in contact with an agent I was using at the time. He finished his career with the Nashville Predators, and they were interested in bringing him on board as a broadcaster. I knew he'd be great at the job.

That same summer, he was competing on the CBC show *Battle of the Blades*. He was making trips to Toronto, and sometimes we would meet up for lunch.

I was at a point in my career where I knew it was time to move on from Maple Leaf Sports and Entertainment. I had been there since 2006 and went from covering hockey to also being a part of the Raptors and Toronto FC broadcasts. I had learned so much, had so much fun, but I felt it in my bones that I was ready for network TV.

I had been approached by the executive producer of *Hockey Night in Canada*, Trevor Pilling, and he wanted to hire me for just ten games to do rinkside reporting: MLSE said no. The following year, he came to me with a full-time opportunity, but I still had to audition for it.

I shared my saga with Wade. I was so nervous for the audition. I was also exhausted. My grandfather had been in and out of the hospital for the better part of a year. His heart was failing. There was a stretch in August where he was in the hospital for weeks and I was going to see him almost daily. My grandfather was everything to me.

August was also when I went into the CBC and did a mock show with PJ Stock. I felt good about my performance. I felt confident. I told my grandfather I was trying to get a job on the very show he watched every Saturday night shortly after immigrating to Canada. He couldn't believe it. When he first came to Canada, he saved up enough money to buy a TV, and every Saturday, the family would come over to watch the Toronto Maple Leafs on *Hockey Night in Canada*. My mom and two aunts secretly loved Bobby Orr and the Boston Bruins, but they wouldn't dare tell my grandfather that.

And now his first grandchild, his only granddaughter, was so close to getting a job on that very same show.

Wade was very encouraging and told me I would get the job; he had no doubts.

The last words I spoke to Wade Belak haunted me for years.

It was August 30, 2011. Wade was coming to town. He was having dinner with people from *Battle of the Blades*, and some CBC executives were apparently going to be there. Wade wanted me to join everyone afterwards. He thought that if I met more CBC people, it would help my chances of getting hired.

His flight landed late. I had worked during the day and spent the evening at the hospital with my grandfather. I needed to get home to my dog, Lola.

Wade called and told me where everyone was meeting up.

"Are you coming?" he asked.

"I dunno. I thought I'd have the energy, but I'm zonked," I responded.

"Come on. Go have a coffee, you'll be fine. I want to introduce you to some people."

I just couldn't muster up the strength to go out. "Dude, I'm sorry. I can't. I have to get home and feed Lola."

"Ok," he said. "Go home, feed her, and I'll send a cab to come get you. You don't have to drive. Don't have to pay a thing."

He was trying so hard to get me to go out. Looking back, I often wonder, Was he asking for help? Did he need the company of a friend? Or perhaps he really just wanted to help out my chances with CBC.

I'll never know.

I sighed heavily, "Wade, I'm just too tired. Let's do lunch tomorrow. Ok?"

He sounded so dejected. "Ok, fine. I'll call you after practice."

We hung up. He never did call. We never did meet up for lunch. Tomorrow didn't happen for him.

*I'm just too tired. Let's do lunch tomorrow.* Those words . . . the last words I spoke to Wade Belak haunted me for years. I can't say they still don't, but I've slowly let go of my guilt.

August 31. I remember that day well.

I woke with a pit in my stomach. I had a strange feeling all morning. I had the day off, and guess what I was going to do that morning before meeting Wade for lunch? You guessed it, I was heading to the hospital to be with my grandfather.

I arrived at the hospital. I made my way to his room. He wasn't there. No family member was in sight either. *So this is why I've had a pit in my stomach,* I thought to myself. Something must have happened to my grandfather; I just knew it! I frantically ran to the nurse's station.

"Matteo Colasante!" I screamed his name at the poor lady. "Where is he? Where is Matteo Colasante!" She quickly got on her computer.

"Was he having any tests done today?" she asked.

"No!"

"I'm not seeing anything in my system. Nothing on him has been reported."

"Then where is he? He's not in a condition to just get up and walk out of here!"

I felt my breathing getting shallower, and just then I heard voices. No, I heard laughter. Coming down the hall was my family. My aunt was pushing my grandfather in a wheelchair.

I respectfully scolded them for giving me a panic attack. Turned out my grandfather had a great morning and was feeling pretty lively, so they decided to take him out for breakfast and some fresh air.

With my heart beating at its normal pace again, we all went back to his room to hang out. My grandfather and I started playing scopa, an Italian card game.

My phone rang. It was my agent.

"*Hockey Night in Canada* want to make an offer. Your dream is coming true."

I jumped up with excitement and messed up the cards. My grandfather wasn't happy about that. When I told everyone why I jumped, he forgave me. It was celebration all around in that tiny hospital room.

But that only lasted a little while.

Thirty minutes later I got a text from Sheri Forde, a reporter with TSN.

"Are you hearing the news about Wade?"

"No, what news?"

"They're saying he's dead."

Dead. I stared at the word. Dead. I truly couldn't process that word. Dead.

There was that damn pit in my stomach again.

I immediately sent a text to Wade. I don't even remember what I said. I was in shock. Maybe I asked if he was still alive? If we were still on for lunch? How did practice go?

I figured if I acted like everything was normal then it would be normal, and Wade would be alive, and we'd still be on for lunch.

I stared hard at my phone for several minutes expecting a response.

None came.

My family felt the energy change in the room. I told them the news.

"But I don't think it's true," I said. "We're meeting up for lunch. I'll figure out what's going on soon."

I called my husband, who was then still my boyfriend. He calmed me down and said he was sure everything was fine.

"Make some phone calls," he said. "You'll get the truth."

I called PJ Stock. I had done my *Hockey Night in Canada* audition with him. He also knew the *Battle of the Blades* crew. I asked if he could look into it for me.

It felt like hours before he called me back, but really, it was minutes.

"Andi, it's true. Wade's gone. They found him in his hotel room. He didn't even make it to the rink this morning." PJ was also in shock.

I was destroyed. I was inconsolable. My family tried. My boyfriend tried. Nothing and no one could make that pain go away. It was visceral.

It was over an hour before I could make my way back to my grandfather's room. I had been in a common area in the hospital simply sobbing.

My grandfather asked, "How old was he?"

"He was only thirty-five, Nonno."

My grandfather's eyes glossed over. "I know my time is coming. But I'm eighty-three. I've lived. He's too young." I cried even harder. How soon would I also be shedding tears for him? Too soon it turned out.

I started at *Hockey Night in Canada* the following month. My grandfather watched me proudly until he passed on November 9.

I became just the fifth woman to be a part of *HNIC* and the first ever woman to be a full-time member of the studio show. An incredible honour. But at the time, I never truly absorbed the history I was making. My heart was broken.

Wade was a special friend. They don't make guys like him often.

## *CHAPTER 19*

# ANOTHER GOOD ONE GONE

Wade wasn't the first friend I had lost.

May 26, 2009, I rushed home to watch the Stanley Cup playoffs and tuned in just as Ron MacLean was giving Canada the news that Peter Zezel, a great hockey player, had passed away.

I was stunned. I knew he had been battling a rare blood disorder for a few years, but he said he had everything under control. I called Mark Osborne, one of Zez's best friends and constant golf buddy.

"Is it true? Is Zez gone?" I asked, hoping Ron just gave the biggest "fake news" report ever.

"He's gone, Andi. He's gone." That's all Ozzy could muster up the power to say because he was so choked up.

How can I describe Zez? He was full of life. Always laughing. A heart so full of love, especially for kids in need. I once saw him pull out a wad of hundreds at a golf tournament that was raising money for a children's hospital and tell the woman selling 50/50 tickets to keep it all.

He later told me that his niece, who had battled cancer, died in his arms.

Zez loved golfing. When he found out I moved to his area of the city, he wanted to show me all the local spots and help me buy some golf clubs. "Andi, we have to get you looking like a pro when you go to all these charity events. We'll work on your swing later!"

He took me to the best bakery in the area, a cheese boutique, a coffee shop, and then we hit up a sporting goods shop where he helped get me a discount on a full set of clubs.

"Not quite sure about my golf game, but at least I'll look good," I said as we chuckled over a San Remo Bakery donut.

Zez would help get me paid appearances at golf charity events as a "celebrity" because he knew I was just getting started in the business and had just bought a condo.

Often, it was Zez, Ozzy, and I rolling up to these tournaments together, and I would have no business being there. We'd be at the range warming up, and watching the two of them was like watching those commercials where the athletes call out all these ridiculous shots . . . and then make them! Closest to that pin . . . hit that sign . . . hit it next to that tree without touching the tree . . . and on and on they would challenge each other.

Every time Zez came to a Leafs game, he would make a point of stopping by the Leafs TV set and saying hi to Ozzy and me. He was always armed with a few jokes and made people all around us laugh.

But I knew his illness made him very self-conscious. The medication he was on to combat the blood disorder caused him to gain quite a bit of weight. Whenever he ran into someone he hadn't seen in a while, he would immediately say, "I don't always look like this. The medication does this to me."

He would do that four or five times a night. It broke my heart.

A lot of laughter left this world when he passed.

Over the years, my husband has bought me some new clubs, but I refuse to get rid of the old ones I bought with Zez. I even recently got them regripped, so I can keep using them.

My golf swing still stinks.

## CHAPTER 20

# MAKING THE LEAP TO NETWORK TV

I was beyond excited to be joining the iconic *Hockey Night in Canada* show. I even received a lovely note from Cassie Campbell-Pascall welcoming me to an elite group of women. I was about to become just the fifth woman to be part of the broadcasts for *HNIC*. The first was Helen Hutchinson. After her came Brenda Irving, Martine Gaillard, Cassie, then me. I never knew I was joining such an exclusive group. After she sent me that note, I was immensely proud.

But it was hard leaving Maple Leaf Sports and Entertainment. All my dreams had started to be realized during my time at MLSE.

Sometimes I wonder if things needed to end at all.

A year before leaving, I had been approached by the executive producer of *HNIC*, Trevor Pilling, to do some freelance work. Cassie was going on maternity leave, and he needed to make some changes. The opportunity emerged for a rinkside reporter position for ten Montreal Canadiens games. Trevor thought of me. Did I jump for joy? Yes! (My neighbour in the condo below was not impressed.) It never occurred to me that my bosses at MLSE would say no. Other than this opportunity being for *HNIC* and for only ten games, the main reason I thought the request would be green-lighted was because all the other on-air talent who worked with me at Leafs TV also appeared on other networks. Paul Hendrick did rinkside reporting for Sportsnet games. Harry Neale and

Greg Millen worked on *HNIC*. Joe Bowen called games on Sportsnet and then went to radio on Saturdays for AM640. How could they say no to me when the precedent had been set?

But. They. Said. *No*.

I was speechless. I presented all the arguments, but they didn't care. I belonged to them, and that was that. To say I felt hard done by is an understatement. Not to mention, the double standard was real. But instead of living with resentment, I told myself they valued me so much that they didn't want to lose me. Even so, I stayed in contact with Trevor.

A year later, he came to me with an offer I couldn't refuse.

"Alright, Andi. MLSE won't let you do outside freelance work. So, how about you leave and come to *HNIC* full-time?" Sold. I took the job.

But leaving MLSE was hard. Mostly because of the people: a *lot* of good people. And one in particular was COO Tom Anselmi. We had been to Haiti together. Afghanistan together. He had been so good to me and was just an awesome guy. I remember the day I went to his office to tell him the news. I was confident in my decision, but the second I sat across from him, I caught a frog in my throat. It took some hardcore inner dialogue to keep from crying. It almost felt like I was betraying him by saying goodbye. Tom was great. He congratulated me and wished me well. But you don't get to his position in life without being a savvy business person.

He knew the details of my deal with the network very well. He knew I was under contract and had a non-compete of ninety days upon resignation. When I resigned, it was already September 2011, and hockey training camps were just days away. Once again, Tom was good to me. He didn't screw me over. He said I could start right away with *Hockey Night*, BUT I had to continue working for Leafs TV for ninety days. I would be given Saturdays off, but I had to host the mid-week games for MLSE. I guess you could say it's because of Tom that I learned how to juggle working at multiple networks at once — ha! We shook on our agreement.

My ego was a little wounded when they put out the standard company email saying I was leaving. I wasn't expecting a parade. I wasn't expecting to be showered with gifts. But damn, at least make the email good . . . I had been there for five years and put some great content together for the Leafs, the Raptors, and Toronto FC, but all that was sent out were two lines: "Andi Petrillo is leaving for *Hockey Night in Canada*. Her last day will be in December."

I mean, c'mon. We've all received those kinds of emails, and they always start with "We're sad to see this person go . . ." or "With heavy hearts we say goodbye to a teammate . . ." or "We wish this person all the best in their future endeavours . . ."

Despite the bland email, one of my producers, Rebecca Waters, threw a going-away party for me. All the people who mattered came.

Years later, I got my answer as to why the email announcing my departure was so curt. One of the higher-ups flat out admitted he didn't want to lose me and was angry. He apologized and admitted they could've handled things better.

At the time, it stung, but in the grand scheme of life, it doesn't change at all how I feel about my time at MLSE. My journey there will always hold a special place in my heart. MLSE took a chance on me. MLSE helped me grow. I will forever be grateful to MLSE.

## CHAPTER 21

# DON

I get asked about Don a lot. Don Cherry is a polarizing character, and hockey fans, to this day, are fascinated by him.

One week on Coach's Corner, it would feel like you were being regaled with stories from your grandfather; the next, he would say something very divisive. Don never played it safe.

I was told very quickly into my *Hockey Night in Canada* days that Don didn't like distractions. He never wore an earpiece because he didn't want to hear someone in his ear. Every little sound bothered him. He needed to be completely focused on his segment. When they rehearsed Coach's Corner, everyone who wasn't needed in the studio was booted out. I had a little desk in the corner where I would prepare for my iDesk hits. One Saturday, I lost track of time and didn't realize rehearsal with Don and Ron was starting. And because the studio was so dark, no one saw me still sitting at my desk.

Once I heard Don's booming voice, I froze. Uh-oh . . . I'm stuck here. I can't move. I can't make a sound. Since I couldn't type or click on the computer mouse — yup, those sounds could be heard — I decided to just sit back and watch them do their thing. I got thirsty. No harm in opening this can of Ginger Ale, right? I'll stifle the noise with my sleeve and open it verrrrrrrry verrrrrrrry sloooooowwwwwwly. Click. *Damn, that was louder than I hoped.* Don heard it. Double damn. He gave a huff and stopped the rehearsal. The floor director yelled, "Quiet on the set! No noise!"

I slid down in my chair and tried to slink under the desk. When Don saw it was me who made the sound, he softened.

Either way, I never got stuck in the studio during rehearsal again.

Don was always very kind to me. We both shared a love for animals, and we talked about our dogs often. He once came across a budgie that needed a home, and he couldn't bear the thought of it being abandoned. He found a home for it with our makeup artist!

He also loved to talk about his first wife, Rose. She was of Italian heritage, like me, and he would always ask if my family made certain meals or had certain traditions, and he would say, "Rose would do that too!" Some nights he would look at my outfit and say, "Hey, Rose used to wear something similar." He always said this in a very nostalgic way.

Despite having a gruff aura about him, Don was friendly and approachable. I still remember him walking around on the last Saturday before Christmas, handing out candy to the entire *HNIC* crew along with gifts. I was a newbie to the team, but he still gave me a one-hundred-dollar gift card to a restaurant. I don't even spend that much on my friends!

Don has said his fair share of controversial things, and one of those times was during my *HNIC* days. In April of 2011, Chicago Blackhawks player, Duncan Keith, made a snarky comment to a female reporter after a game in the dresssing room. Many people began accusing Keith of being sexist. It prompted a ton of discourse in the media, and naturally, a debate about whether or not women should be allowed in men's dressing rooms.

Don went on Coach's Corner and gave his thoughts. One of which was that women should not be in the room.

After his segment, he came to me and said that he fully supports women working in the sports industry and thought the real idiots were the players acting foolishly around them. He didn't want women to be subjected to garbage behaviour. Don also pointed out that while he was the head coach of the Boston Bruins, he was the first coach to let a female reporter into the dressing room. Her name was Robin Herman and she was a hockey reporter for *The New York Times*. She was one of the first female journalists who was granted access to NHL dressing rooms, and Don helped make that happen.

Well, the country went bananas. I received a ton of phone calls from newspapers asking for a comment. I did one interview and said I didn't like what Don said on air, but that he did tell me afterwards what he meant, and I believed him.

The following week at work, Don made a point of coming up to me and once again reiterated how much he supported the work women did in the industry and what a big fan he was of me. I can't speak on his behalf, but based on his behaviour after that Coach's Corner rant, I think he regretted how he said things.

From my experience, older men definitely exist in the industry who aren't quick to — or flat out never will — accept women in the sports industry.

That wasn't Don; he accepted me right away.

I know there are people out there who don't want to hear how kind and accepting Don was; perhaps they don't want to believe it. I'm not telling you these parts of him because I think it will excuse or erase the other parts that have offended people. I'm simply sharing my experiences with him. Don is definitely an enigma.

On the topic of locker rooms, I'd just like to point out that I've been in many pro rooms, from hockey to basketball to soccer. The way they're set up gives players complete privacy. Yes, some of the road dressing rooms can be smaller and a tiny bit exposed. In those cases, I think every media person, male or female, should be mindful of where they stand, so players can be respected. But on the whole, if a player is getting naked in front of media, it's because he chose to, not because he has to. A lot of fans have visions of their dinky elementary or high school locker rooms when this debate comes up. And let me tell ya, pro rooms ain't dinky. Also, some people are under the impression that it's the female reporters insisting on being in the rooms. Nope. Let me share a story with you.

In 2010, Aron Winter became the head coach of Toronto FC. A former player who did some coaching in the Ajax system in the Netherlands, he grew up in the Dutch soccer world, and he had a very European approach to things — including how media was handled. In Europe, media don't go into the rooms. There are conference rooms or other mix zone areas where interviews are done. Aron decided to ban the media from the TFC room but promised to honour accessibility to the players for post-match comments. He told the players that each and every one of them had to go to the fitness room five minutes after the match ended and make themselves available. I was the only woman covering the team at the time. I loved this move. You see, in the dressing room, the players could run and hide. Often, the players would get the PR person to lie to the media and say they were on the physio table or in the shower, and then they would sneak out through a back door and duck out on everyone. But with this new system, *everyone* had to be in the fitness room. I was pinging off interviews left, right, and centre. Three guys lined up on the stationary bikes? Three interviews. Couple of guys stretching on the mat? Make that five interviews. The accessibility was the best it had ever been . . . until it wasn't. You know who complained? The men. The male reporters. They felt it was their right to be in the room. Even though we were nabbing interviews with everyone from bench players to superstars, the male reporters wanted to be in the room. Poof, my five to seven interviews after matches went down to one, maybe three if I was lucky. The hinges on that back door started squeaking as players proceeded to start sneaking out again. Thanks, guys, thanks for nothing.

So do I care about being in the locker room? Yes and no. No, because the goal is to get interviews. I need quotes I can use. I need players to be available and not run and hide in the showers and then take off through some secret door. But it some ways, yes. In my experience, a lot of the best stories I got and the best insight I got of team dynamics came from sitting next to a player in his stall, just shooting the breeze.

I guess I would say this: Whether in the locker room or a separate room, just be respectful of one another. We all have a job to do. It's a professional work environment. Behave yourselves.

I always knew Don Cherry was a superstar. My family loved tuning in to Coach's Corner. Some just wanted to see what he was wearing, and others wanted to hear his opinion on the hockey news from the week. But I didn't quite grasp the magnitude of his presence until I started working in the industry. Every Saturday night in the press box at a Leafs game, every single media member would pile into the hallway during the first intermission and crank up the volume on the TV. Whatever Don said would most likely become headline news the next day. Yes, the next day; Twitter wasn't huge yet.

But it wasn't until I joined *HNIC* that I *really* witnessed his celebrity status.

Every year, *HNIC* puts on a one-day hockey bonanza known as Hockey Day in Canada. One town from across the country is selected to host the festivities for a few days. Features are done on people in the community who have contributed to hockey, events with hockey celebrities are held, minor league hockey games between local teams are played, and it all leads to a massive day on the Saturday, which features NHL games. The *Hockey Night in Canada* talent would be on location for a few days as well. And every time Don made an appearance somewhere, he needed security. In 2014, we were in Lloydminster, Alberta, and Don was being escorted into an event by the RCMP. The fans didn't care. People pushed their arms through the human barricade just to touch him. Kids crawled on the floor between legs to get to him. I thought for sure Don was going to get crushed. But he made it to the stage safe and sound.

Other times on the road, Don stayed in his room, and Ron kept him company. I asked Ron why Don never joined us for a drink at the hotel bar. He said it's because Don knew he would attract a crowd and wouldn't be able to talk to everyone, and he didn't want to make people feel bad. Don also told me that's why he didn't really do autograph sessions. He knew that if he agreed to sign things and take pictures with fans during a certain time limit, inevitably people would leave empty-handed: "You see, Andi, if they say I'm signin' things from two to four, and there's still people lined up after four . . . What happens to them? I don't like that, you see. No one should be turned away. So, if I'm showin' up, I'm signin' till the line is done."

I remember exactly where I was when I heard the news about Don's Remembrance Day rant. I was in Seattle for the MLS Cup Final. Twitter blew up when he commented that people don't wear poppies anymore, and more importantly, he seemed to blame the lack of poppies he saw on newcomers to Canada who didn't respect the sacrifices of our veterans. I knew he wasn't going to come back from this controversy. We all know

Don has immense admiration for our veterans and for those who have lost their lives protecting our freedoms. Don is a proud Canadian. In fact, he got angry with me one night when he asked if I could identify all the provincial flags, and I said I couldn't. (I can now.)

Sometimes I wonder, as with the women in the dressing room comment, if he wishes he had said things differently . . .

*CHAPTER 22*

# THEY WEREN'T SUPPOSED TO KNOW ABOUT THE NEW HOTEL

We've all seen footage of fans going crazy for athletes. When I watched the documentary about legendary Argentine soccer player Diego Maradona, I felt claustrophobic on his behalf. When he joined Italian team SSC Napoli, the poor guy couldn't go anywhere without a crowd around him, completely suffocating his space. A current Argentine great, Lionel Messi, was hounded by crazed fans during the 2024 Copa America. People who booked rooms in the same hotel as the team posted footage of themselves on social media, watching through the peepholes of their doors for Messi to exit his room, and when he did, they flooded the hallway. How frightening for Messi. No space. No peace.

There have been two occasions where I have witnessed people acting crazy, hysterical, even primitive-like, when it comes to celebrities in the sports world.

And yes, I know all about the craziness that followed David Beckham and Wayne Rooney; I watched the documentaries. But I'm talking about my own personal encounters.

I mentioned one earlier when it came to Don Cherry. People — grown men — losing all sense of decorum just to shake his hand.

The other was when Cristiano Ronaldo, the prolific goal scorer from Portugal, came to town.

Toronto FC scheduled a friendly against Real Madrid in August of 2009. MLSE spent over $200,000 installing natural grass for one friendly because there was no way superstars like Ronaldo, Kaká, Karim Benzema, Arjen Robben, and company were going to play on turf.

The day before, I was scheduled to attend a private party with the players, special guests, and Spanish soccer dignitaries to grab some interviews. GolTV, the network owned by MLSE, held the broadcasting rights to the game, and we were told in confidence that the hotel everyone thought the team would be staying at was not the actual one. They did this to reduce the crowds that would hound the players and cause a security nightmare. They made this announcement to us while Real Madrid was mid-flight. They said they waited till the last minute to tell us of the change to minimize any chance of the news getting out. We didn't say a word. We kept the hotel information quiet. But apparently, there are moles everywhere.

Clearly, someone in the know informed someone else, who then informed others, because by the time my camera guy and I arrived at the supposed "secret" hotel, the place was mobbed. I'm talking hotel staff scared to bits as mobs of people stormed the lobby and were spilling out onto the streets. There was not enough security to deal with the amount of people storming through the doors.

We were supposed to get shots of the arrival of the team's bus, but we were getting jostled around by the mob. Security's priority was definitely not to protect the media; they had the team to worry about. When the players arrived, all I could see were people reaching out and grabbing Ronaldo. Random people just touching another human being without his permission. I was dumbfounded. This type of fandom is insane to me. Ronaldo maintained his composure. He had to, or he would've been crushed.

I still can't believe what I saw. Grown men losing all self-control just to sniff Ronaldo or brush up against his sleeve.

I'm all for fandom but not when it makes you act wild like that. For example, I'm a huge Aerosmith fan. When I was ten years old and watching MuchMusic, the video for "Love in an Elevator" came on. I was mesmerized by the dude with long hair wearing a unitard with flames along the side, wailing away. I've loved Steven Tyler ever since. I've seen the band live in concert three times. One time was in Toronto at the

Scotiabank Arena. A friend of mine knew one of the security guards working the event and managed to get us in front of the part of the stage that juts out into a runway. At one point, Tyler planted his foot right in front of my face as he was belting out a tune. My girlfriend, knowing how much I loved this guy, yelled out, "Grab his leg!"

The very thought of doing that was so alien to me. *Touch someone without their permission? Why? That's so weird.*

I was quite content staring at him, completely awestruck.

But these Ronaldo fans didn't think anything was weird or wrong about wrapping their arms around him or grabbing his face and kissing him on the cheek.

The private room where the party was being held before the players made their way to BMO Field for an open practice was far more civil. Although some women who were convinced they were Ronaldo's future wife did manage to sneak in, they were far easier for security to contain and remove.

I was already given the heads up that Ronaldo was doing a bunch of photoshoots and might not be up to doing a sit-down, but I could approach him if I wanted to.

Unfortunately, his shoots and autograph signings went longer than expected. But when I walked up to him, he was very kind when apologizing and saying he didn't have time. His response caught me off guard. He spoke English with a Portuguese accent but used the vernacular of a British person. After all, he had spent over five years with Manchester United.

Almost twenty thousand people packed the stadium for the open practice. The next night, over twenty-two thousand showed up for the game. Back in 2009, that was a big deal for Toronto FC.

The Reds were down 3–0 at halftime, and I interviewed TFC defender Adrian Serioux. He was sucking in air big-time, and I said something like, "What's it like out there trying to defend against that kind of fire power?"

He looked at me wide-eyed and said, "I'm dying. Does that answer your question?"

Toronto ended up losing 5–1, but it was such a dynamic night for so many soccer fans in the city. I had the chance to interview Brazilian great Kaká, and I was pretty excited. I think I asked him what he thought about playing in front of such a big crowd. I cringe now just thinking about it.

This guy was used to playing in front of close to a hundred thousand people in one game, but I was wrapped up in the moment. Like I said, over twenty-two thousand was a big deal for a Toronto soccer club back in 2009.

It was such an awesome night. But man, I'll never forget how scary it was at the hotel with all those crazed fans trying to get a piece of Ronaldo.

## CHAPTER 23

# WHAT KIND OF FEATURE?

On October 5, 2022, I was honoured to be on the panel of the inaugural Spark Summit. It was an event hosted by Canadian Premier League side Forge FC. The event was held at Tim Hortons Field before a match, and it connected professional women in the sports industry with other women aspiring to make the leap into the sports world.

A lot of great questions were asked, and thoughtful conversations about personal experiences were had. One woman inquired of the panel if any of us had ever been asked to do something by our bosses that would otherwise not have been asked if we weren't women. Nothing came to mind. I said no. Being treated differently at times because of gender, sure, but asked to do something beneath me strictly because I'm a woman? Nope.

And then, the next day . . . it hit me.

I don't know why I didn't remember this story at the time. Genuinely forgot? Getting old? Or did I manage to lock it up in that dungeon-like room in my brain along with other shocking memories? I never wanted those types of experiences to get in my way, and I definitely never wanted them to become a crutch that would slow me down . . . or worse . . . make me quit.

So, to the woman who asked that question: I'm sorry I didn't remember on the spot. You're not alone. Here's the answer I should've given.

*Hockey Night in Canada* was in its final season: 2013–14.

It was such an odd time. We all knew there was a very good chance the CBC was losing the NHL rights, but we were also excited and in full "go-time" mode, getting ready for the Sochi 2014 Olympics. As it would turn out, we would be in Sochi when the news broke that we had, in fact, lost the hockey rights.

I knew I was going to be an Olympic host. I had been informed I would be hosting the overnight show with CBC news anchor Andrew Chang. I also knew that I would be a host during the 2014 FIFA World Cup.

With all this in mind, I wasn't satisfied with my iDesk role on *HNIC*. I wanted to do more. I knew I could do more. But our leadership was in flux. Nobody wanted, or perhaps had the motivation, to do anything different. Everyone figured they'd be out of a job soon. It was such a strange feeling. I truly know what being in limbo feels like.

I really wanted to do features with players. I had done them during my years with Leafs TV. The segment was called Xtreme Close-Up with Andi P, and I had done fun things with Toronto Maple Leafs players. They weren't meant to be serious. They were meant to show the players' fun sides. I did yoga with WWE Hall of Famer Trish Stratus and brought Luke Schenn and Garnet Exelby with me. I went to the Ontario Science Centre with Jeff Finger, and we went head-to-head in all the cool challenges they had on the sports floor. I did a scuba diving lesson with Wade Belak and went to the World of Coca-Cola museum in Atlanta with Ian White.

One of my favourites was touring the Harvard Campus with Dominic Moore. He attended university there and played hockey for the school. It hadn't occurred to me to call the school ahead of time to receive permission to shoot on school grounds; I just assumed it was a public space. After a while, we were approached by campus security. They were off-duty cops with very thick Bostonian accents. When I told them what we were doing, their demeanour totally changed. "Dam Moore! Love ya, man! Great hawkey player. I tell ya what. We'll take ya around campus. Where'd ya wanna go?"

*Seriously?* I couldn't believe our luck. I thought we were going to get escorted off campus with an accompanying swift kick in the arse, but Dom's reputation saved us.

"Well," I said, "I'd love to be able to get inside the Harvard hockey locker room and onto the ice if possible?"

"No problem. Hop in the caw."

We finished off the feature with me interviewing Dom at centre ice. It was pretty cool.

Fast-forward a few years, I'm now with *HNIC*, and I wanted to bring these types of features back. I kept asking one of the executive producers to give me a chance to put a feature together.

At the time, the digital space was becoming a thing. It was a place where we could drive viewers to watch full features and read lengthy articles. During the broadcast, we would air a thirty-second teaser and then promote the full piece on cbcsports.ca.

I was finally given the green light to do something.

Next day at Leafs practice, I approached the newest member: David Clarkson. A hometown boy getting to play for the team he grew up idolizing.

Clarkson was awesome. I always try to be as efficient as possible with athletes; I never want to take up too much of their time. And for this feature, I knew I needed to be on the ball. We were visiting three locations in the Etobicoke, Ontario, area: the outdoor rink he played on, the school he went to, and finally the adult watering hole he liked to frequent.

Clarkson never made me or my crew feel like we had to rush. In fact, when we were done shooting, he was the one who wanted to continue hanging out and bought us all a round!

The feature turned out great. We played about a minute of it during my iDesk segment and then promoted the full feature on the website. The digital department was happy about that too.

The exec who had finally given permission to go ahead with the idea was also ecstatic.

Sometimes, you have to keep pushing to show someone what you're envisioning. Once it comes to life, let your hard work do the talking.

I was feeling pretty good about myself. *Perhaps this could become a regular occurrence*, I thought. I wanted to be more than the person who reads highlights every Saturday. Plus, if these features were a hit, then maybe I could do more for the Sochi Olympics!

The exec pulled me aside in the hallway the following week after the feature aired.

He said it was getting a great response, and he would, in fact, like me to do more.

"Excellent! So exciting," I responded. Mission accomplished. But then . . .

He asked, in a very serious tone, "Have you ever thought about doing these features with you and a player in a hot tub?"

Pause . . .

Silence . . .

Did I blink? I don't think so.

Did my heart stop? I think I was suspended in time.

I waited for the punch line . . . he had to be joking, right?

It didn't come.

By now, he realized he had shocked me, but instead of backtracking, he doubled down.

"Well, you see," he said, "I used to work at a music network, and we would always have hosts doing interviews in a hot tub. Huge success."

"Um, yeah," I responded, "that's the music industry. This is sports. Ain't gonna fly."

"Why don't you think about it?" he urged.

"I did think about it," I said. "Answer is no."

He pushed a little more and said it would be good for ratings. I mean, I guess I shouldn't be that surprised. This was the same exec who would text me on Friday nights and ask what I would be wearing on the Saturday broadcast.

I called my producer of the iDesk and told him what had just happened. He couldn't believe it.

"Are you sure you heard him correctly?"

"Um, yeah. I understood him perfectly. I know when someone's serious and when someone's joking. Horrible joke if it was the latter."

"Ok, I have a meeting with him in a few days to discuss this weekend's show. Let me see if he says anything."

A few days later, I get a call from my iDesk producer.

"I can't believe it," he said. "I just got out of a meeting with the exec talking about this weekend's show, and he pulled me aside and told me I should try and convince you of this idea he has about you doing interviews in a hot tub. He was dead serious. I told him there was no way I would do that. This guy is nuts."

We all knew there was no way I would've been asked to jump into a hot tub with athletes if I were a man. This ask was strictly because I was a woman.

But just to be sure. To be really sure . . . I went to Elliotte Friedman. He was doing a lot of sit-down interviews with players . . . features if you will. So, I asked if he had been approached by this exec and asked to don a Speedo and get in a hot tub? After having a good chuckle, he wanted to know why I would ask such a foolish thing. I told him. He was mortified.

I'm not sure if someone had a word with the exec or if he finally came to his senses, but he never asked me about getting into a hot tub again.

Sadly, that year, I didn't do another feature, despite the success of the first one.

Thankfully, that exec was let go. There were and continue to be incredible bosses at CBC. They became aware of his antics and acted accordingly. Like I said, it was a weird time at the network with nobody really wanting to be there because of the loss of hockey. Some strange hires were made to fill positions that real industry people weren't interested in.

Sometimes, I joke about that hot tub request. I can do so because I stood my ground when I said no and had the support of other people. Having support from co-workers and other executives is crucial because feeling alone can be so defeating. But I know there are other women who have been, and continue to be, pressured into doing certain things their male counterparts would never be asked to do. It's heartbreaking and it can be crushing to a woman's confidence; not to mention, it can force her to leave an industry she loves altogether.

So, to the woman at the Spark Summit: I empathize with your experience. And the more we talk about women being asked to show more skin, flirt, or do things men are not expected to do, the more we can hopefully stop this practice.

I've been at the CBC for close to fifteen years, and I've stayed because I love the people and the work we do. Nobody covers Canadian athletes representing the Maple Leaf the way we do: at the Olympics, at world championships, and in all the in-between years when they're competing on their respective sports circuits.

Behind the scenes, I've had some great producers as well.

For my first Olympics in Sochi, a woman named Karen Sebesta produced me; she's a force of a woman. She worked in the trucks during the early days of *Hockey Night in Canada* and had to deal with a lot of crap as a woman. She's shared some stories with me that have left me speechless.

She produced me once again for the Tokyo 2020 Olympics, and then she retired. Sebby was organized, Sebby knew her stuff, and Sebby stood her ground. I feel lucky to have worked alongside her for the time that I did.

Another producer who challenges me to this day is Sherali Najak. I first met Sherali during my Leafs TV days while he was producing *HNIC*. Right away, he became a mentor and was a huge reason why I made the move to CBC.

Before any of my on-air hits, we would spend forever going over the content. It doesn't matter if it's a thirty-second read or three minutes, Sherali always wants to strike the right chord with the viewers and set the perfect tone. He's very creative, and there's always pomp and circumstance around everything he does. When he became the executive producer of the Olympics at CBC, everything felt bigger than life. For Paris 2024, the set was huge, the support staff was incredible, the resources were robust, and inclusivity was at the forefront of everything he did. But with all that grandness comes expectations. Sherali does his part behind the scenes, and now it's my turn to deliver in front of the camera. When you see someone like him work as hard as he does, you want to repay him with a solid performance. Working with Sherali truly is a collaborative team effort.

There are so many other great people at the CBC, and they are a huge reason why I love going to work.

Sunil Thakolkaren was one of the first producers I worked with when I joined the CBC family. I was so green, but we had a great working relationship that continues to this day. It couldn't have been easy for him working with a rookie on a big show, but he displayed a lot of patience with me. I've heard horror stories from other talent about their early days in the industry and how they were yelled at and belittled by producers who weren't willing to help them grow. Thank goodness Sunny isn't that kind of human.

Mike Dodson has been one of my main producers for years, and there's a great trust that has developed over that time. He was my producer during the 2015 Pan American Games, and during one show, we were close to signing off, but we had just received some baseball highlights. There was no time to review them or even write a script for them. They had to get to air pronto before the show ended.

Doddy piped into my ear: "Ok, you're going to have to trust me. I'm going to say the highlights to you. The score, the inning, who the player is, and what's happening. Just repeat after me and then add your own flair, ok?"

"Oh boy, I don't know about this, Doddy."

"Just trust me. You have to. I'm coming to you in twenty seconds!"

Doddy gave me the stats I needed to know, and then I reacted to what I saw. We were flying by the seat of our pants. You have to remember these weren't MLB highlights. There were no graphics on the video feed that could give us the information we needed, and the players weren't well-known MLB names. Not easy, but we did it!

That's how trust between a host and producer works.

It's very rare in this industry that you'll work with just one or even a few producers. Yes, there will be ones with whom you'll work better. You'll be able to finish each other's sentences. And those are the best kinds of TV relationships. There's nothing scarier for a host going live to millions than having a producer who hangs you out to dry. I call producers "The Mother Ship." They are the connection between you and the entire show. I've had many things go wrong during live broadcasts, but I've always navigated through the problems with my producer. However, if I lose contact with my producer, then it's time to panic!

Working at *Hockey Night in Canada* was a dream come true. It's still wild to think I was just the fifth woman to become part of this legendary show, but it also explains a lot of the hate I received. I know it was because of my gender because the online attackers literally would say things like, "Why is there a woman telling me about hockey on *HNIC*?"

But thankfully, as I mentioned earlier, I worked with incredible people who always had my back.

Elliotte Friedman, PJ Stock, Kevin Weekes, and Kelly Hrudey were so easy to deal with and immediately treated me like one of the team.

Ron MacLean answered any question I had and treated me with respect. In fact, whenever panel discussions during intermissions were starting to go too long, Ron would cut things short and get to the iDesk, the segment I hosted, because he wanted to make sure my on-air time was protected. He wasn't always successful — those guys could talk!

But do you know what? I can't remember my first rinkside assignment for *HNIC*. I know it was in my first year with the show — 2011–12 — and I know it was a Toronto Maple Leafs home game. But for the life of me, I can't remember the opponent or who I interviewed that night. I do remember standing in position for the start of the show, the iconic opening soundtrack playing in my ear, hearing Ron's voice, and a few minutes later, he threw to me. No clue what I said. I hadn't been that nervous since my first stand-up at Rogers Cable! Seriously, my knees were knocking.

But if I'm honest, pissing off the knuckle-draggers out there made me feel warm and fuzzy inside. So, although there was a lot going on in my head that night, and that's why it remains a blur, I'm ok with it. In my head it was a magical night . . . why ruin it with facts?

During my time at *HNIC*, I also had the chance to work with some great hockey people during the playoffs. We would often bring in players or coaches who had been eliminated from the playoffs and use them as analysts.

Marty Brodeur was one of them. It's already been established that I'm a goalie-hugger, so hearing him talk about the game and how he was seeing things unfold was pretty cool. He's also really funny. Marty was a lot of fun to work with.

Adam Oates and Barry Trotz were two other guys we used. They both hated being in their hotel rooms, so they would come to the studio early. I was always the first to arrive because I had the early makeup call — I was the rookie — so they were stuck talking to me. But we had some great conversations. Oates loved breaking down a player's game — right down to his head movement. Oates had been David Clarkson's coach in New Jersey; the player was now in Toronto, and Oates went through, detail for detail, Clarkson's role in New Jersey vs. Toronto and how that affected his play. I loved having those hockey chats. It doesn't surprise me that Adam went on to start his own hockey skills business. A lot of NHL players spend their offseason training with him. I can't tell you how many times some men in the industry get all funny around women and don't know how to just talk hockey with a woman. Adam Oates and Barry Trotz didn't have that problem. It was refreshing.

At the time that we had Barry on *HNIC*, he was the head coach of the Nashville Predators. He was the franchise's first coach, and he was pretty open with us about how devastating it was for him not to get to a Stanley Cup Final with the team. He loved Nashville and sang its praises. I can't imagine it's easy to help build a team from scratch, especially one that's in a non-traditional hockey market. I didn't quite know what to expect when I covered a game in Nashville for the first time. When the team got their first power play, I was taken by surprise when all the fans around me started yelling "Fang Fingers!" and raised their index and middle fingers on both hands in the air. I didn't know what I liked more: the Fang Fingers in Nashville or the two Thrasher bird heads in Atlanta that would spit fire after every home goal. Both were very entertaining.

Barry was also very motivational. When the playoffs were done, he gifted us each a book: *Fearless* by Eric Blehm. He said he gave that book to his players during training camp as well. He wanted us to know what hard work and sacrifice were really about and use it to motivate ourselves. I highly recommend the book.

When Barry Trotz finally became a Stanley Cup champion, it was as the head coach of the Washington Capitals in 2018. A very kind man who deserved that great Cup.

This industry can be incredibly rewarding; you meet amazing people and have wonderful experiences. Unfortunately, bad apples still exist. And yes, they will single you out simply because you are a woman. A lot of gaslighting goes on, but when you're asked to don a bikini and get in a hot tub with athletes, there's no denying why you were chosen and not your male counterpart.

I'm not going to tell you that if you stand your ground, there won't be any negative consequences; I'm not going to tell you that many of your co-workers will come to your aid and support you — everyone's situation and outcome are different. I can only hope that by talking more about these sexist actions that still exist, we can shine a bright light on them and not allow them to function in the shadows anymore. The more women who share their stories, the more awareness there will be, the more support will be garnered, and the stronger we will feel.

Don't let the bad apples spoil the abundance of fruit this industry has to offer.

## CHAPTER 24

# GOLD MEDAL CALL

The Sochi Olympics were my first as an Olympic host. There was so much I didn't know about the job, and no matter how much I tried to prepare, I simply didn't know what information was worth knowing, which sports and which athletes I should pay attention to, which historical facts were important, and which stories people wanted to hear.

It was overwhelming.

One Saturday night before going to air with our *HNIC* broadcast, I scheduled some time with Ron MacLean to pick his brain about what it took to be a great Olympic host. His main message to me was that part of this gig is learning on the fly. And once you find your style, you'll get into a rhythm and know what to do.

At the time, I was a little disappointed with that advice. I wanted him to give me a very detailed approach to being an Olympic host. I wanted him to script out how my day would look and the information I needed to seek out. Only later would I come to appreciate his encouragement to find my own Olympic voice. I also quickly learned while in Sochi that there is no etched-in-stone playbook when it comes to hosting the Games.

I also reached out to Scott Russell. He gave similar advice but added, "Andi, remember this: the Olympics are a marathon, not a sprint. Get sleep where you can, eat regularly, and allow your mind to take a break for a little while every day from the Games. If you don't do the above, you'll burn out and the experience won't be a good one."

Sleep, eat, chill . . . seems simple enough, right? Wrong. It was only when I got to Sochi and got into the thick of things that I realized how tough it was to sleep — there is so much stress; how tough it was to stick to a regular diet and not starve — it was too easy to become distracted by work; and how tough it was to calm my mind and not be on high alert all the time — I didn't want to miss any of the action!

In Sochi, I was hosting the overnight show in Canada. My schedule went like this: wake up at 4 a.m., catch the 4:30 media bus to the studio, get my makeup done, have breakfast, do a hit into Ron's show at 8:30 and be on air for my show from 9 a.m. to 3 p.m., have lunch, do some prep work for the next day, try and catch some sports live, try to fall asleep by 8 p.m.

Some days, I stuck to the schedule. But most days, I barely ate and barely slept. About a few days into covering the Games, I was already emotionally and physically exhausted. One day, I got back to my hotel room, sat at the foot of the bed, leaned back with my arms spread out to the side and my feet dangling over the end, and fell asleep fully clothed. The cleaning service usually showed up to clean my room around 4 p.m., and the poor woman, upon finding me, clearly thought I was dead because I woke up to her ear in my face as she was trying to see if I was breathing.

But man, I was having a blast. What an incredible rush it is to be at the Olympics. With all the different time zones around the world, there was always a constant buzz everywhere because people were reporting and hosting shows at all times of the day and night. I eventually got into a groove. I would make my way down to the hotel lobby at 4:30 a.m. to catch the bus to the studio, and the lobby bar was rocking. People were coming back from their shifts just as mine was getting started. It was easy to tell which country other media were from because the jackets we wore bore the colours and symbols of our nations. And that led to a lot of people wishing each other luck when they knew an athlete from that media member's country was competing. One morning, I had quite a few people yell out to me, "Good luck, Canada!" when Mark McMorris was one of the first Canadians to compete in the new Olympic sport, snowboard slopestyle.

And then I had a really cool experience when I decided to attend the medal ceremony for Charles Hamelin, short track speed skater, who had won gold in the 1500m. I was recording the national anthem and watching the Canadian flag rise into the night sky, and I hadn't noticed a circle forming around me. When the anthem was over, everyone started applauding . . . me! Congratulating . . . me! As weird and embarrassing as that moment was at first, it did fill me with pride. My jacket told everyone I was from Canada. And yes, media is supposed to be impartial, but c'mon, it's the Olympics, baby! I will always work hard to tell the story of every deserving athlete, no matter which country they're from. But allow me to lay my cards on the table right now . . . I will always care about the Canadian athlete. My heart breaks when theirs breaks on the biggest stage of their career. And my heart sings when they sore in front of the entire world.

And that leads me to one of the coolest honours of my career.

We were nine days into our coverage when I received a call from CBC's executive producer of the Olympics, Chris Irwin. The Canadian women's hockey team had made it to the semifinals. They were taking on Switzerland. Along with the television coverage they had been receiving, the network wanted to broadcast the game on the radio as well across all CBC's channels. Chris said he knew he was calling me short-noticed, but he wanted me to do the colour commentary for the game, which was the next day.

I didn't even hesitate. "Yes!"

If there's one thing I've never suffered from, it's imposter syndrome. It's a real thing, and I've seen others struggle with it, but I've always believed I was right for a job. And if I'm not completely ready to take on a new task, I have no problem learning on the fly. I never turn down something I want. You can call me impulsive, you can call me presumptuous, you can call me over-ambitious, but don't ever accuse me of not going after what I want or jumping at the chance to do something amazing.

Now, in this particular case, I wouldn't say my confidence made me say yes — I would say the lack of sleep did. I know this because the first words out of my mouth when I hung up the phone were, "Oh shit."

My bedtime was 8 p.m. — the semifinal game started at 9 p.m. I had never done colour before. I had a lot of studying to do on all the players.

I needed to know their bios by the next day while still preparing for my own Olympic show.

Oh shit was right.

I had hosted plenty of hockey panels up to that point, but anyone will tell you that hosting, play-by-play, and colour commentary are unique in their own way and require different skill sets.

February 17, 2014. I finished my show and then sat down to continue my hockey notes. Glenn Healy, former NHL goalie, approached me and said, "So, kid, I hear you're doing colour for the game. You ok if I give you some pointers?"

*Would I be ok? Ah, yes, yes, please. I need all the help I can get!* I hadn't asked for his help because I didn't want to bother him. Everyone's cup is filled to the brim while working the Olympics, so to have him approach me on his own meant a lot.

Heals was amazing. He walked me through the role of being an analyst. Why was that play good? Bad? Why is that player special? He told me when to lay out and let the crowd noise take over and when to raise my voice with excitement.

"Follow the lead of your play-by-play person," he said. "They're calling all the action, and you have to complement them."

That play-by-play person was none other than the great Steve Armitage. After my lesson with Heals, I sat down with Army.

"Don't worry, Andi. I got you. All I ask is that you take my cues. I raise my hand after a play. That means it's your turn to talk. When I raise it again, it means wrap it up."

When we arrived at the Bolshoy Ice Dome, I was so nervous I thought I was going to puke. Army and I walked by the NBC booth where Doc Emrick and former player for the US women's national team A.J. Mleczko were getting ready for their broadcast. We chatted for a bit, and I blurted out, "I've never done this before, and I think I'm going to pass out!"

Doc chuckled and asked if I knew the game.

"Of course I do," I said.

"Then you'll be just fine," he responded.

A.J. said, "You'll be great, just let your passion shine."

Simple words from both of them, but they meant the world. I slowly started to catch my breath.

Canada went on to win 3–1. The Canadians scored all three of their goals in the first period, so after a frenzied start to the game, I was able to find my groove the rest of the way. Army and I made a good team.

The network thought so too. They asked if I would do it again for the gold medal game: Canada vs. America.

Of course I would.

Despite getting only two hours of sleep after that semifinal game because I had to do my show the next day, I was walking on cloud nine. What an amazing experience, and now I was going to call the gold medal game!

I hadn't told any family about the semifinal call; I was too nervous and wasn't sure how it would go. But this time I emailed my mom, and I told her to tell the entire *famiglia* about the final game — that's not a problem for an Italian woman.

February 20, 2014. It was another 9 p.m. start. The storyline heading into the gold medal game was that it was America's time. The American women won the inaugural Olympic gold in 1998, but since then, the Canadians had won every edition. But the Americans were strong; actually, they were stacked. They were led by Meghan Duggan and Hilary Knight; making their Olympic debuts were Alex Carpenter, Kendall Coyne, and Amanda Kessel. That team was scary. But in the group stage, Canada defeated them 3–2. However, every crazy sports nut, myself included, hated that stat. It's this weird, twisted belief that the Canadians "used up" their win in pool play, and now when it matters, the Americans would come out on top.

I know it sounds crazy, but trust me when I say every sport has a similar feeling. Four-time world figure skating champion Kurt Browning once told me that skaters get nervous if they skate a perfect routine in practice during a competition. They have this belief that they "used up" their best performance in training.

The tension between the two teams was palpable right from the first puck drop. Five penalties were called in the first period. No score. Army and I settled into a good rhythm.

Second period, the Americans scored first courtesy of their captain, Duggan. The Canadians couldn't get anything past their goalie, Jessie Vetter.

Third period. The Americans scored two minutes in. Ugh, devastating. In the press area, American journalists were starting to shake each other's hands in a congratulatory way. They felt their team was finally about to end their gold medal drought. I saw all this going on around me but kept my composure on the air. I also felt I kept up my professionalism as well. A lesson I learned that night is that when calling a game, you have to keep your energy up. You have to give the game the justice it deserves, even though "your" team is losing. Plus, it ain't over until the final buzzer.

Time started to tick away. Ten minutes left in the game, and it was still 2–0 USA. Five minutes left in the game, and it was still 2–0 USA. Many Canadians started leaving the arena. The high-fives by Americans to one another increased.

And then, with three minutes and twenty-six seconds left, Brianne Jenner scored for Canada. There's life. Army, instead of lifting his hand to give me the signal to start talking, whacked my arm in excitement. When he wanted me to stop, he whacked it again.

Canadian goalie Shannon Szabados was pulled for the extra attacker. The Americans won a face-off in their zone and sent the puck towards the empty net. The puck missed the net by inches — nay, millimetres! In fact, it hit the post and stayed out. The rink erupted, Army whacked my arm again, I said something, he whacked it to get me to stop.

With fifty-five seconds left to go, Marie-Philip Poulin, who we now have come to know as "Captain Clutch," got the equalizer. The game was going to overtime! I felt like I was having an out-of-body experience. The throbbing in my whacked arm brought me back to reality, however. I sent a text to David Amber, who was hosting the morning Olympic show in Sochi and happened to be one of the people who left early. He couldn't bear to watch Canada lose, so he left with less than ten minutes to go, and he couldn't believe what I was texting him. Canada tied it up. The big man turned around and sprinted through the park to get back to the rink. I feel sorry for anyone who may have gotten in his way!

Overtime. Just over eight minutes in, it was Poulin again. Canada's hero. Poulin got the golden goal, and the Canadian women were Olympic champions. I didn't care how many times Army hit my arm because I was smacking his by then too! It was our turn to get excited in the press box. What an honour to call that game. To this day, I've never had the chance to listen back to that call. I just hope I didn't blow out anyone's eardrums with all the screaming I did.

My mom told me everyone back home listened. My dad was at work that day. His environment as an ironworker could get pretty loud. So, he told his co-workers not to bug him for a few hours as he sat in a separate room listening to my analysis on the radio.

I doubt I'll ever do colour commentary again. But that's ok. I don't think anything could live up to that game.

## CHAPTER 25

# FIRED TWICE IN ONE YEAR

You say *not renewed*. I say *fired*.

Whatever you want to call it, I was dumped on my ass twice in one year.

I remember sharing my ordeal with some younger broadcasters who looked at my career and just assumed it was always smooth sailing for me.

Yeah, right. In this industry, it's always choppy waters.

When I took the job with *Hockey Night in Canada* in 2011, I had a lot of people telling me I was making a big mistake. Everyone was hearing the rumours that CBC was going to lose the NHL rights. The broadcast rights were up in 2014, and they said I would be leaving MLSE for another job that would only last three years.

TSN sports broadcaster and friend James Duthie was my voice of reason. I called him up and said my emotions were all over the place. I had just been offered my dream job, I had just lost a good friend, and now I was being told by some in the industry that accepting a job with *Hockey Night in Canada*, a legendary sports show in this country, was a mistake.

Duthie put it like this: "Let's say everyone is right and it will all be over in three years. You need to use these three years to show everyone who you are, what you're capable of doing, and make connections in this industry. And Andi, how many people can put *Hockey Night in Canada* down on their resume? Not to mention, nothing is guaranteed in this industry. You can't say, 'It will be over in three years, so what's the point?' Trust me, you can accomplish a lot in that time."

On so many fronts, he was right. Especially about no guarantees. As many of you know, shortly after Rogers and Bell became majority owners of the Toronto Maple Leafs, Leafs TV didn't stand a chance going up against the hockey programming on Sportsnet and TSN. Leafs TV downsized big-time and eventually folded.

Duthie made me feel better about my choice. I joined the CBC family and have never regretted it.

September 2012, just a year after I joined *HNIC*, the NHL went on hold. Depending on who you talk to, the league locked the players out; others will say the players went on strike. I simply call it another frustrating year.

When they had lost the entire 2004–05 season, I was ticked off as a fan and as an aspiring broadcaster. Here I was, trying to get a job in hockey, and hockey had disappeared. I felt like my career was being put on hold.

It's a sensitive topic for many players at that time. One of my colleagues at TSN, Mike Johnson, still gets a nervous twitch when you bring up the '04–'05 lockout. I lost a year of trying to advance my career — he lost a year of playing and definitely a lot of money.

But the 2012–13 year ended up being a crucial one for my broadcasting development. I didn't know it at the time because the benefits would be felt a few years later.

With no hockey being played, I was sent to the CBC Sports department to cover high performance sports. CBC had lost the Olympic rights to CTV for the 2010 and 2012 Games, but Scott Russell still hosted a weekend show on the network that covered all these other niche sports and the Canadian athletes who competed in them. I became a reporter on that show. I was covering sports like cross-country skiing, biathlon, and alpine skiing. This was such a foreign sports world to me.

I came from covering major league professional sports: NHL, NBA, MLS. Anytime I needed information on anything, it was easy to find.

Have you ever tried finding info on Finland's top biathlete?

Or the Chinese diving team?

Or even Canada's own athletes who compete in rugby sevens?

The websites for these sports are atrocious, and there aren't enough reporters who cover these events on a regular basis for decent articles with any kind of information. But of course, come Olympics time, everyone wants to know about all the sports and the stars who compete in them.

That's why CBC Sports continues to have a vested interest in telling these stories. No one else in Canada is doing it the way CBC Sports does. We have a saying at the network: We don't want Canada meeting Canadian Olympians for the first time at the Olympics; we want to share their stories all year round.

I became a part of that sports division for a few months during the lockout. I learned so much. When the lockout ended, I was back on hockey.

Fast-forward to 2014, and the Olympics were back on CBC.

I told my boss at the time, Trevor Pilling, that I wanted to be a part of the Olympic hockey coverage in Sochi, Russia.

I'm a firm believer in telling people what I want. How else are they supposed to know? They can't read my mind. If you don't tell people what you want, then you don't put them in a position to help you.

Trevor shocked me when he said, "I see your role being much bigger than just a hockey reporter. I want you to host an Olympic show."

Excuse me?

My heart was racing. As a kid, I remember Terry Leibel popping up on my TV and being totally mesmerized by a woman hosting the Olympics. I wanted to be her.

When I met her for the first time in 2019, I was a complete fan girl around her, and I have zero regrets. There's a saying, Don't meet your heroes. That didn't apply here. She was everything I hoped she'd be. Kind, funny, engaging, and just wonderful.

Trevor believed I could host a show because he saw how quickly I adapted to covering high performance sports during the hockey lockout. I didn't realize it at the time, but the bosses were taking notice of how willing I was to immerse myself in the world of high performance sports.

And then, the dreaded news came. The news I was warned about in 2011. While we were in Sochi and locked into our Olympic grind, CBC lost the hockey rights. *Hockey Night in Canada* was dead. More than sixty years of tradition, gone.

A lot of cuts were made to CBC Sports. I was a freelance worker, so it was easy to simply not renew my contract. I had hosted the 2014 Sochi Winter Olympics. I had hosted the 2014 FIFA World Cup Brazil.

I had an exceptional year in my professional career, and yet, I was dumped. CBC couldn't afford to bring me back. It was over.

Rogers had informed me I wasn't part of their plans. So, while hosting the World Cup, I was also job searching. Not an ideal situation to be in.

I was so emotionally drained. The panic of being out of work was compounded by the loss of my precious Lola, who passed away two weeks before the start of the FIFA World Cup.

But I had to pull myself together. This was the greatest tournament in soccer, and I was about to host it. Another incredible experience for me, even though I wasn't able to fully appreciate it at the time; I was walking around in a haze.

I had a few days off during the tournament after the Round of 16, and NESN flew me out to Boston for an interview. I have American sportscaster Kathryn Tappen to thank for that. She reached out when she heard the Rogers news and immediately put me in contact with some of her old colleagues. I had only met her a few times but knew instantly she was salt-of-the-earth kind of people.

The audition went great. My flight home did not. I was already taking a risk leaving the country in the middle of hosting a major sporting event, but I needed to think about my future. Everything was timed perfectly: fly in for the audition, stay the night, have a wonderful dinner with Sarah Davis, who was still working for NESN before making the move to TSN, fly out the next morning, be back in the host chair for the quarterfinals. Except . . . my flight got cancelled. Damn it. I scrambled hard and managed to get on a later flight. Crisis averted. No one knew I had flown out of the country. But that was an anxiety-filled scare I did not need.

Then, my friend Kevin Weekes made some phone calls at the NHL Network on my behalf. He and I had hit it off during our time together on *HNIC*. Weekesy has a very big heart.

You really do see people's true colours when shit hits the fan.

I'm forever grateful to Weekesy and KT for going out of their way to help me. Even a simple phone call makes all the difference.

It was during this time that Mark Milliere, executive producer of TSN, called me. We met for lunch, and he said he wanted to hire me as an anchor on *SportsCentre*.

When I first wanted to get into sports, hosting the morning or evening highlight shows was my dream. But things had changed. Over the years, I got a taste of what it was like to be a host during live game broadcasts. I was doing what James Duthie and Ron MacLean were doing. I was hosting panels and was part of the action. I wanted more of that. My goals had changed.

I built up the courage to be honest and told him this. To my surprise, he wasn't offended; he completely understood. He agreed my talents were better suited to steering the bus on panels.

He took what I said to heart and said that if any of those opportunities became available at TSN, I would be the first to know.

I felt relieved that he understood. I felt proud that I expressed what I really wanted to do. No woman at that time in Canada was hosting sports panels, but I believed I could do it on a regular basis. But driving home, I still couldn't help but feel like I turned down a great opportunity. Did I just boot myself out of the industry?

After the World Cup, my husband and I took a trip to Charleston, South Carolina, and then visited his family in Philadelphia. It was a wonderful vacation that helped me clear my mind. I didn't think about work because I didn't have any work! I tried not to stress over not having a job.

When we returned, I got a phone call from the NHL Network offering me a position. Phew, the mortgage could still be paid!

The NHL Network studio was located inside the TSN building. And before I even started my new gig, I was already hearing I'd be out of a job in a year. Great, here we go again.

You see, TSN housed the NHL Network because TSN had held national rights. But now that everything had gone to Sportsnet, the NHL wanted to move the network to the United States.

Because of this uncertainty, I signed a contract for just one year.

Shortly after signing, true to his word, Milliere called me and said he had some opportunities for me to host TSN's weekend panels for the English Premier League when the regular host, Luke Wileman, was unavailable. The shows were early mornings, and with hockey happening at night, there would be no conflicts with the NHL Network. The only conflicts were with my sleep! Some weekends, I worked till 1:30 a.m. waiting for the west coast hockey games to wrap up, made my way to a nearby hotel to sleep for what felt like ten minutes, and then headed back to TSN to host a 7 a.m. soccer broadcast. I definitely earned the bags under my eyes.

I had a blast at the NHL Network that year. I met so many amazing people. Good friends Craig Button, Jamie McLennan, and Mark Roe, I met for the first time working there. But there was always a low-grade anxiety over what was going to happen to the network. Would it stay in Canada? Would it relocate to the United States? It ended up moving to Secaucus, New Jersey. Now the big question was, would the network take the Canadian hosts with it?

I got my answer while attending my cousin's wedding . . . in Italy . . . in September 2015.

I point out the month because many of you hockey fans know that's when training camps start. It was already getting very late in the hiring process, and if I wasn't retained by the NHL Network, it would really hurt my chances of finding hockey work elsewhere.

I know it wasn't an easy process for the people in charge of hiring. A lot of things happened last minute, and moving an entire network to another country wasn't easy.

To help with all the chaos, I'd hired an agent who represented Canadians in the States, hoping he could assist if I did in fact have to move.

It was a beautiful Mediterranean night in Naples, Italy, and I was sitting inside a breathtaking eleventh-century castle. My cousin, Valentina, looked enchanting in her wedding gown. The food was endless, and the drinks were flowing. And that's when my agent delivered news via text that crushed me: "They've decided to go in another direction."

I tried to keep a smile on my face at the wedding. I was surrounded by beauty, by family, and we were celebrating a union. But my parents knew I was spiralling.

For the second time in a year, I was out of a job. Life of a freelancer. I thought for sure this time I was done. The sports world was making it perfectly clear it didn't want me.

My mom sat with me all night; my dad was never too far, keeping watch. We half bitched about the industry, half made plans about moving on.

Once again, I was coming off an incredible year professionally. After the NHL season wrapped up, I'd hosted the Pan American Games for CBC. Even though they hadn't renewed my contract on a full-time basis after losing hockey, they still wanted to use me for big sporting events. The Pan Am Games were in Toronto that summer. I hosted the afternoon show. I was proving to everyone I could handle hosting multiple sports at various levels, and yet . . . it wasn't good enough.

The year before, I was coming off hosting the Olympics and FIFA World Cup and wasn't given a new contract.

This time around, I was coming off hosting hockey and soccer panels and the Pan Am Games (for which I won a Canadian Screen Award, but more on that later) and still wasn't given a new contract.

What was I doing wrong? Was I just not good enough?

Under the Mediterranean moon, I said goodbye to sports.

I made peace with a career I believed was over.

Even though I was out of sports, it didn't mean I stopped hustling.

When I got home from Italy, I was like the Tasmanian Devil zipping through the house, finding anything and everything I could sell at a garage sale.

I will always find ways to make money.

Two weekends in a row, I held a sale on my driveway. I think I made over a thousand bucks. I was so proud.

But man, my ego was bruised. I was also in foreign territory: I started working when I was sixteen years old. I worked at the snack stand inside the local hockey rink at the Maple Community Centre, serving coffee to half-sleepy parents at five in the morning on weekends. Since then, I'd held a job, sometimes multiple part-time jobs, right through to this point in my life. Now, here I was, thirty-five years old and out of work.

My husband was incredible during this time. I felt like I was letting him down, but he reminded me that when he first moved to Canada to be with me after retiring from playing in Major League Soccer, he had no job and couldn't work because he wasn't a Canadian resident yet. "You took care of me. Now I'm going to take care of you," he said.

He was working with Toronto FC's academy at the time.

I started coming up with outlines for shows I could pitch to HGTV and the Food Network.

My aunt is Anna Simone, a world-renowned interior designer. Her firm is Cecconi Simone Inc. She had connections with producers at HGTV because she was on a few of their design shows.

I had a few meetings with some producers and was feeling pretty good. (No, I won't share my show ideas because I'm still hoping to one day get them produced.)

And then I received a phone call from an old acquaintance. Nelson Millman. A great dry-sense-of-humour guy. Love him.

I had met him briefly during my time at Rogers Cable. He was good friends with my station manager, Lisa McClean-Stellick. His daughter had needed help with a school project, and I offered to answer some questions for her. I ran into Millman again when I was a guest on Sportsnet 590 The Fan. He ran the station.

Now he was the program director at Sirius XM Radio.

He asked if I wanted to work at the station. Radio? I had no clue what went into being a radio host.

He said they would ease me in. Steve Kouleas, longtime sports host, was hosting a show on the NHL Network's channel. I would just come in on Mondays.

Ok, why not? I had nothing to lose.

Steve is very high-energy and very well prepared. I quickly learned that compiling notes for radio is a completely different beast. Television is structured. Radio is all over the map. You have to be well-researched to be prepared for any direction the conversation might take you. And Kouleas loved going off the rails. It was a lot of fun working with him, but I also sat on the edge of my seat quite a bit!

Shortly after accepting the part-time job with SiriusXM, my former CBC boss gave me a call. He had heard the NHL Network wasn't taking me to Secaucus, New Jersey.

It had been a year since the hockey rights loss, and CBC worked hard to find its bearings again.

He wanted to offer me a job. A multi-year contract.

I thought I was dreaming. After all, didn't the sports world want nothing to do with me? Why were these job offers coming in?

I'd sold furniture and some of my clothes (and some of my husband's, without him knowing) at a garage sale, gone on EI, had met with HGTV producers and desperately tried to get them to like my ideas, and was stressed to the max.

And then just like that, everything was changing.

I was back, baby. A little scarred, a little wiser, but definitely stronger than before to tackle this crazy world of sports broadcasting.

So to all the young aspiring broadcasters out there, I mean it when I say I hope you have a smooth ride in this industry. But the reality is that most likely won't be the case. And I can guarantee that a lot of the on-air people you watch have had their fair share of struggles but keep on fighting. It's not always easy, but no one said chasing your dreams would be.

## CHAPTER 26

# MY BOUNCE BACK SUMMER

The summer of 2015 was the first time I hosted a decently sized sporting event all on my own. The Pan American Games were being held in Toronto that summer, and I was hosting the afternoon show solo. I loved every second of it.

Our studio was right in the middle of the atrium of the CBC building, and it was always buzzing with people. People from different parts of the world came to Toronto to watch the competition, and when they saw my studio right in the middle of the building, they got a kick out of watching a live television broadcast.

I remember the negative talk leading up to the Pan Am Games: "Who cares about this tournament?" "No one will watch." "Traffic will be a nightmare." "Blah, blah, blah."

I was used to it. Leading into the Sochi 2014 Olympics, all the talk was about how we were going to get bombed or kidnapped by the Russian military and never be seen again! The talk heading into Russia by Canadian news outlets gave me nightmares for one month straight before the start of the Olympics. I soon learned this was just par for the course. The talk around the 2016 Rio Olympics was that we were all going to get the Zika virus — I had nightmares about that too. During the Pyeongchang 2018 Olympics, we were apparently going to get nuked by North Korea — once again, nightmares. Even before the Tokyo 2020 and Beijing 2022 Olympics, I had nightmares. Despite doing both of those shows on Canadian soil, I was worried about contracting Covid. Obviously, I didn't want to get it for health reasons, but I also didn't want to go into quarantine and miss out on the Games. Months and months of hard work just thrown away because you've been booted off your show. At the Sochi 2014 Olympics, I remember Bob Costas had to step away from his hosting duties with NBC because he got pink eye — in both eyes! I can't even imagine how frustrated and heartbroken he must have been, given all the hard work he did leading up to the big show. Afterwards, Costas talked about how he felt he let his team down.

During the Covid Games, we tested every other day. I had so much anxiety staring at that solution, praying it remained negative. I didn't want all my hard work to go to waste, and I most definitely did not want to let my team down.

I've come to expect tons of negativity around massive sporting events before they start, and I've also come to realize how quickly things turn positive once the competition begins. People can't help but get swept up in national pride when they see athletes representing their country. There are so many stories of perseverance and family support that people get hooked on the human component more than anything. And that's what happened in 2015.

The talk quickly went from "Who cares?" to "I want to see more of this sport and more of that sport!" We ended up extending my show by an hour so we could accommodate the demand.

My work on the 2015 Pan American Games earned me my first Canadian Screen Award nomination. I was the first woman nominated in the Best Sports Host category. I won that year, and the award ceremony was held on International Women's Day. It was a special moment. I was nervous that night, but clearly nowhere near as nervous as my husband! When my name was announced, he jumped out of his seat before me and gave me his hand to help me up. My grip nearly slipped because his hands were so disgustingly sweaty. After my acceptance speech, I went back to our table and asked him if he was feeling ok. I thought for sure he was coming down with something — who sweats that much just sitting there at a gala?

"Nope, I'm fine. I was just drowning in nerves for you. But I'm totally fine now!" he explained.

As we were getting ready to leave, fellow nominee James Duthie approached with a big smile on his face, but the first words out of his mouth were "Fuck you!"

We're good friends, but that doesn't mean we don't love a little friendly competition.

"I can't believe you won off your first nomination! Do you have any idea how many years in a row I was nominated and each time I watched the award go to Ron MacLean before I *finally* won?"

We had a good chuckle, and then he sincerely congratulated me. I think James is one of the best. To be nominated alongside him is always an honour. I beat him out two other times for my work on the Tokyo and Beijing Olympics, and I remind him of it every time I see him.

But he gets the last laugh. I still have a long way to go to catch up to his nine CSAs!

However, before the Pan Am Games started — before I even won my first Canadian Screen Award — something special that summer had already happened. My hometown of Maple, Ontario, extended an invitation to be part of the Pan American Games torch relay that was making its way through its streets.

There was zero hesitation in my response: "Yes!"

I was so excited to be a part of the relay that I didn't think to ask which leg I was running. When the day arrived, I discovered I was one of eight people running. It was only after we put on our Pan Am gear — special shorts and T-shirt — that I was told I would be running anchor. That meant I would take the torch last and run it through the massive crowd that had gathered outside the Civic Centre for the ceremony. It also meant I had to bring it on stage and light the portable cauldron. Obviously not the real one. That one was lit during the official Opening Ceremony by basketball player Steve Nash.

I'll never forget being handed the torch. It was way heavier than I was expecting . . . I thought for sure the weight of the torch was going to force me to wobble side to side while running, and I was going to light something or someone on fire accidentally! Thankfully, I had police escorts running alongside me, and they kept me going in a straight line.

When we arrived at the Civic Centre and started running through the massive crowd that had gathered, mostly children, I held onto that torch real tight. My core got a great workout. But as is standard, there's always one child who doesn't obey the rules. They were all told to stay behind a certain line, but one kid got so excited that he leapt out in front of me. One of the cops didn't even break stride when he scooped up the kid and plopped him back down behind the line. Phew, no one was going to go up in flames that day.

Now, the real hard part. Once I got on stage, I had to gracefully light the cauldron. My shoulders and traps got the workout of a lifetime as I slowly lowered the torch, trying to hide my shaking arm as much as possible, and lit the flame. An oddly powerful feeling.

Once my responsibility with the torch was over, I was able to relax. It was a beautiful day, a wonderful celebration of sport, and an amazing experience. My family was there to watch as well.

Who knew that those streets where I grew up, rode my bike, walked to and from school, and may or may not have caused some mischief on, would be the very streets where the adult me did something pretty cool.

Summer 2015 was a good one.

## CHAPTER 27

# OLYMPICS AND AWARDS

The Olympics are such a trip. They are the most exhilarating and exhausting shows to work on. But every second is worth it.

In fact, I hope that at some point in every sportscaster's career, they get to work on a major sports tournament. Not just because it's a pretty cool thing to do, but because when you spend a lot of time with the same people, you learn true teamwork. It's very challenging working a large tournament day in and day out: long hours and stressful days, the demands and unpredictability of live sports, exhaustion and grumpiness, and often dealing with some sort of sniffles or sore throat because you're rundown. It sounds awful, but you get through it because of your "teammates." You know who's pulling their weight and who isn't. And you never want to be in the latter category! Everyone's role matters. No matter how big or small you think that role is.

During the Covid Olympics — Tokyo 2020 and Beijing 2022 — I hosted the morning show in Canada. I was on the air at 6 a.m. every day until noon. And that meant I was in the makeup and hair chair by 3 a.m. every day. The coffee cart would come around by 3:15 a.m. Students who were interning with us were in charge of drinks and snacks. And let me tell you something . . . those students played an extremely important role in helping me get my day started! No coffee, no happy Andi or makeup and hair stylists. We relied heavily on that coffee cart.

Big tournaments — and I would even say this is true about covering the playoffs for pro leagues — are a kind of grind that can't be explained but needs to be experienced. You bond with your co-workers, especially since you're seeing them more than you're seeing your family. And the experience really teaches you how to be there for each other and make some damn good TV.

What makes the Olympics extra special is that, on top of all the great competition, you get to experience other cultures. Often, the Olympics act as a postcard for the host country. Historical sites, customs, and traditional dishes are on full display in broadcasts alongside the sports.

I was crushed when I found out I wasn't going to Tokyo or Beijing. Our main studio shows and the majority of our play-by-play we'd all done from our building in Toronto. Of course, I understood the reasoning; but for the first time since I became an Olympic host, I felt disconnected from the host countries.

Sadly, I wasn't in Paris for the 2024 Games either, even though things were back to normal. With the time change, it meant that my prime-time show would air at 1 a.m. local time; there would be no live sport happening and little to no chance of having an athlete come to the studio. The reasoning for not being on location was totally understandable, and with the advancement of technology, viewers sometimes don't even know the difference! During the Covid Games, we used holograms of the athletes for our interviews. They were onsite, sitting in a green screen studio with their eye line teed up at a certain level; mine was at the same level in my studio back home to make it look as if we were staring directly at each other and sitting side by side. I still run into people to this day who thought I was on location because those interviews truly looked like we were all in the same room together.

I get it. I get all of it.

But, in my opinion, the authenticity of it was lost.

And perhaps this is just me having a pity party for one. I'm constantly told that viewers don't care where I am, just as long as they're watching a good show. And maybe that's true. But I can tell you that whenever I do speaking engagements, without fail, I'm asked about my Olympic experiences and what it's like to be there. People understood why I wasn't at the Covid Games, but when they found out I wasn't going to be in Paris, there was always a pause and some sort of offering of condolences.

By the way, being on location isn't about a free trip. Trust me, covering the Olympics is no vacation. It's about first-hand knowledge. It's about seeing the athlete's village myself and describing it to viewers. It's about being in the building and watching Andre De Grasse and Usain Bolt go head-to-head in the 200m in Rio 2016 and telling the viewers how electric the vibe was. They were introduced to the crowd with "Welcome to the Jungle" by Guns N' Roses blaring through the speakers.

Or how one night, I went to the Canadian Embassy in Rio to watch the last Tragically Hip concert. They put up a huge screen TV to host a rooftop viewing for some of the athletes and broadcasters. While on the bus en route to the Embassy, windows down, I heard a massive roar erupt all across Rio. Neymar had just scored the winning penalty kick in the soccer gold medal match inside the Maracanã to give Brazil the victory. What a sound. The hairs on my arms stood up. When I went to air the next day, I was able to share this first-hand story with my viewers and paint a picture of this incredible moment.

In Sochi 2014, ski halfpipe made its Olympic debut, and Canadian Mike Riddle claimed the inaugural silver. He joined me in the studio and gave a heartfelt answer when I asked him about Canadian freestyle skier Sarah Burke. She had advocated for the sport to be added to the Olympic program. Sadly, she never got to be an Olympian as she tragically passed away two years prior in a training accident. It was a proper face-to-face interview, and I know the viewers felt the difference between that and a Zoom or hologram interview.

Not being on location has been in the works for quite some time. It's not just an Olympic thing. Many play-by-play announcers now call games inside tiny voice-over booths instead of travelling with the teams and being in the arenas or stadiums. These announcers are at the mercy of the cameras. Cameras don't show something, announcers don't see it, viewers don't get told about it.

We'll see where this crazy world takes us. But in the meantime, here are some other stories from the three Olympic Games I was able to attend. Some of them are not glamorous experiences, but it's the tough and sketchy moments that people love hearing about!

Sochi 2014 was extremely organized. The rules were strict, and the operations moved along smoothly, mostly because the security detail outnumbered everyone else. I came to realize there were three types of security: the very obvious ones who had *security* written on their jackets, the undercover ones who started to reveal themselves to me after a while, and then there was the military. Needless to say, I felt very safe. The few nights I called women's hockey, I never felt threatened walking back to my hotel in the middle of the night by myself.

There were a lot of stray dogs in Sochi, and I tried to feed them all — Scott Russell as my witness. Our hotel had this beautiful breakfast spread with a lot of cured and smoked meats. I would grab a to-go container and fill it with meat to feed my furry friends. One morning, a few military guys were sitting in their truck as I was feeding a couple of dogs outside my hotel. One got out and started making his way towards me. I prepared myself for an argument. I thought for sure he was going to discourage me from feeding the strays. Instead, in broken English, which took him a few tries before I could understand, he told me there were more dogs around the corner who would love some food, and could I possibly grab some more? I blinked. Stunned. *Could I? Watch me!*

Rio 2016 was a bit of a different story. Lovely people, but way more laid back and a tad bit disorganized. Media buses weren't on time or sometimes just didn't show up. One day, I decided to watch the swimming races after my Olympic show. My co-host for the Rio Games was David Amber. At the last minute, he got pulled into doing mix zone for swimming. It was a late night for both of us. After the races, I went to the bus stop to grab the 11 p.m. bus. The time rolled around, but the bus didn't. Still nothing by 11:15 p.m. It was late, dark, and I was starting to get concerned. Rio during these Olympics wasn't as friendly to pedestrian traffic as Sochi had been. We had been advised by our security detail to take the media buses provided at all times and avoid walking alone — especially at night. My phone was losing juice, but I managed to send David a text that I was stranded. Still no bus by 11:30 p.m., and now my phone was completely dead. I wasn't sure if my text had gone through and if he was trying to call me back. I resigned to the fact I'd be spending the night inside the International Broadcast Centre. But something told me to wait just a bit more before going inside. It was close to midnight when I heard someone yell my name. It was David! CBC had provided him with a driver because of all the running around he had to do, and after he got my text, he tried calling me back, but it kept going straight to voicemail. Clearly, something told him I didn't make it back to the hotel, so he told his driver to keep driving around until they found me. Thank goodness he did that. Now that's a teammate!

That wasn't the only time David came to my rescue.

I knew right away that Rio was going to be a different experience from Sochi, and not just because one was a winter Games and the other summer, but because of how the workers and volunteers approached things. Sochi volunteers were more reserved; Rio volunteers were lively and fun. Sochi security was always professional; the Rio security guard outside our studio was either on the phone or eating, and he would use his gun as an extension of his arm when asking to see our credentials.

*Watch where you point that thing, mister!*

The Sochi workers rarely made eye contact with you, whereas during our site tours in Rio, the workers were constantly catcalling. I'm not trying to say one culture is better than the other. I'm simply pointing out some of the differences that were noticeable to me. That's the joy of exploring new countries!

But there was a real concern about theft in Rio. Times were not good for the Brazilian people. It was quite heartbreaking. David had been in Rio just two years prior to cover the 2014 FIFA World Cup, and he said that things were drastically different.

Even though we bring a lot of our own crew on location for Olympic coverage, we still need to hire locals to help with logistics and other things. A few of the makeup artists were locals. When the Olympics were done, we gave one of them the iron from our dressing room. She broke down in tears. She had never owned an iron before. I had some food and drinks left over in my hotel mini fridge and some CBC swag, and I was told I had to leave a note stating I was leaving this behind for the maid service. Without that letter, they'd be accused of stealing.

One day during our show, we threw to some live sport and I took advantage of the break to use the washroom. I had to go down a set of stairs and down a hallway. The washrooms, like many structures at the Olympics, are not permanent. But these walls were exceptionally flimsy.

It felt like a gust of wind could carry them away, and I'd be left in a precariously funny position. This day, there were three men hanging around the washroom. No passes. No credentials. Looking very suspicious. When they saw me, they tried to get my attention by smiling and being flirtatious. I did not like what was happening. Did I mention these washrooms didn't have locks? My mic packs were no longer picking up a signal; I was too far away from the studio. But those guys didn't know that. I made it very obvious that I was wearing a microphone, and then I put my hand to my ear so they could see my earpiece. I started talking into the mic as if someone was listening. The smiles quickly vanished from their faces. I went to the washroom and listened. They were whispering. I couldn't make out what they were saying, but they didn't sound happy. Who knows what I walked into, but it felt like I foiled something. I didn't break stride to see what they were doing when I exited the washroom; I bolted up the stairs and back to the studio. I told David everything. He was not happy. Without hesitating, he said he was going to check things out. He wanted to at least let the security guard know what was going on. David isn't exactly a small man, and he was most definitely bigger than those three guys I saw. But by the time he got down there, they were gone. They clearly knew I was going to alert someone.

The funny part was that David always brushed his teeth halfway through a show, and before he headed down, he grabbed his stuff. I kept picturing this big buff guy going to confront people who looked to be up to no good with a mini toothbrush and toothpaste in his hand. How intimidating! Ha!

For Pyeongchang 2018, I had another great co-host. Olympic diver Alex Despatie. We hit it off right away. Frick and frack. Two peas in a pod. We were always cackling over something as we got ready for our show. Halfway through the Games, I got really sick. I'm pretty sure a custard tart I ate that was on display at the market and hadn't been refrigerated for days was the culprit. It was a horrible show to host. The location of our studio was not close to a washroom, and I needed to use it every fifteen minutes. To get to the washroom, you had to walk outside in the bitter cold and along a metal platform that became very slippery with snow and ice. After you braved the frigid temperatures, you finally got inside and had to go down two flights of stairs. Ugh, what a wretched night. Poor Alex.

He didn't know what to do. When we weren't on air, I curled up in the fetal position on one of the chairs. Alex sat next to me and kept asking, "What can I do? What do you need? Tell me and I'll do it."

I laugh about it now because he was being such a typical dude. He didn't know what to do unless I told him. But in that moment, when I thought I was going to have an accident live on air and go viral for all the wrong reasons, I wanted to kill him for constantly asking, "What can I do?"

Thank goodness our floor director was a mother. Emily Sit was my hero that night. She didn't need to ask me what I needed; she just knew. She grabbed me dry crackers. She got me hot water with lemon. She made sure my warm booties were waiting for me once I was done an on-camera so I could quickly kick off my heels and get comfortable.

When the show was over and I finally made it back to my hotel room, I was freezing and had the achy body shakes. In Pyeongchang, the common areas weren't heated. They saw it as a waste of energy. So, when you walked into buildings, the lobby and hallway areas felt just as cold as outside. But the rooms were nice and toasty thanks to the heated floors. I moved as fast as I could through the hotel and into my room. That night, I slept on the floor with my body face down, soaking up the radiant heating. How glamorous.

The next day, I felt a bit better. During Pyeongchang, I also hosted hockey for the Canadian men's games. The arena was about an hour away from the broadcast centre, so I had a local driver assigned to me on hockey nights. His name was Che. He wanted to practise his English, and that led to some great conversations. Time in the car flew by! When he found out I was sick, he went to the pharmacy and bought me a bunch of local remedies. I don't know what was in that Korean candy, but I swear it worked instantly! Our Korean hosts were very warm and welcoming and always willing to help. Che was a good example of that.

After three Olympics working alongside co-hosts, CBC entrusted me with my own show for Tokyo 2020 and then again for Beijing 2022. It was a dream come true and another step in my career. All the great Olympic hosts have their own show — a solo mission. I didn't take this honour lightly. At the previous three Olympics, my hosting duties were split. But now, I was responsible for a six-hour show all on my own. For Tokyo and

Beijing, I hosted the morning show, which meant I was live on the air by 6 a.m. every morning. Wake-up call was around 2 a.m.; I'd be in the makeup chair by 3 a.m.; production meeting at 4 a.m.; start getting dressed at 5 a.m., and then make my way to the set to start getting mic'd up. A gruelling schedule all on its own, that was made a little more challenging a few times because of soccer. The sports calendar was so messed up due to the pandemic that during the Tokyo Olympics, which were held in the summer of 2021, the CONCACAF Gold Cup tournament was happening at the same time. I hosted these games for OneSoccer. The Canadian men's team made it out of their group and advanced to the semifinal, meaning they played two games while the Olympics were on. For me, that meant a few almost all-nighters. I would host my Olympic show until noon, do as many notes for the next show as possible, then make my way to the OneSoccer studio, host the game, head back to my hotel room, shower, close my eyes for forty minutes, then head back to the CBC building for 3 a.m. One of these crazy shifts had me host the Canadian men's semifinal match against Mexico, which they lost, then head into work and host the Canadian women's soccer team and watch them win their Olympic quarterfinal match against Brazil. My emotions were all over the map for those twenty-four hours!

It happened again during the Beijing Olympics. The Canadian men's team had a World Cup qualifying game against El Salvador the night before our opening show.

As an admitted functioning stressaholic, I actually enjoyed the challenging schedule!

But I have to say, doing a summer and winter Olympic Games six months apart was brutal. I knew the time I needed to prepare for the Olympics, but I never realized how much time I needed to recover from one. Finding my energy for Beijing so soon after Tokyo was very hard.

I can't believe that up until 1992, the summer and winter Olympic Games were held in the same year. Yeesh.

Thank goodness the sports calendar is back to normal.

After that crazy year, I booked a two-night getaway at a spa. My husband had to work, and it was hard to coordinate our schedules, but he told me to book it anyway and get in some good rest and relaxation. Shortly after booking my trip, I received notice that the Canadian Screen Awards were being held that same week. I was a nominee in the Best Sports Host category for my work on the Tokyo Olympics.

The Canadian Screen Awards were still being held virtually because of Covid. So, on the night of the awards ceremony, I enjoyed a nice dinner at the hotel restaurant, went for a little walk, and then made my way back to my hotel room and logged on.

I truly didn't think I'd win. I had one CSA under my belt, and it's a cherished one. At the 2016 awards ceremony, CTV news anchor Michelle Dubé presented me with the award for the Best Sports Host category.

But then the following year, I wasn't nominated. I did eventually earn two more nominations but lost out to my good friend James Duthie. I began to think that I had caught lightning in a bottle that year. Maybe I wasn't that good? It's amazing how quickly you can start messing with your own head. But the thing is, I didn't feel sorry for myself. I was annoyed that more women weren't being nominated and winning. There are so many incredible women in the sports industry who are hosting big events and delivering on a consistent basis in this country. I thought my winning in 2016 would open the floodgates. It didn't, and that's what disappointed me the most.

So, when I settled in for the announcement of the 2022 winner, I was genuinely shocked when I heard my name. As much as you continue to believe in yourself, there really is something special about being recognized by your peers. I didn't mean to flex in my acceptance speech when I said I was currently at a spa, but I didn't know how else to explain the mood lighting and soft flute music playing in the background!

The following year, I was nominated again. This time, I thought for sure I would *not* win. I was still the only woman to win in the category, and that meant no woman had ever won back-to-back Best Sports Host CSAs.

The awards ceremony was back to being held in person, but sadly, I couldn't attend; the national women's soccer team had a match on the same day at the same time.

The executive producer at CBC Sports, Paul McDougall, called to ask what I thought of Brenda Irving going up and accepting my award if I won.

"I'm not going to win, Paul. But yes, I think that would be special," I responded.

"Don't be so sure you won't. You killed it during the Games. I think you might be surprised."

Paul is one of those executives who has always had my back. I first met him in 2010 when I was still working at MLSE and was given a tour of the CBC studios during the 2010 FIFA World Cup. He was producing one of the shows, but he still made time to answer questions, and I remember thinking, *This guy is intimidating!* I wouldn't say much has changed — ha!

The thing is, Paul doesn't have time for nonsense and always makes room for common sense. He pushes you to be better. He challenges your ideas to make sure it's what you really believe and want to say on air . . . And he's always game for a scrappy yet healthy debate. Paul has trusted me to front many big events at CBC Sports. And many times, he sees the value in something before you do. That was the case when he suggested Brenda represent me at the CSAs.

Turns out he was right. I did win. And seeing Brenda — a trailblazer in the industry, a hard-working woman who has knocked down many doors for women like me — up on that stage accepting that award felt like a beautiful full-circle moment. When I saw her a few days later to thank her for stepping in, she didn't get mushy. Nope, not Brenda. She threatened to kill me for making her get up on stage and have the spotlight on her. That's Brenda: never wanting the attention for herself.

I have three CSAs. The first woman to win one for Best Sports Host, the first woman to win back-to-back, and the first woman to own three. I proudly display them in my house. And another proud moment came in 2024.

I wasn't nominated. But another woman was. And another woman won. TSN's Kate Beirness was named Best Sports Host for her work on the Canadian Football League.

I would be lying if I said my ego didn't enjoy being the only one for many years to have won this award, but that kind of self-serving joy fades pretty quickly. I started looking around and realized I was alone; that's no fun at all. As I've gotten older, I've come to recognize that while personal accomplishments in the industry are self-satisfying, it's the progress one makes for others that becomes gratifying.

I used to be the only woman to have won Best Sports Host, and now I have company.

I hope these are the floodgates I thought would open up back in 2016. There are so many more great women in this industry who are deserving of recognition.

# CHAPTER 28

# DON'T PUT ME IN A BOX

I'm an only child. Go ahead, make your jokes. We're weird, we're entitled, we're spoiled, we're lonely, we're anti-social . . . blah, blah, blah.

We are who our parents raise us to be. (Ok, totally a wee bit spoiled.)

My parents raised me to be very well-rounded. I don't know if it was a conscious effort or just something that came naturally, but because I was their only child, I did everything, not just the things that are considered feminine. I learned how to do the laundry *and* cut the grass. I learned how to cook *and* check my tire pressure. I took dance lessons *and* played soccer. The traits of masculinity and femininity were always blurred in my household. I did what was considered girl things and boy things.

And because of my upbringing, it was natural to see myself belonging to an industry that was male-dominated. That type of environment never felt foreign or intimidating to me; I always felt right at home.

But there are certain people who can't wrap their heads around a woman having masculine traits, and that can lead to oppressive assumptions.

They assume women are too fragile, women are too prudish, women are innocent, women are sensitive, women aren't interested in sports. And that last part can quickly morph into "Women don't know anything about sports, and they don't belong in sports."

Female athletes have many stories of gender bias so outrageous that the first reaction is to laugh. An example is women's ski jumping at the

Olympics. The event finally joined the Olympic program in 2014 at the Sochi Games, even though the men had been competing in the discipline since 1924. The reason? Men truly thought a woman's uterus would fall out when she landed after jumping that high and far. You laughed, didn't you? So outrageous. But these are real oppressive battles that women have had and continue to have.

No one ever thought my innards would come flying out of my body, but based on the assumption that men and women need to be categorized neatly under masculine and feminine columns, I was given a hard time on quite a few occasions at work.

My first assignment when I was hired by Leafs TV was to cover the Leafs pre-season intrasquad game known as the Blue and White tournament. When I made my way down to the dressing rooms to do the postgame interviews, the security guard stopped me. I thought it was because he didn't see my credentials, so I showed him that I totally belonged there and needed to get into position quickly for my live hit. He flat out said, "I can't let you back here because you're a woman."

I was stunned. By the way, this was 2006, not 1956.

I started to panic because I was minutes away from going live. The security guy wouldn't budge, but I continued to make a stink, and when he saw how agitated I was getting, he got on his walkie-talkie and asked someone what to do. I could hear the voice on the other end sound equally as baffled as I was: "Is she with Leafs TV? Then let her through! They have the rights to the game; she has access to the area!"

I could tell the old security guy wasn't happy, but he was told he was in the wrong. I made my live hit, a little breathless, but I made it.

And by the way, not all men think like this. I want to make that perfectly clear. In fact, many of my male co-workers have come to my defence when it was obvious I was being targeted. An example of that would be when we were on the road travelling with the Leafs and I'd be standing alongside the boards watching practice with Joe Bowen, Dennis Beyak, Paul Hendrick, and Jim Ralph, and without fail, at almost every road rink, security would approach me. "Are you lost, miss? Do you need help, miss? Can we see your credentials, miss?"

One time we were in Tampa Bay taking in practice, and what do you know? Security came up to me, just me, and asked to see my media pass.

The guys had had enough. They all started asking the security guy why he hadn't asked to see their passes. They all cheekily showed him their credentials to make a point. At least the security guy had enough sense to show some embarrassment.

I was at a party with some friends, and a guy flat out told me he doesn't listen to women on sportscasts because they never played pro. "The guys know what they're talking about because they played at a high level, the women never did," he said.

Was this guy for real?

I proceeded to list off male sports hosts, male reporters, male play-by-play announcers, and male insiders who had not played a sport at the professional level. Most of the former professional athletes fill analyst and colour roles. But the majority of everyone else is a passionate fan who went to broadcasting school and turned their passion into a professional broadcasting career.

I also pointed out how Cassie Campbell-Pascall, legendary hockey player who captained Canada to wins at the Olympics and world championships, was brutally criticized when she became the first woman to do colour on a *Hockey Night in Canada* broadcast.

"So don't tell me, buddy, that you don't listen to women because they don't have the 'playing' credentials you claim they need to have. The majority of men in the industry don't have those very credentials, and when Cassie, a better hockey player than every guy watching her from their couch, was belittled and attacked on social media, we both know it's because she's a woman. You're making assumptions based on gender, not knowledge of the game. Period. Your bigotry is suffocating."

I'd clearly had a few drinks and was brave to go on this rant, but to the guy's credit, he listened to me slack-jawed and then apologized. He actually apologized.

"Wow, I'm sorry. I totally assumed every guy who was in sports broadcasting played sports at a high level."

Nope.

But not all men are like this guy. I've made this point before to other men when they've said something similar, and they just shrug their shoulders and dismiss me. They don't care that I just debunked their reasons for why they don't accept women in sports broadcasting. That tells me that no proper sense is used when they cast their judgment: They simply see a woman, and that's that.

When I was hosting the 2014 FIFA World Cup, an article was written about CBC's talent covering the tournament. I was the only woman on the broadcast. All the men received glowing reviews. I, on the other hand, did not. I wouldn't have had a problem if the writer had based his judgment on my work, my knowledge, or my presentation. I took issue with his criticism because he assumed I knew nothing about soccer. The writer said I had no business hosting soccer and should go back to the hockey arenas from whence I came. My blood boiled when I read the article. Thankfully, I didn't have to respond because readers came to my rescue. Many of them pointed out in the comment section that I had covered Major League Soccer for years before joining *Hockey Night in Canada*.

An old friend, Dave Cadeau, used to be the director of programming at Sportsnet 590 The Fan radio station. He told me when one of his male reporters gave an update and screwed up, listeners didn't have a problem with it. They just figured the guy was having a bad day, and *we all know what he meant to say because he's clearly qualified*. But Dave said when one of his female reporters mispronounced a name or got a stat wrong, his phone lines would light up with complaints.

The man gets the benefit of the doubt, but not the woman.

Remember, masculine and feminine traits are just that . . . traits. They are not qualities bound by some unbreakable magic to gender.

If you're still shocked to learn that women love sports and are knowledgeable about sports, then I'm about to blow your mind when I tell you there are men out there who don't watch sports and couldn't tell you what an offside is in hockey or what a cycle is in baseball.

Oh, and having been an Olympic host since those 2014 Sochi Games when women started competing in ski jumping, I can confirm that all uteruses have remained intact.

## CHAPTER 29

# MEMORABLE ENCOUNTERS

I've been blessed to cover and interview some of the greatest athletes of my generation. But there's still something special about encounters with legendary athletes and even broadcasters who came before.

It's a different kind of dynamic. I don't feel like a journalist interviewing a subject; I feel like a grandchild happily being regaled by stories of yore.

Back during my Leafs TV days, we had a room up in the press box where we would keep equipment, and our camera guy would watch the game from up there. During intermissions, I would make my way to the room just to shoot the breeze with him. However, that room had a little two-seat sofa in it, and Mr. George Armstrong had discovered it. Armstrong, who'd been the captain of the Toronto Maple Leafs the last time they won the Stanley Cup, was working for the team and would be at every game. He too would make his way to the room during intermissions, and he would drape his massive 6'2 frame over this tiny couch. We didn't dare tell him to leave because, quite frankly, we didn't want to. He was hilarious, always cracking jokes. He would also complain quite a bit about the team; the Leafs weren't exactly doing great things at the time. He loved to tell us about the bench-clearing brawls they used to have and that the only way the refs could get a handle on things was to have the arena play the national anthem: "No way any of us gents would disrespect the anthem! We'd all stop and salute the photo of the Queen that was hung at one end of the arena!"

Johnny Bower was one of the first legends I met in my young career. I was still working at Rogers Cable and was hosting a local charity event, where I was seated next to "the China Wall." I remember watching him reach into the breadbasket and thinking he didn't need goalie gloves; his hands were huge! He must've grabbed five of those dinner rolls in one scoop.

Johnny was such a gentleman. He shared a few stories with me. He said he remembered clearly the day Tim Horton asked him to invest in this coffee shop idea he had. Johnny wanted to, but he didn't have the money.

He also recalled a story when he asked Harold Ballard if he could keep his goalie pads. At the time, the club owned the gear. He said Ballard asked for an absurd amount of money, knowing full well Johnny couldn't afford it. When telling the story, Johnny looked down and got sad when recalling the price, but then he looked up with a little spark in his eye and said, "It's ok, now I can go to the Hockey Hall of Fame and see my pads anytime I want."

At least he was able to chuckle about it.

There were countless other Leafs events throughout the years where I would run into Johnny, and when he talked to you, he made you feel like you were the only person in the room.

I was on vacation when the news of his passing was made public.

When I returned home, my furnace had gone on the fritz, and my pipes froze. I had to boil water in a kettle and take it to the tub to bathe. I did whatever I had to do to get ready for work the day after returning because a ceremony was being held at the Air Canada Centre for Johnny Bower. There was no way I wasn't going to be there to say goodbye.

Billie Jean King was always a figure bigger than life. I watched her on TV, listened to her speeches, followed her advocacy for gender equality in sports, and even watched the Hollywood movie about her life and the lead-up to the famous Battle of the Sexes tennis match between her and Bobby Riggs.

So, when I heard I was going to be interviewing her during the inaugural Professional Women's Hockey League draft, I was very nervous.

The draft was live from inside the atrium at the CBC building. Billie Jean was going to be my guest right off the top of the show. There was a lot of commotion around the set because the "Periwinkle Carpet" was right beside it. It was lined with loud, adoring fans as the players walked it and signed autographs. Family members, agents, team representatives, and other media were all running around. Safe to say there was a lot of chaos, but even so, I spotted Billie Jean King in the crowd as she was making her way to the set. A little over five feet tall, seventy-nine years of age, not moving too quickly, but none of that mattered. Her presence was massive. Every single person — man, woman, and child — made way for her as she walked. I'm a huge believer in energy fields. It's what connects us to each other and the Earth. And there is no denying how powerful Billie Jean King's energy is. But she didn't intimidate. She was very warm and genuine. We had a great conversation about how hard it is to start a league and how proud she was of the female hockey players for sticking together when it was so easy for things to fall apart.

I interviewed Billie Jean again on January 1, 2024 — the inaugural game of the PWHL between Toronto and New York. She had a massive smile on her face, remembered my name, and was so kind when she said, "Andi, this league is going to help so many players and coaches and everyone else in the game. But I really hope it helps you too. Women deserve to be working in this space and have a voice in sports too. I really hope it opens doors for you. I hope it opens more doors for women in broadcasting."

And she meant it. She wants to help, always.

I also thought it was hilarious to see her so nervous when she found out she would be reading Toronto's starting lineup in the dressing room to the players. This fearless woman, who has stood up to so many ignorant and sexist people in the world, was staring intently at a little notepad with the players' names on it. "Andi, I can't mess this up!" she said.

I first met Bobby Orr at a charity event. The "man flying through the air" (a nod to his legendary photo) was standing right in front of me. I told him that my mother and two aunts adored him. My grandfather was a diehard Leafs fan, but they loved Boston because of him. He asked for the addresses of all three and within weeks my mom and aunts called me freaking out — Bobby had sent each of them an autographed photo.

Jim Ralph, former goalie, radio analyst, and my good friend, attended the charity gala with me. There wasn't a Leafs game to cover that night, and many of the players were also at the event. When it was time to take our seats, I made my way to the table while Jim went to the washroom. There was one other person at the table when I sat down. He didn't look up when I took my seat; he was reading something. I sat there in silence, looking around at all the people. Bobby spotted me and made his way over. He leaned in and asked quietly, "Has this gentleman introduced himself to you at all?"

"No. But it's ok. I'm a people-watcher anyway!" I replied.

Bobby was not pleased. "Ok, let me handle this."

He made his way over to the guy. "Excuse me, sir," he said. The man looked up, and his eyes lit up when he saw that it was Bobby Orr. "My name is Bobby —"

"Oh yes, I know who you are!" the man interrupted.

Bobby kept going but in a friendly manner. "This is my friend, Andi. She's sitting all alone. I don't know about you, but when I see someone sitting alone so close to me, I don't ignore them."

The guy sheepishly introduced himself to me, and we made some small talk before the other guests started arriving at the table.

"See, so much better!" said Bobby. He winked and walked away. Bobby wasn't rude to the man, but he made it perfectly clear that the man was being rude to me.

I continue to see Bobby at events. He's had a lot of surgeries, but he'll always make himself available at golf tournaments to greet fans. I can't imagine the kind of pain he's in, especially with his knees, but he always has a big smile on his face when he greets me. Bobby Orr, quite the gentleman.

Brian McFarlane is the voice I hear in my head whenever I'm having a nostalgic hockey moment. One winter, my husband and I took an overnight trip outside of the hustle and bustle of the city. We went for a walk one beautiful crisp morning and came across a young girl skating on a frozen pond, working on her stick handling, her chocolate lab happily chasing her around the ice, trying to steal the puck. We stopped to soak in this picture-perfect Canadian moment. Narrating the scene in my head was . . . Brian McFarlane. I love his voice, I love his cadence, I love his passion for the game. And I love his kindness. When I was working at Rogers Cable, I decided to do a documentary on road hockey during the winter months and how it was like a rite of passage for so many Canadian kids. Frozen faces, frozen toes, makeshift nets, rules always changing, neighbourhood dogs barking at the action as you and your friends pretended to be your hockey heroes; and then running inside, dumping your wet, snow-covered mittens on the vent to dry, and racing to the kitchen because you knew a cup of hot chocolate with marshmallows (the small ones, please) was waiting for you on the table. Who better to paint this picture than McFarlane? I took a chance and reached out. I was in luck! He would be in town soon and would be more than happy to stop by the studio and do an interview. I couldn't believe it. He was such a legendary voice on *Hockey Night in Canada* for decades, and yet, I didn't have to ask twice to get him to come to a local station with limited viewership and sit down with a rookie no-name host to talk hockey.

He was fantastic. I'm so proud of that documentary. Brian McFarlane's ability to make the cold come to life, to have the joy of the game course through your veins as if you just finished playing, through his tone, through his words . . . it made my documentary whole. And then my luck doubled: Wendel Clark was kind enough to lend his voice to the project as well.

Years later, I would encounter McFarlane again. This time it was at an event in which I was being honoured by Sports Media Canada with the George Gross–Don Goodwin Award for Outstanding Sports Broadcasting. He made a point of seeking me out to congratulate me. We reminisced about the first time we met — almost twenty years ago — and I thanked him for being so kind with his time. Those are the moments that stay with a young broadcaster who's just trying to make it. Meeting people like Brian McFarlane so early on can be inspirational and motivating. Seeing him at that event all those years later was such a beautiful full-circle moment for me.

I've never had the privilege of working with Brian Williams — the godfather of Olympic hosting — but he has been kind enough to go out of his way to compliment my work.

When CTV/TSN was announced as the rights holders for the 2010 and 2012 Olympics, Williams joined that crew; our paths never crossed at CBC because I joined the network in 2011. When CBC regained the

Olympic rights for Sochi 2014, Brian sent me a lovely note wishing me luck. He was thrilled when he found out I would also be hosting the Rio 2016 Olympics. It's special having someone like that cheering you on.

Years later, at the 2022 Sports Media luncheon where I was honoured, he too was honoured with the Career Achievement Award. As special as his words have been to me over the years, it meant the world to see him make a beeline for my parents at the event and tell them how much he loved my work. My parents were beaming with pride; he made their night. I could tell my mom was really in awe of meeting *the* Brian Williams, and he lived up to the billing.

I'm not quite sure I have the words to describe what Scott Russell has meant to me.

I know it could not have been easy for this accomplished, award-winning veteran sportscaster to be paired with me as a co-host every weekend on CBC. Scott was and still is an expert when it comes to high performance sports coverage. When Scott announced his retirement in 2024, saying that Paris 2024 would be his last Games, it felt like the end of an era. I feel so lucky I was able to see him in action and learn so much from him for close to a decade before he decided to unplug his microphone.

When I joined *CBC Sports Presents* in 2015, which was called *Road to the Olympic Games* at the time, I had only one Olympic Games as a host under my belt. My knowledge paled in comparison to his.

Every weekend, I watched him. I observed. I emulated. I became a true apprentice. In the beginning, I followed his lead. I have no problem saying I wasn't his equal at the start. I had a lot of learning and catching up to do. Eventually, I gained his trust, and we became true partners on the show.

Scott taught me how to see the Olympics through the eyes of the athletes. "Andi, there's nothing wrong with praising champions. They've earned it. But for many of these athletes, this will be the only Olympics they ever compete in. There are only three medals up for grabs, and they'll most likely go home empty-handed. But that doesn't mean they don't have a story we need to tell," he said.

Scott taught me that an athlete's hometown matters. People from those places love cheering on their own. He taught me to learn the names of family members who are in attendance, rooting for their loved ones. Families sacrifice a lot too, and sometimes a simple name recognition goes a long way. Along with acknowledging which part of the country an athlete is from, Scott also taught me that giving a shout-out to where a competitor trains is also special. Mentioning the club or school they belong to means the world to the other athletes who train alongside them. Scott would say, "Remember, it takes a village."

He also taught me about context. For example, an athlete may have missed out on a medal, but they might have finished the highest they ever have before in a competition. Perhaps they set a personal best. Or maybe they just recovered from a horrible injury, and just competing at the Olympics was a miracle.

Medal and non-medal winners have stories worth sharing — Scott taught me that.

So, when I was asked to select someone to introduce me when I was honoured with the Sports Media Canada Outstanding Sportscaster Award, it was a no-brainer to say Scott Russell. His introduction made my parents cry. Not a surprise from my mom, but definitely a shock from my dad. That's how great an orator Scotty is. More than anything, he puts so much passion into everything he does.

When we co-hosted the closing ceremony of the 2015 Pan American Games, he warned me that when the flame was extinguished, he would take his headset off and need a moment. "I get choked up. The flame represents so much: the spirit of true and fair competition, hopes and dreams, accomplishments and defeats. When it goes out, a chapter closes. I take a moment to acknowledge, appreciate, and mourn," he explained.

The Olympic Games mean so much to everyone involved. The sacrifices, the heartbreaks, the friends who become family, the hard-fought triumphs. Once you understand all these things, truly understand and feel them in your soul, it can be very emotional. When we co-hosted the closing ceremony for the Rio Olympics in 2016, I understood. Scott and I both needed to take our headsets off and have a moment when the Olympic flame went out.

Scott loves dancing on set, even though he has two left feet! I would get annoyed every time he blasted country music on set, but I got the last laugh on that one. Scott put in a request for him and me to present an award at the Canadian Country Music Awards before the 2018 Olympics. He said it would be a great way to promote our Olympic coverage, but we all knew he wanted to rub elbows with the singers. Well, it turned out Scott had to work another assignment that weekend, and I, who knows nothing about country music, got to go to all the festivities and present an award. I still tease him about the wonderful time I had.

It's an honour to have worked with one of the best; it's an even bigger honour to call Scott Russell a dear friend.

## CHAPTER 30

# TSN STORIES AND FRIENDSHIPS

I was at TSN from 2014 to 2021, and I had a blast.

When I accepted the job at the NHL Network for the 2014–15 season, those studios were out of the TSN building. So, when Mark Milliere offered me the opportunity to host some English Premier League games as well, it was easy to do. Well, almost easy.

One Friday night, I got the late shift at the NHLN. Once all the west coast games wrapped up, I was off the air around 1:30 a.m. The next Saturday, I was hosting my first EPL match for TSN, and I had to be in for 6 a.m. Gross. Needless to say, the makeup artist had their work cut out for them. Except, there was no makeup artist! The scheduling somehow got messed up, and when I showed up at 6 a.m. looking like death, I stayed looking like death. Oh no, my first show for TSN, my first time working with Kristian Jack, and instead of feeling excited, I felt — and looked — like I just walked out of a UFC ring.

One of our camera operators, Samantha, quickly dug through her purse and found some lipgloss and mascara.

I begged the director, "Please, no single camera shots!"

Either way, I still got a few tweets from people saying I looked tired — thanks, Captain Obvious.

KJ was pretty awesome. He knew it was my first go at hosting the EPL. Even though I had hosted World Cups and covered Major League Soccer for years, it's always daunting when you're working with a new crew for the first time. I wish I could say I was awesome to him. Poor KJ had just had some sort of foot surgery and was in a cast, hobbling around on crutches. During the game, he had to hop across the studio to let someone know what highlights he wanted to break down during the half. On his way back, in the dark studio, he misjudged the distance of the cable on the ground and planted his crutches right on top of them. His crutches gave way and slid forward with his legs still behind him. It happened so quickly. As he was going down, he made eye contact with me, sheer panic in his eyes, and I responded by . . . laughing. Like, point a finger and burst out "Bahahaha" kind of laughing. KJ managed to maintain his balance and stood there steadying himself. I regained my composure and apologized profusely. What the heck was wrong with me? I blame the lack of sleep.

Thank goodness KJ forgave me. (I think?) We still joke about our first meeting.

I'd like to say that was the only time I went to air looking like I had just rolled out of bed. The next incident is more on the sombre side of things.

On the day Gordie Howe passed away, I happened to be at the studio early. The morning radio show had a Leafs segment every Friday, and they rotated through guests. That day, they asked me to be on. Their show ended, and I had a few hours to spare before my radio show started. I definitely wasn't dressed for TV.

I was sitting outside the TSN 1050 studio, having my breakfast, when the news came down about Gordie. I was gathering my thoughts on stories I wanted to share about him for my show when I saw Ken Volden, vice president and executive producer at TSN, pacing the halls. I was mid-bite into my breakfast sandwich when he made his way over to me and asked if I was busy.

"Not for another few hours," I replied.

"Good," he said. "I need you on the *SportsCentre* set ASAP to talk about Gordie Howe."

"Ahhhhh, I dunno. I don't have any on-air clothes, and I've never done a show in there." I was a little panicked.

"It's ok, let me worry about that. But I really need your help. None of our regular on-air people are available this early in the morning, and we need to be on the air *now*!"

I was whisked away into the makeup and hair chair, and Ken showed up with someone's blazer he snagged from CTV News, which was way too big for me, but he didn't care. He hovered over that poor makeup artist to make sure she wasn't wasting any time. You see, Sportsnet was already going live with the news of Gordie's passing. TSN was late.

I walked into the studio with rushed hair and makeup and wearing a blazer with shoulder pads that made me look like a linebacker; but I reminded myself this moment wasn't about me. I got over myself pretty quickly. I learned fairly early on in this business that you can't take yourself too seriously if you want to remain sane.

I gave it my all talking about a legend of the game who I'd had the pleasure of meeting. He was kind, he was funny, he was Gordie Howe. We first met at an event held at a hospital that specialized in brain research. Gordie had donated a lot of money. Afterwards, he kindly asked me to join him and his group for lunch. He reminisced about his playing days, and I soaked it up.

After all the chaos and commotion of going to air, it finally hit me that he had passed away. Once the show was done, I allowed myself to get a little emotional.

After the KJ and Howe experiences, I learned a valuable lesson: Never leave home without makeup in my purse and a blazer with a set of heels in my trunk. You never know when live TV will come calling.

Craig Button and David Poulin are two salt-of-the-earth people, and I just adore them. They appeared on a lot of *Leafs Lunch* shows with me. Radio is a different beast from television, and I would argue radio is harder. You're vulnerable because you're offering up opinions, and that opens the door for people to agree or cruelly disagree. Your topics are somewhat planned in radio, but there's a lot of ad-libbing based on the direction of conversation. You better know your stuff if you want to have meaningful and entertaining conversations on radio. TV is way more scripted, and you can be better protected. Radio is like being dropped in the wilderness with an axe and one match: Good luck! And working with Craig and Pouly made me want to be better.

There's the good old saying: I've forgotten more than you'll ever know.

That's the best way for me to describe those two. You're not pulling the wool over their eyes. They've been around too long, know too many people, and have experienced so many things in hockey that they don't have time for people who aren't prepared.

Pouly is a natural-born captain. He has that presence about him. Work hard, be prepared, respect others, and control your emotions — that's Pouly.

He made you not want to disappoint him. And that's why it's no surprise I learned an important observation from him. When we had conversations about players wanting a better contract, more ice time, more of a leadership role, Pouly would always point out, "There's a difference between *demanding* something and *commanding* something. To demand is lip service. To command is to show with your actions."

Pouly was all about command. The consummate pro. And what a good guy. My husband is a Philly boy and was completely starstruck when he learned I'd be working with a former Philadelphia Flyer who was the captain, no less!

When my husband was having an incredible season with Toronto FC in 2017 as the goalkeeper coach, Pouly would send him a message every game day during the playoffs. They kept winning, so he kept sending! Oh, and that's something else Pouly likes to say: "I'm not superstitious, I just like rituals."

Ha! Yeah, right. But what a guy.

When my husband and I moved into our new home, which was right around the corner from Pouly, he and his wonderful partner, Susan, were our first guests. I had nothing to eat in the house. But Pouly and Susan brought the wine and snacks, and we had a great night.

Craig is a great storyteller. I'm pretty sure he was born at centre ice somewhere. Hockey is in his blood. His dad started central scouting, and his mom worked for the Toronto Maple Leafs under Harold Ballard. He can spot a superstar before the superstar realizes it. I could listen to him break down a player's skill all day long. And Craig can be spicy, just like me. We had some good debates on *Leafs Lunch*, and I loved that he didn't back down or let me off the hook. He never treated me with kid gloves, and he pushed me to be better. If you're going to challenge Craig on any hockey topic, you better have done your homework.

Like Pouly, Craig had some sayings I still think about regularly, and they centre around hard work.

He would often say, "There are a lot of experts out there with no expertise."

I love that saying. It reminds me that experience matters. Getting your hands dirty matters. Being in the trenches matters. And also taking the time to develop your skills, apprentice, observe, and grow matters. Too many people want to be the loudest voice at the table right out of the gate, and they often have the least amount of experience.

Craig also shared this story about what it takes to win.

A coach asked his group, "Who's willing to pay the price to win?"

Everyone's hand went up.

The coach continued, "Who knows what the price is?"

Hands stayed down.

If you haven't figured it out by now, Craig is all about gaining experience and working hard. No shortcuts. If you work hard, you'll have his respect for life.

A little story: One Thanksgiving, I invited him over, and because the majority of my family would not be eating meat, I made celery root steaks. No meat, lots of veggies. The guys on *OverDrive* — Bryan Hayes, Jeff O'Neill, and Jamie McLennan — teased him endlessly about having a Thanksgiving with no turkey. But forever the gracious gentleman, Craig praised the food and the experience. However, we meet up at restaurants now!

Gord Miller is one of the best play-by-play people out there. His calls alongside Ray Ferraro were my favourite broadcasts. Gord is also funny as hell. His facial expressions and the way he laughs at his own jokes make me chuckle every time. He would try to come across like a crusty guy on air during *Leafs Lunch*, teasing me about something, but it was all in jest, and he has a heart of gold. The way he adores his daughter, Blair, tells you that Gord supports strong women, and even though he plies his craft in the men's game, he is a huge advocate of women's sports. In fact, I remember he lost it on Twitter one time at a guy who tweeted at him during the Women's World Championships. The guy said something along the lines of how he felt sorry for Gord having to do play-by-play for the slow and crappy women hockey players. Gord wouldn't hear it.

He responded professionally but definitely told the guy to take a hike while praising the women.

People also loved our brother/sister banter on air and would get in on the fun by choosing sides. One Leafs training camp, Gord and I carpooled to Gale Centre Arena in Niagara Falls. I hate being late, so I said we had to leave two hours before call time. He likes cutting things close and wanted to leave with one hour to spare. Who would've thought that argument would strike such a chord with our listeners, but it did! The early arrivers versus the latecomers.

I got my way, and we left early. When we parked our car at the arena, a police cruiser pulled up behind us. We both were a little confused. Gord hadn't run a red light, and he wasn't speeding. What was going on?

We got out, and Gord said, "Good morning, officer! Everything ok?"

The cop had a big grin on his face and responded, "I've been waiting to see what time you guys would get here. Judging by your early arrival, I guess I know who won the fight!"

Bob McKenzie and Darren Dreger are known as the "Hockey Insiders," and rightfully so. They have tons of connections, and they work hard at fostering relationships. Bobby and Dregs were also very helpful during my nights filling in for James Duthie on Leafs broadcasts. Dregs is such a good storyteller, and we had some good laughs on *Leafs Lunch*.

One day, I had to bring my dog, Pepper, to work. My husband was out of town, I was catching a flight right after work, and I didn't have time to go back home to get her, so I brought her to work so I could drop her off at my parents' house on the way to the airport. She was in the studio, lying at my feet, during that day's *Leafs Lunch* broadcast. But here's the thing: Pepper gets very concerned when a human raises their voice and starts moving their hands around. Dregs was passionately sharing a story and flapping his hands up and down. Well, Inspector Pepper had to make sure everything was ok. She got up and started jumping on Dregs, scratching at his legs and arms, trying to calm him down, and he's trying to stay animated while also trying to shake her off. It was during the first hour of the show, which was simulcasted on TV, so people could see Dregs talking and some black furry thing popping up from under the desk, trying to get him to relax. Mike Johnson, the other analyst in the studio that day, and I couldn't ignore Pepper anymore and burst out laughing. It goes without saying I put Pepper on a leash during the first commercial break.

I first met Bobby Mac when I was still with Leafs TV. We were at morning skate one day when he was sharing with me all the places he'd worked. I'd always known him as an accomplished hockey analyst on TSN, but he'd worked hard to get where he was. He chuckled after reciting his resume and said, "Yeah, I guess I've worked at a lot of places. But here's something I'll share with you — I always tried to find a job that paid me more and had me work less. The longer you're in this industry, the more of a break you deserve."

Those words stayed with me and mean more to me now that I have a few decades of experience under my belt. Slowly but surely, my work/life balance is shifting. It used to be 90/10 in favour of work, and that made me happy. Currently, I would say I'm at 70/30, with the scale still tipping more towards work. Every time I make a move to ensure my happiness and my sanity, I think of Bob's advice.

I have a lot of respect for Bob. So, when I received a call asking if I'd be interested in sharing my story in his book, *Everyday Hockey Heroes*, I was extremely honoured.

There's a saying in sports: Offence gets the glory, but defence wins the game.

The same can be true when talking about sports broadcasting: The on-air talent get all the recognition, but the crew behind the scenes make sure the show makes it to air and looks good. So, I want to take this time to give love to my girl, Stephanie Apolito. She started working at TSN on *Off the Record* and has been a part of TSN 1050 since its launch. She produced Hayes, O'Dog, and Noodles on the original *Leafs Lunch* show and stayed on when I took over. Now, she oversees the whole shop. She's had to deal with all of us crazy on-air folks, and she's the mastermind behind a lot of the great content the radio shows pump out. She consumes games, is on top of all the storylines, and she overprepares to ensure her host feels confident that all the stats and info are correct before the microphone is turned on. There are so many great women behind the scenes directing and producing shows, and Steph is one of them.

But Steph's timing is horrible. During Covid, when we were doing shows from home, she would always call me to discuss the lineup just as I was getting out of the shower.

One time, she asked, "Would this be easier if we FaceTimed?"

I laughed out loud, "Nope, I'm butt naked."

"Again! Why don't you ever have clothes on when we talk?" She was laughing.

"You're the one who calls me," I said. "I'm beginning to think you're doing this on purpose!" I teased.

I wish I had the chance to work more with hockey writer Kristen Shilton when we were both at TSN. She was a guest a few times on my radio show, and she always shared a ton of knowledge. I love her dry sense of humour as well, and it didn't surprise me when she moved on to write for ESPN.

Tessa Bonhomme and I kept missing each other when it came to doing shows together. When I left Leafs TV, she joined the network. At TSN, we never worked on the same shows. But then finally our paths crossed when I hosted the inaugural Professional Women's Hockey League game between Toronto and New York, and she was one of my panellists. One of the coolest hockey photos, in my opinion, is of Tessa wearing sunglasses with the Canadian flag on them, a cigar in her mouth, beer in hand, and the gold medal around her neck that she had just won at the Vancouver 2010 Olympics. Tessa is a true advocate for women's hockey.

Cheryl Pounder became a regular at TSN after I left. I love watching her on their hockey panels. Her knowledge, her delivery, her energy on air are everything I love. But we did get to work together when we covered the inaugural PWHL draft. It was an emotional day for her, a trailblazer in the sport, seeing this league get off the ground. Her analysis that day was top-notch. But her toughness behind the scenes impressed me even more. We had rehearsals the day before the draft, and after a few hours, we were getting hungry. I made my way to one side of the stage that had a few steps. I knew the steps were there because I had done many shows on this particular set, but they're difficult to see in the dark. When Cheryl heard I had some food waiting for us, she came running over, but she didn't see the steps. She toe-punted them and went flying. I tried to catch her, but it happened too fast; she smacked her face on one of the steps. But Cheryl, the tough hockey player, got up laughing. I asked if she was ok, and she said she was just embarrassed, so we all proceeded to have a good chuckle. She was lucky she didn't chip a tooth or get concussed. But then we resumed rehearsing, and blood started soaking Cheryl's sock. She had cut her leg in the fall. I started freaking out, but Cheryl just kept laughing: "It's nothing . . . I'm fine. I'm just happy I'm not whistling through my teeth!"

Good times, great people, and friendships that will last a lifetime.

## *CHAPTER 31*

# DON'T BE AFRAID TO PIVOT

Leaving TSN was hard. It was such an honour to represent that network. I loved my job, and I loved the people. But I had to go.

When I joined TSN on a full-time basis in 2016, I was in heaven. I was hosting *Leafs Lunch* Monday through Friday. I was James Duthie's fill-in for Toronto Maple Leafs games, and he and I would split panel duty during the Stanley Cup playoffs. That's when I learned of Bob McKenzie's jujube weakness. We would take turns purchasing snacks from Bulk Barn and I was specifically told that Bobby Mac got his own stash of jujubes. Those snacks saved us during long overtime nights. Not the healthiest food, but who cares when it's triple overtime and you're starving? I once had a plate of Funyuns onion rings with a side of sour keys to get me through a late night. Delicious.

I also continued my soccer coverage with them and began doing more Major League Soccer broadcasts. I was still part of their English Premier League panels and their FIFA World Cup coverage for both men and women.

So, you can imagine my shock when new leadership came in and said they didn't see me as part of the TSN television family.

I was heartbroken. But I loved the people I worked with on the radio side at *Leafs Lunch*, so I kept going for a few more years. However, I was beginning to wonder where I fit in at the network.

In the summer of 2021, I left. This was a very difficult decision for me. Firstly, I worked so hard to become a part of TSN, and even though I knew I was making the right decision, I still felt like I was throwing something great away. I mean, who leaves TSN? But I knew there was no more growth for me. And as a freelancer, I had to decide where to funnel my energy. It was a scary decision — very rarely are decisions in this industry easy — but I guess I would say this to all the aspiring journalists: It's ok to make a move that you feel is right for you. Sometimes we can get caught up in the hype of something, but if it's not working for you, you have to pivot. Just because you saw your path going one way doesn't mean you can't take another path to get to the same destination.

Be amenable, be brave, and stay focused.

The other reason why the decision to leave was difficult was because I felt the weight of responsibility. Responsibility to all the young women aspiring to become radio sportscasters. It's a special accomplishment when you become the first at something — when you smash the glass ceiling. But with that achievement comes a continuous duty to represent and prove that your group — in my case, women — belong. Many on-air people care about their legacy and the doors they've opened for the next generation. The thought that you could now be the reason why that door closes leaves you riddled with guilt. If I left *Leafs Lunch*, would that send the message that women can't do this job? Will I be turning back the clock? How long will it take for another woman to sit in this chair?

I struggled with all of these feelings because I don't take the power of representation lightly. I know I'm not alone in these thoughts. I recently spoke to a good friend who holds an executive position in a professional sports league and is the only woman in the entire league to currently hold this position. She wants to leave, move on, but she's scared she will close a door for other women.

But at some point, you have to trust the process. Trust the progress and all the hard work women have done and continue to do in the sports industry. It was time for me to leave. Thankfully, the door did not close. Julia Tocheri was named as one of the hosts to step in for *Leafs Lunch* on TSN 1050 radio and at one point Sportsnet 590 The Fan hired Ashley Docking; currently, Ailish Forfar is one of their radio hosts.

Trust the process.

Even though that particular chapter of my career came to a close, I took some incredible memories with me from my days at TSN.

For one night and one night only, I was a TSN Hockey Insider . . . by complete fluke. I got a phone call from a family member who said they were going to be doing some work on the home of a Toronto Maple Leaf. She didn't really know hockey, so she couldn't remember his name. She had been dealing with his wife. I had gone through almost the entire roster before she stopped me: "Yes! That's the guy! Nikita Zaitsev!"

At the time, Zaitsev was in the middle of contract negotiations with the Leafs, and everyone was trying to figure out what the term and salary were going to be.

"Hmmm, if you're doing work for him, I wonder if that means he's staying in Toronto for a while," I said.

"Oh yes," she jumped in. "They are going to be here for at least seven years."

Bingo.

Turns out the Insiders had the AAV (annual average value), but they didn't know the term. I immediately called up Darren Dreger and told him what I heard. TSN had a broadcast that night, and even though he wasn't on it, Bob McKenzie was. Dregs relayed the message to Bobby Mac, who in turn called his source with the Leafs to get confirmation on the seven years. He was given the affirmative. So, the next intermission, Bobby made the announcement.

It was pretty cool to see that all come together and know I played a small part. But of course, I naturally walked around like a bigwig. I cheekily asked Dregs about the next TSN Insider Trading meeting and if I should bring coffee.

"Nice try, kid," he replied.

My time as a Hockey Insider was very short-lived. That's ok. That gig is tough. I've seen those guys in action. I'm more than happy to sit back and tune in to their show for all the updates.

I have incredible memories covering soccer for TSN as well, and a lot of that is thanks to the success of Toronto FC. I began covering TFC in 2009 when I was still under the MLSE umbrella. Along with Leafs TV and Raptors NBA TV, the company launched their own soccer channel: GolTV Canada.

To quote Shaquille O'Neal, the team was "horra-awful" in the beginning.

Things really started to turn around for TFC when MLSE finally brought someone in who understood soccer: Tim Leiweke. And the team started to heat up during my time hosting MLS on TSN.

In 2015, TFC made the playoffs for the first time but was promptly eliminated in the first knock-out game by country rivals CF Montreal.

The following year was an incredible ride. The partnership between Jozy Altidore and Sebastian Giovinco really blossomed. Toronto won the Canadian Championship for the first time since 2012 and became the first Canadian MLS team to make it all the way to the MLS Cup Final. But first, the Eastern Conference Finals. Toronto FC vs. CF Montreal, who were known then as the Montreal Impact. It was a home and away series, and the first game was held in Montreal. That game has become known as the night we literally watched paint dry.

The game was a big deal because it was the furthest both teams had gone in the playoffs — semifinals — and the first time two Canadian teams were contesting for the Conference title. Montreal normally plays out of Saputo Stadium, just over a nineteen-thousand capacity. But this match-up was so huge that Montreal moved the game to the Olympic Stadium, affectionately called "The Big O." They announced a sell-out crowd: 61,004.

The players, from both teams, were none too pleased about the move. The stadium was built in 1976 for the Olympics and was in need of major repairs. The pitch was turf laid over concrete. The ground was hard as a rock and hard on the players' joints. The day before the match, the TSN crew of me, Luke Wileman, Kristian Jack, and Steven Caldwell took in practice. We were standing with then TFC media relations guy Mike Masaro. Giovinco didn't like speaking to the media because he wasn't comfortable with his English yet, but he made a beeline towards us when he saw us arrive. Hands on hips, huffing and puffing, he said, "Look at this! How can we play on this?" He then proceeded to start ripping up a corner of the turf. "Look! Look! This is not right. Tell people about this. Write it. Say it on the TV!" Before any of us could respond, he put his hands back on his hips, turned, and stomped away. Masaro broke the silence when he quipped, "Can't speak English, my ass!" We all burst out laughing, but we also all agreed with Giovinco.

The next night was game night. We invited Carl Robinson to be a part of our panel as a special guest analyst. He had played for Toronto FC and was currently the head coach of the Vancouver Whitecaps. We were doing our pregame show with warm-ups going on behind us. During one of the commercial breaks, Carl leaned over to KJ and said he didn't think the goal lines were painted properly. The measurements appeared to be off, and he noticed the goalkeepers and coaches starting to count their steps. Turns out the 18-yard lines were completely off. They were too narrow! This was all discovered with about twelve minutes till kick-off. Unbelievable! At one point, Montreal player and once Chelsea great Didier Drogba popped his head out to see the situation and had an absolute look of disgust on his face.

They had to repaint the lines, and we had to wait forty-five minutes for them to dry. Our show went longer than expected as we literally sat there and watched . . . paint dry.

I use this experience as an example when speaking to aspiring journalists about being prepared for anything. Often, you do a ton of work and probably use 5 percent of it in a show. But the reason you do so much research is to be ready for the unexpected. When the show went an extra hour, none of us on set missed a beat because we were all properly prepared. You never know when something unexpected is going to happen and you're called upon to do some serious tap dancing.

Toronto won the Eastern Conference title that year and faced the Seattle Sounders in the Cup Final. The game was held in Toronto at BMO Field on December 10, 2016. It was friggin' cold. Factor in the stadium being right along Lake Ontario, and that lake breeze made it feel like the North Pole. That night, the city had wind, snow, and sleet. The game went into penalty kicks, and when Kristian Jack returned from being on the sideline, his hair looked like it had been electrocuted then frozen into place. But I had a completely different experience that night from KJ and my two analysts, Carl Robinson and Greg Sutton. Unlike them, who believed they were going to freeze to death, I thought I was going to die from heatstroke. TSN brought this massive fan that pumped out heat. It was so huge we had to rearrange our chairs on set to make room for it. It found a home right beside me. When we turned it on, it felt great. I was nice and toasty. But after a few minutes, Carl and Greg said they still weren't feeling any heat. We kept it running, thinking it would eventually reach them but . . . nope. This thing the size of a tire was just blowing hot air about two feet in front of it. By the time halftime rolled around, I was sweating like I had just done a cardio workout while the guys had their coats zipped up. They had their scarves, hats plus earmuffs, and gloves on. I had no hat, no scarf, no gloves, and my coat was unzipped. I would've found it funny at the time if I wasn't on the verge of passing out.

When the game was over, I checked Twitter and saw fans commending me for being a "true Canadian" and "tough as nails" because I wasn't as bundled up and "soft" as the guys were when it came to the cold. Little did they know I had the Sahara Desert blowing up my wazoo.

Don't worry, Mother Nature froze me out before that night and plenty of times afterwards. In December 2013, I worked the alpine event in Lake Louise, Alberta, where Lindsey Vonn skied in her first race since returning from her knee injury. I stood outside for hours in minus 36-degree Celsius weather; I had icicles on my eyebrows, eyelashes, and hair. I also worked the Snow Rodeo in Alberta, snowboard halfpipe and slopestyle. That was the first time I learned what a polar vortex is. I spent hours in temperatures that felt like minus 52. My phone died immediately, and my fingertips were in agony within two seconds of taking them out of my gloves. My husband came with me on that trip because the event went through New Year's Eve, 2021 to 2022. He came to pick me up at the end of the day, and I was so frozen I couldn't bend my joints to get into the car. He hoisted me in as if I were a cardboard cutout.

Every day was full of laughs at TSN. A big reason for that was my *Leafs Lunch* producer, Stephanie Apolito. Even if I came to work cranky — you know, after another Leafs early exit from the playoffs — she always managed to make me giggle about something.

I was crushed when I heard the news of *Leafs Lunch* getting cancelled. It was the summer of 2023, and I was in Las Vegas for soccer. I was covering the Final Four of the CONCACAF Nations League tournament because Canada was in it. A bunch of us media folks were at Canada's practice when the news became public. We couldn't believe it. How could a Leafs-crazed city like Toronto lose a show that dedicated two hours every day to Leafs talk? It prompted us to discuss the ever-changing landscape of journalism. When it comes to radio, car manufacturers like Volvo, Ford,

BMW, and Tesla are just a few who have said they will be eliminating AM radio from their dials.

That's why I think Sportsnet's decision back in the day to put *Hockey Central at Noon* on TV was brilliant. It was such a novel concept in the early 2000s, and I was hooked. I loved watching Nick Kypreos, Daren Millard, and Doug MacLean yell at each other! Radio was adapting, and simulcasting on TV was a huge step towards reaching a wider audience. When TSN radio launched, it did the same thing. To this day, I have people coming up to me saying they had *Leafs Lunch* on the television at work every day. Eventually, our radio shows were turned into podcasts. People who couldn't listen or watch live had the option to download the show later in the day.

Sadly, when budgets come calling, there will be victims.

I really hope more women can see themselves hosting sports talk radio or a sports podcast. When I was announced as the permanent host in 2016, I became the first woman in Canada to host a daily sports talk radio show. That ruffled a lot of feathers with the knuckle-draggers out there, but I know I inspired young girls; I had fathers and uncles reach out to me on Twitter to tell me so. But I know radio and podcasts can be intimidating for a lot of women. In October 2020, Sean Fitz-Gerald of *The Athletic* wrote a piece about the challenges women faced in sports radio and why so few worked in the medium. It wasn't until I saw the responses to the article that I felt compelled to respond. I don't normally care about degenerate comments, but this hit close to home. I felt it was my duty to lend my voice to the narrative. Here is the Twitter thread I put out on October 21, 2020:

> Hmm, so here's the thing. I don't like taking to twitter to talk about women in sports media. Too personal and complicated a topic to try and explain on this type of medium. But based on Sean Fitzgerald's recent article that has spurred the conversation today, I will say this: women love sports. Women watch sports.
>
> Women are knowledgeable in sports. Women spend money on sports. Women play sports. And women talk sports. Want to see more women? Change comes from the top. Since the topic is radio, I'll stick to that medium. I was

> 10yrs into the television business before Nelson Millman called me and asked if I'd join the NHL Network's radio station as a part-time host. Shortly afterwards, Jeff MacDonald offered me a full-time job at TSN 1050 hosting *Leafs Lunch*; a gig I've held going on 5 years. Sure, some ass-backwards people have tried to get me off the air because they don't want to get their sports from a woman (boo friggin hoo) but the leadership at the top didn't care. Didn't listen to hollow voices. Do your homework, be prepared, have fun — that is the message from up top. And yes, there are women out there who aren't good enough. Plain and simple. And they shouldn't get the job over someone else. But that's not the problem. It's that there are too many women who ARE GOOD ENOUGH and they're not being given an opportunity. Fix it. From the top. Top top top. I will forever be grateful to Nelson and Jeff. In fact, when I asked Jeff back in 2016 why he was taking a chance on me his response was encouraging: *I'm not taking a chance, I'm hiring the person I feel is best for the job.*
>
> That's another thing, stop seeing hiring women as 'taking a chance', see them as the right/qualified people for the gig. I've had to learn this type of thinking too after years of being made to feel like I was intruding on someone else's space. From the mamas who bring their kids to practice/games to the women practicing and playing to the ones going on TV/radio talking about practice and games . . . we're not intruding, we helped build this space, baby."

TSN and TSN 1050 radio played a huge role in making me the sportscaster I am today. I will always be grateful for the memories and lasting friendships.

## CHAPTER 32

# SUMMER HOCKEY FUN

Joe Thornton is the reason why I developed an obsession with watching *The Maury Povich Show,* and Marty St. Louis is the reason why I almost broke my ankles.

In the early 2000s, during my Leafs TV days, a producer I worked with at MLSE also had a production company. He had been hired to shoot instructional hockey videos for Kellogg's, and the videos would be sold in cereal boxes.

The two hockey players were Joe and Marty, and then, little ole me was the host.

The first summer, we shot ball hockey videos. I had interviewed Joe and Marty as part of media scrums after games, but this was totally different. We were together all day, shooting, joking around, and getting to know one another. I was pretty nervous, but the guys were great.

That summer was also the first time I saw someone get smoked by a camera.

The shooting location was a house with a massive driveway. A ton of kids were part of the shoot. We were doing a jib shot — a jib is a huge camera you see on an extended arm that creates those beautiful sweeping shots — and the kids were all sitting down in a line in front of the goalie net. The producer wanted the jib to sweep over the kids from behind and end right in front of the net. The kids were told many times — don't stand up, stay seated, don't pop up, sit down at all times. The crew told them, their parents reminded them, and everyone said they understood.

And just as the jib swooped through the air over the heads of the seated kids . . . one pops up and is in the process of saying he has to use the washroom when the camera knocks him silent. Dear Lord, child. We all froze. But the kid got lucky. He was fine. No blood. More embarrassed than anything.

But man, that could've been worse.

The following summer, we were in a hockey rink, and there were no kids. Less to worry about.

That summer was way more fun because the three of us and the crew were now comfortable with one another. We picked up where we left off. The only problem was now that Joe and Marty knew me well, they had no problem teasing me.

Right away, they were not happy with the dressing rooms situation. They had to share a small space while I had a massive room with a couch, television, and Nintendo Wii all to myself. Joe, who's 6'4, was the first to speak up: "This won't do, Petrillo. From now on, this will be my room."

In the end, the room belonged to all of us: me, Marty, Joe, and our makeup person.

One day, it was my turn to shoot some solo on-cameras. When I came back to our room to kick off my skates, Joe was sleeping on the couch. It was close to 1 p.m., and I wanted to watch a show I'd been watching since I was ten years old: *Days of Our Lives*. Yup, a soap opera. It's my guilty TV pleasure.

So, I tiptoed into the room, grabbed the TV remote, and changed the channel.

He had been watching *The Maury Povich Show*, and there were about ten minutes left in the program.

Just as quickly as I changed shows, I heard, "Put Maury back on. I need to know who the baby's daddy is."

I just about hit the ceiling with fright. I swore I heard Joe snoring — he was out. But there he was, eyes open, wide awake, and he wouldn't take no for an answer. We had to know the DNA results.

So, we sat there watching the drama unfold before our very eyes, and I'm embarrassed to admit — I got hooked. For years after that day, I would watch Maury. I finally understood Joe's obsession: I just had to know who the baby's daddy was.

Marty wasn't hooked on TV shows, but he loved a good joke.

I had never played Nintendo Wii before and didn't know how the controllers worked. I had just gotten off the ice, still had my skates on, and saw Marty playing. I asked him to show me how to play the tennis video game, and he told me I had to run as if I was playing for real.

Like an idiot, I ran side to side, still wearing skates, trying to hit this video game ball while waving the controller around like a real racket. My fault for not taking off my skates, and Marty was having a good chuckle watching me destroy my ankles and almost face-plant the wall.

I learned the hard way that I didn't need to run around like that.

I also learned quite a bit about Joe and Marty.

Joe is very laid back. Very cool and easy to get along with. That's why it didn't surprise me at all that the young guys on the Leafs adored him. Auston Matthews even chose to bring Jumbo Joe as his guest on one of the Toronto Maple Leafs mentors trips.

Marty always took his scenes during the Kellogg's shoots very seriously. He wanted to make sure he was explaining things properly and giving the best advice possible. And that's why it doesn't surprise me that he became an NHL head coach. I'm sure there are people in the Montreal Canadiens organization who can also attest to Marty's humour!

Those two summers were a ton of fun. It's always nice when you get to see the athletes outside of their work environment. You get to know them better and see who they really are. Hopefully, they get to see that not all media are big bad wolves!

# CHAPTER 33

# RELATIONSHIPS ARE HARD

A woman working in a male-dominated industry and interviewing athletes, often on the road, who are in peak physical condition? Yeah, that doesn't often go over very well with that woman's potential suitors. So, it's no surprise that young aspiring female broadcasters ask me how I handled work and my dating life. I tell them the truth: It was damn hard, it was heartbreaking, it was exhausting, but I eventually found someone who supports, trusts, and encourages me to always chase my dreams.

But let me tell ya, there were a lot of frustrating relationships along the way. Please don't let someone else's insecurities derail you from the path you've chosen. It's a path you're passionate about, it's a goal you've dreamed about, it's a life you want to live. Only step away because *you* have decided to follow another road. Never let anyone guilt you out of following your dreams because of their jealousies.

When I found out I got the job with Leafs TV and would be travelling with the team on their charter plane to every single road game, I was dating someone. Shortly before starting the job, a group of us went to a Buffalo Bills game. A friend of my boyfriend was making small talk with me and asked where I worked. I told him about my new job, and he immediately stiffened up and said, "If you were my girlfriend, I'd never let you take that job. No way in hell I'm dating a girl who hangs around pro athletes all the time."

Good thing I wasn't his girlfriend. Unfortunately, I knew all my boyfriend's friends thought this way, and I have zero doubts they were feeding his insecurities with their own.

Anytime something funny happened at work, I would share the story with him, and he always looked uncomfortable.

"Darcy Tucker said something hilarious today," I would share.

Barely an acknowledgement.

"I think I'm finally getting Mats Sundin to trust me."

Blank look on his face.

"I have a long road trip coming up."

Grim look followed by a miffed grunt.

My work schedule with Leafs TV was demanding a lot of my time, but I did have the upcoming Valentine's Day weekend off. I was planning a nice evening out with my boyfriend.

With a few weeks to go until my time off, I was on a road trip with the team when I got an email from my boss asking if I could now work that weekend. The network had added some shows, and they wanted me to front them. My heart sank. I knew my boyfriend wouldn't understand, and it was a conversation I didn't want to have. Maybe I'll tell my boss no? That didn't sit right with me.

I was stressing out over what to do, so I decided to blow off some steam in the gym before responding to the email. Joe Bowen was in the hotel gym riding the bike. I told him my predicament. He thought about it for a second and then asked, "How often does Valentine's Day come around?"

"Every year," I responded.

"And how often does a chance come around to impress your boss and show you're serious about your career?"

"Umm, not that often."

Great advice. I worked that weekend and felt great; I went out for dinner another night with my boyfriend.

Bonsie was always giving me advice. He could see my potential, and he wanted to make himself available to me anytime I had any questions — about navigating the industry and dealing with relationships affected by it.

One of those lessons came on my very first road trip with the team. We arrived in Boston, and the media crew of Bonsie, Dennis Beyak, Jim Ralph, Harry Neale, and I all agreed to drop our bags off in our rooms and meet back in the lobby fifteen minutes later, at 4:15 p.m. I settled into my room, did some refreshing, changed my clothes, then went back down. It was around 4:18 p.m. I didn't see anyone else and figured I was the first to arrive. I waited for about ten minutes and then felt something was wrong. I sent a message to the group asking if the meet-up time had changed. The response was, "Nope, we're already at the pub around the corner from the hotel. 4:15 is 4:15."

When I finally met up with them, they teased me about being late. But to make sure I didn't feel too bad, they had a drink waiting for me.

Bonsie belted, "If the bus leaves at 10, you show up at 9:30!"

I was also told, "The news starts at 6 p.m. . . . not 6:01 p.m."

I was never late again.

My relationship problems persisted that first year with Leafs TV. One weeknight, the Leafs had a game in Buffalo. When it was a one and done game against the Sabres and no other travel was required, the team would bus it over the border. On these occasions, I would drive myself and not be on the bus. I decided to drive up earlier than everyone else because I wanted to see if I could get in some good shopping. After giving my credit card a workout, I hit the hotel gym and then took a long, hot shower. When I got out of the shower, I saw that I had missed more than ten calls from my boyfriend. All I could think was, *Oh no, who died?* As I was holding the phone, he called again. I barely answered hello when he went off asking where I was, who I was with, was I lying, etc. A crazed tirade. I couldn't get a word in. Finally, I was able to answer his questions: "I'm in Buffalo by myself, the team hasn't arrived yet, and neither have any of the other media members."

His paranoia completely turned me off.

I didn't feel like I could share my world with him because he didn't like my world. Obviously, that relationship didn't work out.

Another person I dated had dreams of playing in the NHL. After a while, it became evident he resented me for having a job covering the very league he wanted to be in.

One night during dinner, he said, "No offence, but women really shouldn't be covering men's sports."

Um, yeah bro, offence totally taken.

He still kept in contact with guys who played in the minors and knew NHL guys, so he was always hearing stories. One time, I was driving home from work, and he called me and said he had heard an NHL player from another city had a girl he liked to call upon when he was in Toronto. I sat in silence on the other end of the phone, waiting for more to the story. Maybe he knew the girl? Maybe he thought I cared about this gossip?

And then he asked, "Is it you?"

"What the hell?" I spat. "Are you serious with that question? Is that what you think of me?"

I knew he was never going to take me seriously as a broadcaster; he was never going to respect my hard work or support my dreams. In his eyes, I was just a chick working around guys all day.

And then there are other times when the relationship causing you a problem isn't even yours!

I heard a story once about a golf tournament a few decades ago that former NHLer Rick Vaive was hosting. He ended up being criticized for not inviting women. When he was interviewed, he doubled down and said there was no way the wives of the players would allow their husbands to play with other women. Had I not had a similar experience, I would've said he was full of crap and criticized him for coming up with such a lame excuse.

I worked with this one guy in particular who would never come out for drinks with the crew after a show. We always asked, he always said no. But I could tell he wanted to join us; there was always something strange about the way he said no. One day, I flat out asked what was up with him. He was a former pro hockey player who was all about team bonding, and yet, he always stiffed us. Finally, he caved and told me the truth. He said his wife wouldn't allow him to go out after our shows because I was there. If there were no women, then he could go. I was the problem.

"Ludicrous!" I said. "There's a whole crew of us, not just me and you!" It didn't matter to her, and this guy didn't feel like creating issues at home, so he avoided going out with the gang if I was there.

Sadly, romantic relationships aren't the only relationships affected when chasing your dreams. This industry is tough. Especially in Canada, where the market is small, the networks are few, and the top on-air positions don't open up often. Hard work and dedicating a lot of time to your craft is essential to progress, especially early on.

When I knew I wanted to get into broadcasting, I dove in headfirst. I volunteered at Rogers Cable York Region a few days a week, and on Sundays, I did the traffic updates for SkyWorks traffic. My shift started at 5 a.m. No one was in the studio. It was just little ole me in my track pants, a sweatshirt, and a baseball cap; this was before radio was on TV, and you could show up looking like you just rolled out of bed. I fired up all the computers and listened to the police monitors for accidents or road closures. After compiling my notes, I would give traffic news from Toronto to Niagara and all around cottage country. I was in my early twenties, and while friends were partying late on Saturday nights, I was going to bed early.

My work/life balance has changed over the years. My friends heard a lot of "Sorry, can't make it," but the supportive ones stuck around. Unfortunately, I lost a good friend who I had known for decades because she didn't understand my dedication. The night before the biggest gig of my career, hosting the Sochi 2014 Olympics, she sent a multi-page email about how I didn't pay attention to her or appreciate her — I was always too busy at work. On the eve of my debut in the host chair — a chair I had worked years to sit in ever since I saw Terry Leibel on my screen — I read an email that both infuriated and saddened me. We grew apart. She couldn't find a way to support me, and I couldn't find the time to be there for her more.

This industry still demands a lot of one's time, especially during big events like the Olympics, World Cups, and world championships. I still have to pass on a lot of social gatherings. The key is to surround yourself with people who understand you and love you. Find friends who totally get your jammed-up schedule and won't make you feel guilty for working a lot. Find a partner who is confident in themselves and, in turn, wants you to share your work experiences with them because they trust you. My parents know there's a good chance I'll be working on their birthdays or on Mother's and Father's Days; but that's ok, we celebrate on another date and enjoy each other's company just the same.

I get it, relationships are hard. Especially when you're chasing a career versus a job. And especially when you're a woman covering men's sports.

Yeah, relationships are hard, but not impossible.

## CHAPTER 34

# FINDING LOVE

I've only cried twice when watching sports. Both times were tears of joy.

In my younger years, I had only two emotions when watching sports: pure elation or pure anger. But as I got older and had more connections to the teams and players, the floodgates wanted to open.

When Italy won the World Cup in 2006, all I could think about was partying.

When the Toronto Maple Leafs lost Game 7 to the Boston Bruins in the first round of the 2013 playoffs after having a 4–1 lead, I was so angry I couldn't speak.

I'll share with you the second and last time I cried. It was recent. At the Tokyo 2020 Olympics, which were held in 2021, the Canadian women's soccer team finally won the gold medal, and it choked me up. I had become emotional a few days earlier when they defeated the Americans in the semifinals. It was the first time since March 2001 that the Canadians beat their neighbours to the south. A solid twenty years later, they got the job done. American star Megan Rapinoe was so shocked after the match that she said, "I don't think I've ever lost to Canada. So, it's a bitter one." And she was right. She joined the US national team in 2006; she had never lost to Canada in her career. That tells you how big of a deal that win was for Canadians.

But I didn't cry after that game. There was still work to do. We had the gold medal game to get through, and boy, did it ever take our emotions on a rollercoaster ride. Canada defeated Sweden in a shootout, and it was complete mayhem in the Olympic studio. For those Olympics, I was hosting the soccer matches with former national team goalkeeper Karina LeBlanc as my analyst.

When Julia Grosso scored the game-winning penalty kick, my mind went back to May 2009 — when I first started covering the women's national team. It's crazy the number of thoughts your brain can process in such a short amount of time. But I thought of that first camp. The women were in Toronto for a friendly, and I went out to practice and interviewed Christine Sinclair, Kara Lang, and Melissa Tancredi. I loved the vibe, the players were awesome, and I was hooked. That also meant I had been riding the emotional ups and downs with this team for over a decade by the time the Tokyo Olympics rolled around. From the low of the 2011 World Cup with just one goal scored, the infuriating refereeing in the semifinal game against the US at the 2012 Olympics, to the bounce back in the bronze medal game and standing on the podium. Like the rest of the country, I felt the energy that came with hosting a World Cup in 2015. The team made it to the quarterfinals but couldn't recover after allowing early goals to England. At the Rio 2016 Olympics, they stood on the podium again, but they weren't happy with bronze. Canada had beaten Germany in the group stage, but the rematch in the semifinals went the other way.

Canada was ready for gold. Their motto heading into the Tokyo Olympics was "Change the Colour."

So, when they finally did it, it was all those memories and the tournaments in between that came flooding to my mind. I was doing ok, holding back my tears — after all, I still had an Olympic show to do! — until I looked over at Karina, who wears her emotions on her sleeve, and she was sobbing. That was all it took for my floodgates to open up as well.

I managed to get my act back together by the time we went to air; Karina was still choked up. What a softy!

The very first time I cried was December 9, 2017. I remember the minute too — 67th. It was the MLS Cup Final between Toronto FC and the Seattle Sounders. Many of you may be thinking I cried because Toronto won the MLS Cup. After all, I started covering the club in 2009 and travelled around with the team for years, covering one deflating season after another. But no, you'd be wrong. I cried because of my husband — Jon Conway.

Jon and I first met in April 2010. He had just been signed by Toronto FC to be one of their goalkeepers. The first time I saw him was on a road trip. We were making our way to Salt Lake City, Utah, and for the first time, the team was travelling charter. I can't remember the reason why, but MLSE got approval from the league to do so for scheduling purposes. It wasn't until out of necessity during the pandemic that MLS started flying their teams charter. Up until 2020, the teams still travelled commercial, much to the chagrin of MLSE. I remember talking to COO Tom Anselmi about it, and he was pushing hard right from when TFC entered the league in 2007 to fly charter. But other owners didn't want to cough up the money.

Having travelled charter with the Leafs, I told the TFC guys they were in for a treat. Every seat was premium economy, the middle of the plane had a buffet for when you first boarded, and once in the air, they did a meal and drink service. The guys were stoked. Imagine our surprise when we pulled up to the tarmac and saw what looked to be a toy plane. The engine was so small that we, in fact, had to stop halfway through our flight to refuel in Des Moines, Iowa. Geez. The guys were chirping me hard: "Where's that premium economy plane you said we'd be getting, Petrillo?" "I'm starving over here; these crackers won't do." "My shoe doesn't even fit in the aisle!"

I felt horrible. I'm not sure why we got such a small plane, but apparently, it was better than flying commercial for that particular trip.

Jon is 6'5 and a solid 230. He barely fit onto that little aircraft. I'm being serious. When I looked back and saw him, his knees were jammed up against the seat in front of him and his head was slightly tilted because the roof of the plane was so low! My field producer leaned over and said, "Toronto got themselves a cute goalkeeper!"

I admit I thought the same but couldn't stop laughing at his uncomfortable situation.

The next day, after breakfast with my TV crew, we saw Jon in the hotel lobby chatting with the goalkeeper coach, Mike Toshack. They were sitting on one of the sofas. We went over to say hi to Tosh and made our introductions to the new goalie.

"Hi, I'm Andi. I host all the TFC games on GolTV. Nice to meet you," I said.

And like a pure snoot, he responded, "Oh hi, I'm Jon Conway," and then turned his body to face the other way on the couch.

Ouch. I guess the conversation was over.

He would later tell me he did that because he was so nervous when he first met me. He thought I was beautiful, and he didn't know what to say. To which I promptly responded, "You're lucky I'm not easy to offend because that first impression was atrocious."

We barely spoke to each other that year. But I saw how hard he worked. He was near the end of his career, and he was definitely brought in to be a veteran presence. He helped the team win the 2010 Canadian Championship. It didn't surprise me at all that, after he retired, TFC saw his value as a coach and mentor. He first began coaching in their academy system before being promoted to the first team in 2014.

Back to 2010, where sadly, TFC once again did not make the playoffs. However, at that time, MLS was still hosting the MLS Cup Final on neutral grounds. In 2010, Toronto was chosen as the host site. The players were asked to stick around for the festivities. I hosted a lot of the MLS parties on behalf of MLSE, and that's when Jon and I started running into each other quite a bit.

Jon also lived next to the Scotiabank Arena, and on his way to get groceries, he would knock on the window before I went to air with a Leafs pregame show to say hello. Our studio set was visible from the outside.

He did this a few times a week. Sometimes he'd knock on the window during commercial breaks to get my attention. It was actually very endearing. Later in our relationship, I asked him how many times he would grocery shop in a week. He said just once.

"But wait a second, you would stop by multiple times when I was working to say hello!"

He laughed. "Didn't you notice that half the time I was just walking around with an empty bag? I used it as a prop so it wouldn't look like my sole purpose was to come say hi to you!"

We started talking, we enjoyed each other's company, the Cup was awarded, and then Jon was gone. He's originally from Philadelphia. We kept in touch while he was gone, and I just knew something was different.

I remember talking to my mother in my younger years after every heartbreak and asking her, "Will I ever find the one?" And I'm sure you've all been told something similar: "You'll just know!" Well, I just knew. And just as I was counting down the days to Jon coming back to town, he got traded in the offseason to Chicago. I remember that day. I was going to visit my grandparents, and as I parked in the parking lot of their building, Jon called.

"You heard the news?" he asked.

"I did. Congrats!" I said, trying to sound excited for him despite being disappointed.

"Yeah, thanks. Kinda sucks for us though, doesn't it?"

"How so?" I said, playing it cool.

"Well" — he hesitated — "I kinda like what we've started."

*Phew, he feels the same way.* "Yeah, me too," I said.

Then there was a long pause.

Neither of us really wanted to be the first to admit we had strong feelings for the other one. We had just been getting to know each other, and now we were being thrown a long-distance curveball.

I broke the silence. "I would like to continue talking if you want to as well."

"I do! I would love that."

"And Chicago isn't that far," I continued. "We can visit each other."

"Exactly. It's a plan!"

And that's what we did. At least once a month, we'd see each other. On the nights there were Raptors games, I only had to host the pregame show and didn't have to stick around for postgame. So, I would do the show until 7 p.m., hop into a cab, have them take me to the airport in downtown Toronto (Billy Bishop Airport), and by 8:30 p.m., I'd be on a flight to Chicago. I'd spend the weekend, come back home, then count the days until I got to do it again.

At the end of the 2011 season, Jon retired. He entered the league in 2001. He was part of it during its infancy when players made peanuts and had no rights. The league is built on the backs of men like my husband.

Even though he was ready to retire — his back and his knees told him so — it was a tough transition. When I hear players talk about how hard retirement is, I get it. I don't just sympathize, I empathize. When the spouses of players talk about their pain and feeling helpless during this transition, I nod my head in understanding so hard I can hear my neck crack.

For a good year, he felt lost.

And then, at the end of 2012, he was offered a job with Toronto FC's academy. He loved that job. Jon's a motivator by nature. Seeing other people succeed with his help is what makes him happy.

Near the end of the 2014 MLS season, the coaching staff for TFC's first team had been let go, and Greg Vanney, the academy director at the time, was promoted to head coach. He brought Jon with him as his goalkeeper coach.

All of our friends and family were over the moon. But Jon and I think alike. As happy as we were for this promotion, we looked at each other and practically said simultaneously, "Coaches are hired to be fired."

But such is the life of being a pro coach, and Jon dove in headfirst.

It was a dive that lasted ten years. An incredible run. And there were plenty of ups and downs that I lived through right alongside him.

I've already spoken of the 2016 Eastern Conference Finals between Toronto FC and the Montreal Impact, as they were known then. The first time two Canadian teams went head-to-head that far into the playoffs. It was a home and away series, which means away goals matter. For those not familiar with the age-old soccer rule, it's simply explained like this: Away goals count for more. It's a way of breaking a tie if one should come about.

It wasn't at the 2016 Eastern Conference Final Leg 1 that I cried. But I came close. And I didn't come close because I was sad TFC was losing. I'm all for a good match, no matter the teams. That's the broadcaster in me speaking. But the wife in me that night was crushed. TFC were down 3–0 in the game, and the majority of the 61,000 plus in attendance cheered for TFC's demise, which meant they were cheering for my husband's failure. I'm not saying they shouldn't have been booing their opponent or they shouldn't have been elated that their team was winning — that's sports. The atmosphere was electric. It was intoxicating to witness as a broadcaster. But again, as a wife, the energy in the Big O that night was going towards crushing all the hard work and dreams of someone I love.

Sports are wild that way. What a mind screw it is for a losing team who has a massive fanbase mourning a loss right alongside you, but then there's this equally massive fanbase dancing on the grave of your season.

I felt helpless for him that night. I wanted to run across the field and shield him. All those people hated his team, the logo he represented, and him. It was overwhelming. Toronto lost the game 3–2. Despite the loss, those two away goals were huge. In Leg 2, the scoreline was the same after ninety minutes but reversed. This time, it was 3–2 for Toronto, which meant extra time. TFC would go on to win and make the MLS Cup Final for the first time in franchise history.

My husband and the club would go on to lose the final to the Seattle Sounders. It was a hard-fought match. Scoreless after regulation and extra time, it went to penalties. But no, I didn't cry then either. I was experiencing a lot of emotions for the first time. Experiencing the highs and lows of the sports world as a broadcaster is completely different from doing so as a life partner. While I was able to stay professional at work while covering the games, I was emotionally drained when I got home and started to see how the game unfolded through my husband's eyes. What a trip that was.

But 2017 is when I cried.

I covered the regular season for TSN but sadly was not able to do the Conference Finals or MLS Cup Final. The Pyeongchang 2018 Olympics were just over a month away, and my weekends were tied up with CBC Sports coverage. But that meant I could truly enjoy the game in the stands as a fan. I went to the final with my parents. They never missed a game and were just as devoted to Jon's happiness as I was.

It was a rematch between Toronto FC and the Seattle Sounders. December 9, 2017. That's the night I cried for the first time watching sports. It came in the 67th minute. Jozy Altidore scored to put TFC in the lead. I jumped up to cheer, but instead, the sound that came out of me was a croak. The emotions that overcame me shocked me. I didn't see the tears coming — but they did. I just knew in my bones that my husband was going to win the championship. All the memories of hard work, of days he was never around because he was on road trips, of missing out on birthdays and weddings and get-togethers with friends, of losses along the way and friendships made, came to mind. Alex Bono was the goalkeeper for

Toronto, and Jon had been high on him right from the get-go. He pushed to have TFC draft him and built a bond with him that's strong to this day. I knew it meant everything to Jon to see Bones get the job done that night. It ended 2–0. My husband was a champion. So yeah, I cried when that first goal went in. That goal was the pretty bow wrapped around years of hard work. It was the bow on top of a love story that rode the crazy wave of professional sports.

There you have it; 2017 and 2021 were the two times I've cried during a sporting event. But I have a feeling more tears are in my future.

I have to admit that as I'm getting older, I'm starting to get more emotional around storylines that emphasize the process of an athlete's or team's journey. The results don't always tell the whole story. The journey has become more important to me. Watching Andre De Grasse win the 200m Olympic title in Tokyo after battling injuries for so many years got me choked up. Watching Nick Taylor win the Canadian Open in 2023 and becoming the first Canadian to do so since 1954 got me choked up. Watching the Canadian men's national soccer team qualify for the 2022 FIFA World Cup, you guessed it, choked up. Watching the women step onto the ice for the inaugural Professional Women's Hockey League game on January 1, 2024, extremely choked up. In 2024, Cavalry FC of the Canadian Premier League finally won the North Star Cup, and head coach Tommy Wheeldon Jr. shared with me the struggles he went through that season: lost a player he had coached in a motorcycle accident, his father-in-law passed away, and then he had to put his beloved dog down. When I saw him and his wife on the pitch celebrating their win, I ran over to give them a big hug. The longer I've been covering sports, the more the human story intrigues me. The story of perseverance, of failure, of getting back up and fighting, of being able to bring an entire country together by wearing the flag proudly on their heart; each of these athletes and coaches has their own story worth telling. I only hope I can do their stories justice when I share them.

My husband and I continue to navigate this crazy world of sports together. I even persuaded him to come over to the "dark side" of broadcasting and call games for the CPL.

We are each other's biggest fans. And the ultimate teammates.

## CHAPTER 35

# EQUALITY OF LANGUAGE

We were getting ready to go to air with women's rugby sevens. I was on set at the CBC with my rugby analyst, World Cup silver medalist Andrea Burk. Andrea and I were looking at the monitor and watching the players take to the field. These rugby players were absolutely jacked. So strong and powerful.

I thought back to the day before when I had been on the air hosting men's rugby sevens. The language we used around those athletes focused on their physical makeup just as much as their skill. It's very common in men's sports to talk about the athlete's height, weight, size of their legs to generate power, and size of their hands to hold a rugby ball, football, or basketball. But when it comes to describing female athletes, we shy away from those types of physical attributes.

I turned to Andrea and asked her why. She shrugged her shoulders and said she didn't know.

"When you were playing, would it have bothered you if someone talked about your weight and height? I mean, being a physical presence in the sport of rugby is an advantage," I said.

"I wouldn't have had a problem at all. But people just never mentioned those kinds of things, so I never really thought about it," she responded.

I proceeded to tell her I was envious of women who were around 5'9, 180 pounds or more, and just knocking people over left and right on the field. Those strong bodies, just like on the men's side, should be celebrated. If we did that more, then perhaps incredible athletes like Ilona Maher wouldn't have been cruelly attacked for her strong body during the Paris 2024 Olympics. The American rugby sevens player shared the torment she received, and it was infuriating. It made me happy to see the support Ilona received not just from the sports world but from many people around the world who celebrated her athletic frame. She was even invited to compete on the reality show Dancing with the Stars and finished in second place!

I really started to realize how differently we talk about women's and men's sports. Not just about their physiques but the type of analysis, criticism, and expectations we give as well.

I started to pay more attention to the language I was using when talking about female and male athletes. I was embarrassed to discover I treated them differently.

I remember being at a party and talking to some guys who weren't supportive of women's sports. I asked them why.

One guy's answer stood out: "It's not the athletes I have a problem with because they're definitely talented, it's the commentary around women's sports that I can't stand. If a woman has a shitty performance or a team was horrible, people make excuses for them. If they were men, people would be dissecting everything that went wrong and would call for heads to roll!"

He wasn't wrong. I caught myself doing this.

Now, in all fairness, female athletes have been fighting for decades to have their space on the sports stage. Highly skilled, hard-working, talented female athletes have been ignored for simply, you know, being women. The last thing they needed in their fight for equality was for people like me to go on air and point out everything they did wrong.

However, people are finally beginning to give them the respect they deserve. Sponsors, investors, and television networks are finally making women's sports a priority. I'm very proud to work at three networks that treat men's and women's sports equally. At CBC Sports, we offer equal coverage for male and female athletes. At OneSoccer, the women's national team has every single one of their games aired with a proper studio show, just like the men's national team. Amazon Prime entered the hockey space, airing both NHL and PWHL games.

Women's sports have come a long way, and I feel we're at a turning point. Part of that turning point is for sportscasters and sportswriters to change their language. More and more women athletes have said to me that while they appreciate being "protected" by soft commentary, they also feel it gives their critics the ammo they need to say that women are weak and can't handle the same type of criticism as men.

Now, I'm not talking about abuse. Nobody, man or woman, deserves to be abused for a performance or a result. That's just despicable. I'm talking about proper analysis and constructive criticism.

I'm talking about equality of language. Here are a few examples . . .

Before the start of the inaugural Professional Women's Hockey League, I had the chance to chat with Toronto's head coach, Troy Ryan. I asked him about the coverage the league was going to receive. All three networks in Canada — CBC, TSN, and Sportsnet — would be airing games, plus many more in the United States. Were he and his players ready for all the attention and the possible scrutiny? He didn't even hesitate with his answer: "That's actually something we've talked about. This league will have more eyeballs on it than the previous leagues that have failed. They know they're entering the spotlight, and they know it won't be positive all the time. They're ready for it, and they welcome it because they just want to be treated the same as the men. They don't want to be coddled."

When the first trade happened in the PWHL, someone suggested in our storyline production meeting that we talk about how hard this is on the player, how she has to leave family and friends behind, how unfair it was that she was getting ready to attend a Super Bowl party and instead had to pack and uproot her life. I pumped the brakes on that angle. Sure, being traded often sucks, but this is something male players deal with all the time, and nobody wants to hear about how difficult it is. There's an understanding that it's hard on them and their families. But with the number of trades that happen every year, our analysis would turn into one big offering of condolences — and fans don't want to hear it. Instead, fans want to know why it didn't work out with the first team, what the player can bring to their new team, and how the player will fit in with their new teammates and coach.

During the 2024 PWHL season, there was a massive trade that saw Toronto send their 2023 2nd overall pick and top defender, Jocelyne

Larocque, to Ottawa. When Larocque did her first interview after the trade, she said she was shocked by the news but then very matter-of-factly said, "But that's pro sports."

That's right, it's professional sports. Female athletes know it; there's no need to coddle them. On the next PWHL show on CBC, our panel broke down the trade the same way we would have an NHL trade. I then tuned into a panel hit between TSN's Kenzie Lalonde and Cheryl Pounder, who both call PWHL games, and they were breaking down the good and bad of the trade in the same way — my heart was singing.

There was another incident that involved the Canadian national soccer teams. Heading into the 2022 FIFA World Cup, the Canadian men entered a labour dispute with the federation. They even boycotted a game. Needless to say, there was a lot of turmoil and distraction heading into Canada's appearance at a men's World Cup for the first time since 1986. With that kind of time between appearances and the labour issues, you would think there wouldn't be a lot of pressure on the team. But this is men's sports. Alphonso Davies was criticized for taking a penalty kick and missing, coach John Herdman was criticized for getting lineup selections wrong, and people were saying certain players were too old and needed to go. Some of the soccer fans reading this right now might be thinking, *All fair analysis.*

Now let's look at the women. They too entered a labour dispute with Canada Soccer. They threatened to boycott a tournament. Just like the men, they entered their World Cup in the summer of 2023 with a lot of turmoil and distractions surrounding them. Just like the men, the women's star player, Christine Sinclair, missed a penalty kick. Head coach Bev Priestman's tactics were not working. And Canada had a horrible showing in their final group stage game that saw them exit the tournament early. When I went to air and talked about the women's performance the same way I did the men's, the public responses were completely different. People were raging: "Don't you know the women are going through a hard time? Their federation is screwing them!" "They're completely distracted! How dare you say anything bad about Sinclair!" "You're anti-feminist!" That last one really chapped my ass. Not only was it categorically wrong, but the irony was that my equality of language was me being a feminist! Both national teams were going through the same thing, and yet the commentary around the men stuck to their performances, and for the women, excuses were being made. And here's the thing: I'm totally fine with the reasons that were being given for the women if the same ones were being made for the men. But they weren't. Different language. Different treatment. That's not equality.

Plus, I hate the practice of coddling and making excuses. It makes women look weak, and they definitely are not. To suggest otherwise makes my blood boil.

My PWHL analysts — Hailey Salvian and Saroya Tinker — and I gave gender-equal commentary throughout the season. We talked about it before the start of the year and were very conscious of our language. We didn't want the women's league to be treated like a kid's league. These are professionals with a lot of pride, and not to mention many of them are world and Olympic champions, and they deserve to be talked about the same way we would talk about the men. We talked about the great Marie-Philip Poulin, captain of the Montreal Victoire, rightfully getting booed in Ottawa because that's pro sports, baby! We were complimentary and critical of the number one draft pick, Taylor Heise, and we didn't hold back when a player wasn't pulling their weight. And you know what? Not one player or team called us crying over our analysis. Not one player complained that we were being too mean or unfair. And most definitely, no one called and accused us of being anti-feminist. Women athletes are tougher than some care to admit.

I know there are many people out there who don't agree with my approach. They'll argue that men deserve harsher criticism because they still make way more money. But let me ask you this: When women compete in their leagues, are they not still expected to win the title? When they compete at a World Cup, the Olympics, or a world championship, are they not still expected to win the trophy? Are the pressures on women, as for men, still not the same? Women athletes expect just as much from themselves as the men do. I would argue that my use of equal language isn't what needs to change, the salaries do. And that will come. A lot of male athletes who competed during the early days of their leagues will also tell you it took time for their salaries to rise. My husband is a great example of this. Major League Soccer started in 1996, and his first year was 2001. His salary was $24,000. Twenty-five years later, we've seen the introduction of the Designated Player rule in MLS, and we see teams having multiple players on their roster earning millions of dollars. They earn that money off the backs of players like my husband, who helped build the league. Women will also achieve this kind of growth with proper investment. In fact, we're already seeing it in the National Women's Soccer League. In August of 2024, the league announced a new Collective Bargaining Agreement that raised the salary cap and players' earnings and will see the majority of players earn a six-digit figure. The league also became the first in North America to do away with the draft, and players have more control over trades. The league was founded just eleven years ago and is already making leaps and bounds in the sports world. In fact, in September of 2024, according to Sportico, a digital content platform that specializes in the business of sport, the average NWSL franchise is valued at $104 million. The most valuable club is Angel City FC at $250 million.

The Professional Women's Hockey League dropped the puck on their inaugural season on January 1, 2024, and they did so with a Collective Bargaining Agreement already in place. The PWHL became the first professional women's sports league in North America to have a CBA signed before competition even began. With this kind of structure in place, the league is able to maintain financial sustainability while also having a few players on each team earning a six-digit figure right out of the gate.

The women's game is growing, the money is starting to follow, and that's because the quality of the product is there. Now it's about switching how some people still see things.

There's a mentality that still persists, and it drives me mad. It's the belief that supporting men's sports is seen as an investment, whereas supporting women's sports is seen as a risk.

Thankfully, that way of thinking is becoming obsolete. During the PWHL season, I got emails every week announcing a new sponsor.

People can't wait for the launch of the Northern Super League, and founder Diana Matheson has talked about compiling data that shows the financial benefits of supporting women's sports.

The first WNBA game in Canada in 2023 sold out, and a year later, it was announced that Canada would get a team in Toronto starting in 2026. That announcement garnered huge headlines and created a lot of hype.

Investors, sponsors, networks, and online streamers have all jumped onboard the women's sports bandwagon. This isn't a passing fad. People are seeing the value both economically and culturally in supporting women's sports.

And what sports fan doesn't love a new team or player to cheer for? Let's go!

## CHAPTER 36

# USE WITH CAUTION

Social media . . . Do we have to talk about this? Ugh, unfortunately, yes. It can make or break your career, depending on what you post. It can also make or break your soul, depending on how successful you are in gaining control over it and how much you allow it to affect your life.

I've already shared some instances of horrible things said to me through this medium. For many of us, this kind of negativity is something we've come to accept as normal — how sad. For a while now, I've been talking about deleting my platforms. And who knows? By the time this book is published, I may have done just that! I doubt it though. For the simple fact that many potential brand partnerships rely on posting, hashtagging, replying, and overall engagement on social media platforms.

I was late to the social media world. Mostly because I'm a very private person, and I never understood why anyone would care about what I was eating or when I was washing my hair. I've never had a Facebook page, much to the chagrin of my friends.

During my Leafs TV days, co-worker Monika Platek was telling all of us about this new platform called Twitter. It was the future of communication. And it mattered how many followers you had.

"But who are the people following me?" I asked. "Complete and utter strangers? Why do they care what I have to say? Why do I care if they agree with me or not?"

The whole concept was just so bizarre to me, especially since the majority of people in the Twitter space were faceless and nameless.

*No thanks, Twitter isn't for me.*

I think I was the only one in my friend group and at work who didn't have Facebook or Twitter.

The Beijing 2008 Olympics were the first where the power of Twitter was recognized in the broadcast world. For the first time, people had the ability to receive real-time updates. Up until that point, networks controlled the release of stories and competition results. And not in a nefarious way; they controlled it because there was no other avenue to post things. Plus, when sporting events were happening in places with massive time changes — Beijing was fourteen hours ahead of Toronto — a lot of the action happened when most of Canada was sleeping. So, newspapers, radio shows, highlight shows, and any other shows would all post their articles or go to air when the citizens of their country were awake. If a race happened at 2 a.m. ET, you wouldn't know who won until the sports shows went to air in the morning or the newspapers hit the stands. Twitter turned this whole system on its head. Now, if a race happens at 2 a.m. ET, you'll see the results by 2:01 a.m. ET. Heck, you'll even get a proper play-by-play of it, depending on who's watching live and if they're quick enough to tweet the action.

During the Beijing 2008 Olympics, I was still working for MLSE but was able to freelance at CBC Sports. This was the first Games I covered. My shift was from 5 p.m. to 3 a.m. ET. Anytime a Canadian competed, my job was to voice the highlights of their competition. These voiced-over videos were no more than a few minutes long. The videos would then get sent to the mobile phones of people who signed up to receive these updates. I remember a few people saying, "This gig of yours won't be around for the next Olympics. People are already getting their info faster on Twitter!"

And they weren't wrong.

But the good news for me was that I didn't plan on doing that gig again.

I don't remember this conversation happening . . . again, my shift was from 5 p.m. to 3 a.m., and I got a little giddy some nights . . . but according to a co-worker, I pointed to the television one night while Ron

MacLean was hosting and said, "That's going to be me one day. I'm going to be an Olympic host."

A very ambitious declaration, and I'm grateful every day for it coming true!

In 2011, I caved. I created a Twitter account. Not because I wanted to but because I was told to by my new bosses at CBC Sports. At this point in the broadcast world, having a Twitter account was a must. The number of followers someone had mattered. Mostly because it was another platform for networks to advertise their programming.

The first show I did when joining CBC was a hockey show called *Game Day*, and I co-hosted it with PJ Stock on Saturday nights before the start of *Hockey Night in Canada*.

Our first show, I was full of excitement. Not only was I joining the *HNIC* crew, but I was finally entering this digital space that was taking over how we communicated with viewers. However, my Twitter excitement was quickly quashed.

During our first commercial break, I checked Twitter. Big mistake. The first tweet I saw was this: "What the hell is a woman doing on my TV on a Saturday night talking hockey? Get back in the kitchen and cook me a meal."

I felt the blood — and joy — drain from my face. My body went cold, and my heart started beating quickly. At this point, I had been covering hockey at both the junior and NHL level for seven years, I had paid my dues and earned my stripes, and this is how I was still being treated? This is how some people still viewed women in sports? PJ knew something was wrong because my entire demeanour changed, but I told him I was fine, and we carried on. Next commercial break, I just had to check the message again. I wanted to respond. The message was . . . gone.

Where did it go? Had I imagined it? Remember, I was completely new to Twitter and didn't know things could be deleted. After the show, I finally told PJ what had affected me, but now I couldn't find it anymore. He's the one who told me the guy probably deleted it because, hopefully, he realized it was a horrible thing to say. But it didn't matter. I had read it, the damage was done, and clearly, I have not forgotten about it.

It was the first of many insulting tweets, and it's not even close to being the worst one. But because it was the first and it happened so soon into my

Twitter foray, I was skeptical of social media right out of the gate. I mean, there were and probably still are people who take pride in getting blocked because they harass others and say the nastiest of things. And there are co-workers of mine who take pride in *not* blocking these weirdo people. They would say to me, "Andi, you have to take the good with the bad."

Like hell I do. I don't have to welcome negativity into my life at all. I don't have to welcome sexists, racists, bigots, or just plain old idiots into my life. Honestly, what a dumb thing for people to say: *Welcome crap into your life! You have to!*

What were these co-workers of mine smoking?

Don't get me wrong, I love a good, healthy debate and even constructive criticism. But that's not what I'm talking about here. Plus, I still feel like Twitter isn't the place for the above. The art of debating has been lost. We quickly resort to yelling, name-calling, or just outright dismissing people because they don't agree with us. As for constructive criticism, I still take it with a grain of salt on Twitter because that type of evaluation comes from people who genuinely care about you and want to see you improve. My family, friends, and boss give me constructive criticism. Why would an absolute stranger on Twitter care?

I have zero issues blocking people. I block away gleefully! In fact, in 2018, I turned off my Twitter mentions. A big thank you to Gord Miller for encouraging me to do that. He speaks my kind of language: "Andi, you don't have to listen to the opinions of strangers. Just turn it off."

I turned my mentions off just before the Pyeongchang 2018 Olympics, and those were the first Games where I was able to pick up my phone without any anxiety. I hadn't realized how much my phone had become a source of pain to me. There was always this fear I would read something hurtful. But with my mentions off, I could breathe again. There's something special about knowing there are losers out there going out of their way to make you feel bad but have no clue they're yelling into an empty room because you're not there! Ha!

Because of that first night on *Game Day*, I learned early on not to check Twitter while I'm live on the air. At the 2014 Olympics in Sochi, I always knew when my co-host, Andrew Chang, checked his phone. His whole attitude changed. I told him my trick and encouraged him to do the same.

Even when I joined *Leafs Lunch*, and radio is very interactive with listeners, I told my producer I would not check my phone during shows. Even when we would do Twitter polls and I needed to check to get updates on the results, I made her do it for me. I wasn't always like this, but I didn't like how Twitter was making me feel, and I was trying to come up with tools to help me master it and preserve my sanity.

And while both men and women in my industry are equally attacked on these platforms, there's no denying the sexually demeaning and all-out rape undertones that accompany attacks on women.

There have been countless studies done on the abuse female sportscasters and athletes receive on social media compared to their male counterparts. Without fail, the findings show the attacks men face are often about sports results, coaches' decisions, and analysis. The toxic posts towards women attack gender, use sexualized language, and contain sexually violent content.

Sexually degrading women is still a weapon of choice to show dominance.

Here's a revolting example for you that was sent to me after Bryan Trottier was a guest on my radio show:

> Slavic Supremacy: Who's dick did this privileged white woman suck to get this job? Of the thousands of males out there that earned and deserve this job, they find a pussy do a mans job? So, I am to believe this vagina loves Trottier and Hockey more than a man?

And don't even get me started on the numerous inappropriate photos I've been sent that I never asked for.

Along with Gord's encouragement, another deciding factor that went into turning off my mentions on both Twitter and Instagram was one night when I received a lot of . . . compliments. Yup, you read that right. My husband and I were going out for the night, and I posted a photo of myself. My husband told me I looked beautiful, but here I was, constantly checking my phone to see how many strangers were complimenting my look. How embarrassing. My mood was being dictated by what people I didn't even know were saying. Wasn't it enough that I felt great about the way I looked that night and that the man I loved was also telling me how great I looked? That was the switch-flipping moment for me: Just as I shouldn't feel bad about myself because of something a stranger said, I also shouldn't rely on their words to make me feel good.

By the way, I was also a late bloomer when it came to Instagram. It was 2014, and I was working at the NHL Network. I was at the desk with former NHL goalie Jamie McLennan, and he turned to me and said he liked the latest photo I had posted on Instagram.

"Pardon? I don't have Instagram," I responded, baffled.

"What do you mean? I've been following you for months, and so have others!"

He then showed me "my" account, and my jaw dropped. Someone was pretending to be me and was taking photos I was posting on Twitter and putting them on this Instagram page. So, out of necessity, I had to create my own *real* page so people wouldn't continue following an imposter.

Social media has its benefits; hence, why I still have Twitter (now called X) and Instagram accounts. They provide a platform to promote shows I'll be on, events I'll be covering, and basically any on-air work I've done. It's also how I can collaborate with businesses and brands. I'm now at a place where I feel I'm in control of these spaces. I decide when to let people into my life and when to keep my life private. The journey to get here wasn't easy. Ego is a bitch, and it's always tempting you to read what people are saying in response to one of your posts, to care about what they're saying, to have your day or your life affected by what strangers are saying, and to tempt you to respond. But now I trust myself to not get lost in that digital space, and I remember who I am and who truly cares about me in the real world. That's why I was comfortable with turning my mentions back on with Instagram — not Twitter, there's no hope for Twitter. But I turned them back on with Instagram so I could work with brands because of metrics that matter to them when I'm promoting their product.

I acknowledge that I was already a strong woman in my thirties when I entered the social media world. I can't even imagine what young and easily influenced aspiring broadcasters must go through when they're attacked through their phone.

The best advice I can give is this: Don't be afraid to turn it off. You don't have to read the comments, and you sure as hell don't have to accept what's being said.

If you want a real and honest opinion about the work you're doing, then go to your boss! Talk to your executive producer and ask them about areas in which you can improve, things they want to see you do more of, and things they love about your work. They are the ones who will help with your growth and also the ones who decide if you get to keep your job or not! Ha!

Honestly, if I had listened to all the haters when I started working at . . . well, name the job — Leafs TV, *Hockey Night in Canada*, and most definitely when I became host of *Leafs Lunch* — I would have believed that I was getting fired the next day. Thankfully, I've worked with some smart executives who don't get tangled up in that social media space.

And if you don't want to take my word for how beneficial it is to step away from social media from time to time, then perhaps listen to people who are far more famous than me.

Canadian tennis player and US Open champion Bianca Andreescu has talked about her struggles with social media and needing to block it out.

American gymnast and three-time Olympic champion Gabby Douglas has stepped away from social media, citing mental health concerns.

The most decorated gymnast of all time, Simone Biles, has admitted to detaching from her social media platforms to protect her health, and she definitely turns them off during competitions.

Australian swimmer and two-time Olympic champion Ariarne Titmus doesn't have a Twitter account and says she always shuts down her other social media platforms during competitions so she can focus. She admitted that even positive comments can be overwhelming because she can easily get swept up in them.

And there are countless more athletes and celebrities who have talked about their "breaks" from Twitter and Instagram.

When Mitch Marner was in his rookie year with the Toronto Maple Leafs, he was very much in his honeymoon phase with the fans. After one morning skate, I got to chatting with him about Twitter. I asked how he was being treated on it, and he said it was great. He was being shown so much love. Pretty sure I snorted when I told him to proceed with caution. And I'm pretty sure he looked at me like some old woman who had no clue what she was talking about. Fast-forward to his contract year, and he was quite vocal about how the fanbase ruthlessly attacked him on social media while he was negotiating a new deal, and it was a terrible feeling.

I've dedicated a lot of pages to this topic, and I know it's not just people on TV who are victims of the horrible things people say to one another — it happens to everyone. Yes, people who have the spotlight are easy targets. A lot of the anxiety that accompanied me while getting ready for shows had to do with my anticipation of what nasty things people were going to say about me, about my performance, my analysis, my clothes, my body size; and once I learned to control all that, I was able to breathe again and love my job. But just about everyone gets attacked, and it's heartbreaking. I have a friend whose son was crippled by the stress of being bullied online and was hospitalized. It was sad and extremely angering. We no longer think or perhaps care about the consequences our words have on others.

And we also have this twisted notion that people with money deserve to be attacked. Yes, there are well-compensated athletes living more lavish lives than you and me. And there's no doubt they're better at dealing with pressure than you or me as well. But I would also argue their world is like living in an insane pressure cooker. They're constantly stressing over being their best, pleasing their teammates, pleasing the fans, pleasing the sponsors, pleasing, pleasing, pleasing.

Money doesn't turn them into robots. They're still human. They most definitely have the same emotions and feelings as you and me.

I'm willing to bet that a lot of people who say, "Too bad, so sad. This athlete needs to suck it up because they make a lot of money," are the same people who'll wisely state, "Money can't buy you happiness" when they hear of something tragic that happened to an athlete.

So, which one is it?

One day on *Leafs Lunch*, we were talking about the new player the team had just acquired — Brian Boyle. Once we were done analyzing the player and talking about what he brought to the team, I made a pretty innocent comment about how trades continue to be hard on families. I didn't harp on it. I didn't even call for trades to be abolished. I simply said that one day, a player is saying, "Bye honey, see you tomorrow!" He packs one change of underwear for his road trip, and the next thing he knows, he's not seeing his family for months. In Boyle's case, he had a two-year-old at the time, and his wife was around seven months pregnant, and they were back in

Florida. I simply said, "Man, this has to be tough on Boyle. I'm not sure if his wife can travel, and it'll be tough being away from his toddler."

The amount of demonic people attacking me on Twitter, saying, "Who cares about him missing his family because he has enough money in the bank?" astonished me. What does money in the bank have to do with quelling your emotions about missing your family? I never understood this way of thinking. It's this twisted belief that people with money deserve the abuse they take on social platforms. It's like, if someone was born with incredible athletic ability and they're getting paid a lot of money because of it, they must be humbled at every chance.

There are properly trained psychologists out there who can analyze this way of thinking far better than me, but the giddiness some people get in watching people fail is astounding. In a mental health talk, Canadian soccer player and Olympic champion Jordyn Huitema was asked about social media. This was her response: "Over the years, the hate has grown, for sure. I think as you're accumulating more followers, there's going to be people who dislike you, and there's going to be people who want to see you fail. Or they love to see you fail, and they thrive on it, and they love it."

What was once good old-fashioned booing and cheering at games has now morphed into something very dark because of social media. Players lives are being threatened, and their family members are being attacked through their social platforms. There's just an all-out disregard for the well-being of another human being.

What happened to us?

I wonder if the negativity being spread in the social media arena has led to a change I've noticed with many athletes during interviews.

Of course, this isn't every athlete, but it's enough of them for me to notice a difference.

Here's what I mean: When someone won a major trophy, accomplished something big, or was honoured for their achievements, I would interview them, and we would talk about the people who have supported them throughout the years. Family, friends, and youth coaches were always thanked. The interviews and acceptance speeches had a positive vibe to them.

Now, I'm noticing more and more athletes starting things off by calling out their haters, bringing attention to the people who didn't believe in them instead of those who did.

What's happening? Why so angry? I can only guess it's the constant exposure to hate. And when it's coming through your phone — something we all have attached to our bodies — there's no escaping the hate. It follows you everywhere.

I don't blame athletes for putting up walls. I only see a small sample of what they're exposed to on social media; I can't even imagine what's said in their private messages.

But this is a sad trend I'm noticing. More and more athletes talking about the abuse they receive. Some say it motivates them, and some say it has crippled them.

Either way, "the haters" are getting attention, and I — pardon the pun — hate it.

I don't want to hear about the people who didn't believe in you — I want to hear about the people who did.

I don't want to hear about the people who tried to drag you down — I want to hear about the people who helped you.

I've always believed the sports world to be a microcosm of the real world. And if I can feel the anger, the hurt, and the hate in the sports world . . . what is actually happening in the real world? It's a very scary thought.

*CHAPTER 37*

# DECIDING WHAT TO WEAR ON TV IS HARDER FOR WOMEN

Sigh.

This is a tough one for me. Television is a visual medium, and on-air people are often told what to wear by executive producers. And women, especially, are crucified by the public for what they choose to put on. This can be an all-around very touchy subject because people express themselves through their fashion, and when you challenge their clothing, it can feel like you're challenging their identity.

Here's a sad truth: A woman's sports knowledge is judged quite a bit by what she chooses to wear. As baffling as that sounds, many women can attest to this. Not to mention, their character is also judged by their outfit. Based on a woman's clothing, there are people out there who will judge whether or not she's a "slut," "bossy," "a horrible mother," "uptight," "smart," or "a good girl."

A woman could have just quoted stats to support an amazing argument or just given great analysis, but so many people will miss it because they're focused on her blouse or the length of her skirt or "Is that ring on her finger too gaudy?"

Buttoned up too much? Take some clothing off. Showing too much? Put some clothing on.

It can be exhausting, confusing, and many women become anxious over their on-air clothing decisions.

Women, more so than men, are harshly judged by what they wear.

So, it's no surprise that I get asked a lot by aspiring female broadcasters what they should be wearing on TV.

While attending sporting events has become very fashionably casual for fans with their jeans or joggers and jerseys in the stands, our clothing still needs to be professional.

I always tell these young women to wear what they're comfortable wearing. I tell them to ask themselves what makes them feel good, what makes them feel like they're in control and have power, and yes, what makes them feel beautiful.

I didn't always nail my fashion. Some will say I still don't!

But when I get dressed for work, I ask myself three questions: Do I love what I'm wearing? Am I dressed appropriately for the occasion? Will other women like what I'm wearing?

Yup, you read that right. I don't dress for the male gaze. I dress for myself and other women. The reason why I also love dressing in clothing I think other women will like is because I see it as a compliment when someone wants to wear what I'm wearing. After all, imitation is the greatest form of flattery.

But it wasn't always that way. I had to break free from the belief that women in the sports industry were simply eye candy for the male sports fan. And sadly, some women, whether they realize it or not, are stuck in that unfortunate belief system.

There's this brilliant scene in the movie *The Devil Wears Prada* where Anne Hathaway's character snickers at Meryl Streep's character as the latter is putting together a fashion look. Streep looks at Hathaway and then dives into this brilliant rant about how Hathaway thinks she's wearing something that makes a statement against the fashion industry, but she, in fact, is wearing something the fashion industry created for her years ago. You can look up the scene on YouTube — it's titled "Stuff." I've watched it over and over and have it memorized because it's so damn true. Like I said, brilliant.

So, I'll say this about what to wear: Ask yourself if *you* truly feel fantastic in that outfit you put on or if you've been led to believe that you can only feel beautiful if the male audience likes what they're seeing on you. If your answer is a confident one that it's all you — then you do you, baby. You go to work, and you rock it. But if what I just asked gave you pause, made you wonder, then don't be afraid to explore your fashion identity a little further.

I'm sure some of you are reading this and thinking, *Holy crap, how is any of this relevant to sports knowledge?* It's not.

But do you have any idea how quickly people will still dismiss a woman's knowledge of sports simply based on her clothing?

Do you know that a male broadcaster can wear the same suit for an entire year, and no one will notice, but a woman's on-air outfit is continuously scrutinized?

An Australian anchor literally tested this theory in 2014. He wore the same suit on air every day for one year (with the exception of the days his suit needed dry cleaning), and no one said a thing. But his co-host — a woman — received constant judgment about her clothing. No one said a thing about what he was wearing; he was judged solely by his reporting. But the woman's reporting was rated by the sweater she chose to wear that day.

It's crazy the role wardrobe plays in judging men and women. A man could wear the most boring or most outrageous outfit, and no one would question his credibility. Oh sure, people will comment on his outfit — see Don Cherry and the late Craig Sager — but his credibility is never challenged. Yet a woman's clothing is directly tied to her credibility . . . Isn't that crazy?

Sexism and gender inequality, applied through fashion, is alive and well.

One night, while working at *HNIC*, I wore these very nice leather pants with a complementary blouse. Two people started attacking me relentlessly on Twitter. I was a slut, I was a horrible role model to young girls, my father must be ashamed of me, and it went on and on. All because I was wearing leather pants. I was speechless. I didn't know that an innocent and quite stylish pair of slacks would make me the victim of that kind of vitriol.

Other times, according to viewers, my clothes made me look too fat, too short, or were too tight, too baggy, or the wrong colour. Someone once tweeted at me and said I shouldn't wear red nail polish because it made my fingers look fat. Another said I wasn't allowed to stand in the "power stance" because a woman in a dress should be more demure. That comment made me spit my drink out through my nose. Me? Demure? Now that's an oxymoron!

And here's the thing: whenever I didn't feel comfortable in what I was wearing, when I knew deep down inside I wasn't dressing for myself, those types of comments greatly affected me. That's when I knew I had to take control of my sanity by embracing my own style.

And no, women dressing in turtlenecks and suits and being completely covered doesn't mean they're more professional or knowledgeable than the women who like wearing dresses.

I'll let you in on a little secret: I love wearing dresses on air! I mean, I wear anything that makes me feel good, but from a practical approach, dresses are just easier for me on air. You see, we have to wear two audio packs while doing a show, one wireless pack for the microphone and another one for the earpiece, so the control room can communicate with us. These audio packs can be uncomfortable. When I'm wearing a pantsuit, the audio person will clip these packs on the back of my pants. No big deal, right? Until I forget they're there, go to the washroom, and both packs go swimming in the toilet. A few times, I've returned from my bathroom break holding these packs in my hand, sheepishly approaching the audio person and explaining to them what had happened. The first question they always ask before taking them back is, "Pre- or post-you-know-what?"

When I'm wearing a dress, it's just easier to clip these packs onto my bra strap. Washroom trips are easier; I don't have to bother with constantly tucking a top into my pants, and there's little to no adjusting required.

Now that you know this about me, you can imagine how infuriated I was when an article was written about my outfits, and I was never once approached for comment by the author.

I was working for TSN during the men's 2018 FIFA World Cup. A writer from one of the national newspapers was invited to spend the day with the crew to observe our coverage and then write an article about it. He interviewed all the on-air talent except for me. I didn't think much about it at the time. The next day at work, I was walking through the halls on my way to get a coffee when two higher-ups at TSN stopped me and asked if I was doing all right. I thought they were making customary pleasantries, and I responded by saying I was great.

"No really, Andi," they pressed. "We want to know if you're doing ok after what was written."

What the heck were these two talking about? They went on to tell me about the article and how the author took the liberty to "defend" me by accusing TSN of putting me in dresses to simply entertain the male viewer. He went on to say that it was a shame my role had been reduced after I hosted the World Cup in 2014 — a part of the article I didn't disagree with — but the fact he had an entire day to talk to me and never did? That really bothered me. He had every opportunity to approach me and ask me how I felt about a reduced hosting role. He had every opportunity to ask me about my wardrobe. If this man had just walked ten feet from his chair to the one I was sitting in, he could have included my voice in his article instead of speaking on my behalf. He would've learned that I chose my own clothing.

What this writer didn't realize was that by trying to say I deserved a bigger role or perhaps more respect, he was the one who actually reduced my presence to a pile of clothes. He's the one who brought attention to what I was wearing.

And he never once thought to ask me about it.

To the women out there, I'm not sure if I answered your question about what to wear or if I've confused you even more. I guess I'll just repeat what I said earlier: Wear what makes you feel special and has you walk out of the house with a bounce in your step.

To others reading this who are having a tough time comprehending why clothing is so important and causes so much anxiety for women, I'll say this: Pay attention to your thoughts when watching a woman on air versus a man. How much are you judging the appearance of each?

TV is a visual medium. All of us want to look good while doing our shows, and many of us even want to be fashion-forward. Fantastic. The point of this chapter and my train of thought is to caution against reducing women to nothing but what they wear and, more importantly, to caution against outright dismissing their intelligence based on their outfits. No one likes double standards.

However, there is one thing when it comes to clothing that affects both men and women working in the sports industry equally, albeit comically. Beware the colours you choose to wear on game night! It doesn't matter if you love that green outfit. If one of the teams you're covering that night has green as part of their colours, fans will accuse you of supporting that team. It's trivial, for sure, but it can be very annoying having your socials blow up with people talking about the colour of your outfit, your tie, suit, etc. and associating it with your supposed support for one of the teams playing that night instead of listening to your analysis. Some former players turned analysts will do this on purpose and wear the colours of their former team, and that's cool. It's intentional, and they're ok with the attention. But could you imagine if longtime Calgary Flames captain Jarome Iginla did a broadcast on a night the Flames were taking on the Edmonton Oilers, and he showed up wearing a blue and orange tie? Or if former Montreal Canadiens goalie Carey Price went on air during a Habs vs. Leafs game noticeably wearing blue and white? Oh boy.

I went on the air one night during my *HNIC* days and wore what I thought was a really nice black and gold dress. Little did I know I set off a firestorm within the Leafs fanbase. According to them, I was actively cheering for the Boston Bruins.

I just liked the dress. Sheesh!

I remember during the Tokyo 2020 Olympics, former national team goalkeeper Karina LeBlanc and I were getting ready to host the gold medal match between Canada and Sweden. Karina put on this yellow dress that just popped on her. It was stunning. She decided that was the dress she wanted to wear. I had to be the one to burst her bubble: "I know you're going to think this is stupid, Karina, but you can't wear that dress. Yellow is Sweden's colour. Of course, everyone knows you bleed red and white, but I'm telling you right now, you will get people messaging you about the colour of your dress. It will piss you off. And it's a distraction and an annoyance you just don't need."

She understood completely.

While we're on the topic of clothes, let's talk body image.

More and more men are courageously talking about their own body issues, and I commend them for asking for help and drawing attention to the struggles men usually try to battle secretly.

But in my experience, in the world of broadcasting, a woman's weight is fair game to criticize over that of a man's. Oh sure, retired male athletes who put on some weight get teased by former teammates, but it's usually done with a playful tone. In fact, the former athlete himself will joke about needing new suits and the fear of picking something up lest his pants should rip. We all chuckle, viewers included, and we move on.

But a woman who is deemed to be on the heavier side is ridiculed, belittled, and judged unfit to be on television.

Like many teenagers, when I was going through puberty, I started to become more aware of my body and, hence, my image. Of course, I had moments where I was uncomfortable in my own skin, but I never hated myself. I had a very healthy relationship with food. I was athletic, and I was confident.

And then . . . I landed a job on TV. Suddenly, my curvy body was called "fat." My athletic frame was "butchy." The chat sites and social media platforms gave space for nasty people to be . . . well . . . nasty. Even my voice was attacked. One girl said she'd rather drive a knitting needle into her ear than listen to me. Whoa, whoa, whoa, girly, we're supposed to be allies and stick together!

I was a very happy size 8 for most of my life, but apparently, that size doesn't read well on TV. Things are starting to change now, thank goodness, but women still take criticism surrounding their weight more than men.

Sadly, my once-healthy relationship with food deteriorated when I got into TV. I never developed an eating disorder, but man, was I ever hard on myself. Ate too late? I would stress all night over needing to wake up early and work out to burn it off. Ate dessert? Skip dinner the next night. Enjoyed some pizza? Salads for the next week.

I started to work out and change my diet, but it wasn't sustainable. Sure, I dropped to a size 2 or 4, but I was training as if I was getting ready for a fitness competition. It was never going to last as a day-to-day routine.

I knew early on it was a mental game I was playing with myself, but it took me longer than I would've liked to control it.

If I had let my workout and diet go and my body was attacked online after a show, I would sink into a depression.

If I had a run of excellent workouts and healthy eating and my body was attacked by viewers, it didn't affect me because I felt great. I knew it was all in my head. But when your insecurities are being exploited, it's not the easiest of battles to win.

I've been fortunate to never have bosses tell me I need to lose weight or look a certain way. Although, I did have a camera guy early on in my career tell me I needed a boob job if I wanted to go far in the business.

All the criticism I've received about my body has come from viewers. And social media has allowed them to enter my safe space.

But I'm proud to say my relationship with food is so much better.

I'm definitely more disciplined heading into big events, but I do that for fun. If the athletes have to hunker down and get ready for a big event, I stand in solidarity with them in my own version of hunkering down. We're all getting into peak form together!

When I'm feeling particularly critical of my body, I remind myself that this very body saved a life. Yup, it sure did. It was the summer of 2009. I booked a trip to Greece. The tour group set sail on a massive pirate ship that took us to a remote island for the day. The ship had to anchor a fair distance from the shoreline, and the captain said he had lifeboats that would take us the rest of the way. He then said, "But for those of you brave enough, you can always jump off the side and swim to shore!"

I immediately went to the edge and peered over. It was like jumping off a ten-metre platform, perhaps a little higher. I asked the captain if there were any sharks.

"No, the water is too warm," he said.

Wonderful. I took off my bathing suit cover and jumped overboard! Three guys joined me — the rest took the lifeboats.

From the ship, the water didn't look too bad. But once we were in the ocean, it was very choppy. For every three strokes forward, it felt like the waves pushed us back five! Knowing I was the one who led the charge, I cheekily quipped, "Whose bright idea was this?" I heard the guy behind me chuckle; then, a few seconds later, I heard gurgling and then . . . silence. I turned around, and he was gone. I let the waves carry me up and down, hoping they were doing the same to him and eventually I'd see him. Nothing. I looked ahead, and the other two guys were too far in front; they had no clue that one of us had gone under. I had taken swimming lessons all my life and even took lifeguard courses. But as comfortable as I am in water, as trained as I am in water emergencies, this scared the hell out of me. I plunged into the ocean and desperately tried to see something. The saltwater burned, but thank goodness it was fairly clear, and I spotted him suspended underwater. Lesson 101 when approaching a drowning victim: Be prepared to kick them and then quickly slide your arm through their arms along their back so you can push their chest up. Drowning victims, understandably so, panic. They will grab onto anything to help them stay above water and get air back into their lungs. They go into survival mode. Knowing this and taking into account this guy was bigger than me and could've easily knocked me out, I went in prepared to knock him out first! I approached feet first, and it was a good thing I did. His eyes found me, and true to form, he reached for me. I kicked him in the stomach, got behind him, slid my arm through the back of both of his and then kicked to the surface. Who knows how long all this lasted? It felt like an eternity. When we got to the surface, one of the other swimmers was there, looking frantic. He had turned around at some point and didn't see either of us, but all he could do was tread water and pray because he didn't see where we had gone under. When he did spot us, he swam over and helped me bring the other guy to shore. I had one arm, he had the other.

We asked the guy who almost drowned what had happened. Why would he follow us overboard if he couldn't swim all that well? He said the opposite was true. He's a very good swimmer. But the waves exhausted him by constantly crashing into him. He thought he could catch a breather by trying to swim underwater for a bit — avoid the waves. But he said his body gave up. He was so tired and had zero energy to kick to the surface. He said he accepted that this was how he was going to die until he saw me.

"I was so relieved to see you," he said. "And then you kicked me!"

We all had a good laugh over that. Needless to say, I didn't pay for another drink for the remainder of the tour. *Opa!*

So, anytime someone attacks my "chubby" arms, I remind myself that they lifted another human out of the ocean. When someone says my hips are too wide, I remind myself of the power they generated to kick through the water and get us to safety.

Remind yourself how powerful your body is. Remind yourself of the amazing things your body has done and can do.

Sadly, just as I've finally conquered the weight war, I'm now entering the "wrinkle" battle that, once again, affects women way more than men in my industry.

Honestly, between our clothing, our body, and our face, I can only think of one thing to say: Leave us the fuck alone.

## *CHAPTER 38*

# LET WOMEN AGE ON AIR JUST LIKE MEN

It was 2010, the year I turned thirty. A significant milestone. Every year I'm alive, I consider it a blessing. But some people get so weird when they hit another decade; they get depressed. Not me. I read Oprah Winfrey's book *What I Know For Sure* and there's a part where she said she tells people her age proudly because there are far too many who never reach that age; they're gone too soon. That resonated with me. I don't see getting older as a bad thing.

When it comes to the broadcasting industry, some will say age does matter because I'll probably be replaced by a younger woman. What an absolute and utter bullshit mentality to have. I see a lot of older men on my TV. Are they being told the same thing? No. I don't let my age be a hindrance, and I sure as hell don't allow anyone else to do so either.

*But Andi, you can't control the decisions made by executives!*

Yes, I can, and yes, you can. And how we do that is by talking about it. Bringing it to the forefront. Calling out ageism. We need to change our attitude. When men get older in this industry, they're seen as experienced, credible, and worth every penny in their new contract. When women get older in this industry, they're seen as washed-up, too expensive, and easily replaceable by someone younger and cheaper.

The "threat of age" was manufactured by the industry, and women were the ones left suffering. For years, we've been made to believe that once you hit a certain age, you better start looking over your shoulder for the younger woman who's about to replace you. This, sadly, ends up turning women against one another when we should be fostering beautiful mentoring relationships. Instead, older women see younger women as threats. Older women end up ignoring younger women or treating them rudely. In turn, younger women are made to believe they've been brought on board to replace older women. Instead of seeing the experienced woman as someone with mounds of knowledge that can be shared and having wisdom to help navigate this tricky and exhausting landscape, she is reduced to an obstacle that the younger woman must eliminate.

How sad. How horrible. How infuriating!

It's a form of lateral oppression. This is when a marginalized group, in this case, women in the sports industry, bully each other so they can look good in front of their male counterparts.

And some men in this industry, whether consciously or not, enjoy pitting women against one another.

I was working at Leafs TV, and I was only in my mid-twenties. We had recently hired a woman a tad bit younger than me. A couple of male co-workers turned to me and said, with sly grins on their faces, "Ooooo, Petrillo, you have some competition now! You scared?"

What in the actual hell were these two morons talking about? The look on my face must've said it all. Their stupid, sly grins were gone.

"Why would I see her as competition?" I challenged.

They had no answer.

"Is it because we're both women? Because there's only room for one of us?"

That's when the backpedalling began. "Petrillo, we're just messing with you."

"Did anyone mess with you when we hired another guy?"

Conversation over.

I knew exactly where their mentality came from. They too were a product of deep-seated beliefs that women in the sports industry were often regarded as token hires. Not to mention, at that time, women entering the sports space were still seen as a novelty. People felt the need to describe women in the industry using their gender. For example, they would make a point of saying, "This is so and so, a female sports reporter" or "This is so and so, a female sports host."

It was to the point that I even believed I had to include my gender in my job title. One day, I was hanging out in the office of my producer, Mark Askin. I had just returned from an afternoon at a local high school talking to kids about careers. When I told Mark they had introduced me by saying "female sportscaster," he was not impressed.

"Wait a second, kiddo. Why did they have to say 'female'? It's pretty obvious you're a woman. Why feel the need to point it out? When Joe Bowen walks into a room, do you think he says, 'Hi, I'm Joe Bowen, a male sportscaster'? You bet he doesn't. You're a sportscaster, period. And you should be respected as such."

It was an epiphanic moment for me.

We continue to differentiate women in sports, even when it comes to the naming of professional leagues. You have the NBA, and then you have the WNBA. You have the NHL, and then you have the PWHL. You have MLS, and then you have the NWSL. I get it, the men's leagues launched first, so you knew it was men competing. But I think we've arrived at a point where gender in the title isn't necessary. That's why I was pleasantly surprised when Diana Matheson named her new women's soccer league Northern Super League.

For so long, when a woman "made it" and was able to have a career in sports, she was tagged as being the token female amongst the men. Those women worked damn hard to get to that spot and most definitely took a lot of shit along the way. I can see why they wanted to hold on to this coveted position because they were always told there's only so much room for women here.

Enough. That's simply not true. And it never was.

I often ask women, "Do you want to be a lone token in this industry or part of a treasure chest full of gold?" My answer is always — Gimme, gimme all the jewels!

In 2024, NFL host Charissa Thompson did an interview where she talked about some older women in the industry who were cruel to her in the early days. She vowed to never be like that once she became a veteran broadcaster. Mentalities are changing, and it starts with us recognizing and quashing the old and tired messaging that there's only so much room for women and that we're not allowed to age on air the same way men do.

So, to the young women: Stop seeing older women as people you need to replace.

To the older women: Stop seeing younger women as threats and take them under your wing.

There's more than enough room for all of us.

And to the men: Don't create a toxic work environment based on what is so obviously sexist and ageist. What an antiquated way of doing business.

It's a vicious cycle that needs to end. And I think it is. More and more women are coming together, lifting each other up, mentoring, and being all-around supportive. More and more men are entering the industry who have been exposed to working with many women, women in influential positions as well, and they don't see it as threatening.

Women like Hazel Mae, Brenda Irving, and Martine Gaillard in Canadian television are breaking the mould, whether they're aware of it or not. As I'm writing this, I'm in my mid-forties, which means women over the age of fifty who are still holding on-air positions catch my attention. They continue to be role models and trailblazers. They give me hope that our attitudes towards women aging on TV are changing and that someone like me has a chance to continue holding a prominent role in the sports industry past fifty years of age if I so choose.

But frustratingly, there is still more pressure on women to remain youthful-looking and the same expectation is not put on men. In fact, it's almost like wrinkles and grey hair on men in the industry are welcomed because they present a credible and wiser look: *Believe what I'm saying because my aged and weathered face tells you I've been doing this a long time and know more about sports than you do.*

Women, on the other hand, arc told they look haggard and are no longer attractive. Our looks and our youth still take precedence over our knowledge and wisdom, and that needs to stop. And I do believe it is. More and more executives are respecting a woman's experience in the industry and coveting it. As I get older, my bosses seek out my opinion on various things in broadcasting, acknowledging the importance of the years I have under my belt. And I can also say I'm being given more prominent roles on shows because I've earned it. You see, many of the decision-making positions at networks were held by men, and they created this ridiculous belief system that older women needed to be replaced by younger ones.

Many men who currently hold these positions are not following that old mentality. More importantly, these decision-making positions are being filled by women and they're helping to change our attitude towards seeing women age on television.

But despite some of this progress, we still have a lot of work to do. I'm referring to Lisa LaFlamme and Christine Simpson. Both women were still in their prime and doing great work on TV, yet both women were dismissed by their networks with very little reason given. Two incredible female broadcasters being let go in their late fifties is disheartening to fellow female broadcasters.

I read this brilliant quote from music icon Cher that really resonated with me. She said, "We're held to a different standard than men. Some guy said to me, 'Don't you think you're too old to sing rock 'n' roll?' I said, 'You'd better check with Mick Jagger.'"

It's time to send the message that women can age on television, and we need to put that message into regular practice. No matter our age, there's more than enough room for us.

## CHAPTER 39

# XENNIALS

The evolution of women in the sports industry would make for a great case study. If I were to simplify it into three generations, I would say this: The women who broke glass ceilings are The Cautious Ones; coming up the ranks now are The Unapologetic Ones; and then there's my generation, The In-Betweeners. We're both.

Of course, these are broad strokes — not everyone will subscribe to these categories — but I've been doing this a long time, and I know the majority of what I'm about to say is undeniable. Because I'm the living embodiment of both.

The Cautious Ones are tough as nails. They were the "firsts." There were no trails when they started — they blazed them. But they were also taught to believe everything they earned was, in fact, given to them, so they should be appreciative and not ruffle any feathers. Tough, yet insecure. They worked in fear. Fear of being replaced, fear of not being respected, fear of being taken advantage of. Many of these women were given the crap gigs and the longest hours, but they did it because they didn't want to lose all they had accomplished.

They don't really ask why, and they'll bend over backwards so as not to disappoint . . . or be replaced. I find that to be their biggest fear — replacement. Consequently, another fear risks coming to fruition — being taken advantage of. It's a vicious circle, and it's the only one many of them know. Their whole identity is wrapped up in their work.

Men of this generation exhibit a similar fear. Although, I would say it's more of a concern than a full-blown fear of being replaced. And that's because men have been told it's ok for them to grow old on TV. Women need to be young. And guess who we humans have a losing streak against? Guess who we will never defeat? Father Time.

This ties into my previous chapter about ageism. The fear of being replaced, of being told you can't grow old on TV as a woman, makes The Cautious Ones more guarded against younger women. You can even argue it has made some of them mean and standoffish to the next generation of sportscasters.

The Unapologetic Ones know their worth. They subscribe to the theory, "Work Smarter, Not Harder." They ask why when told to do something, not because they don't want to work, but because they want to know that their hard work has a purpose. If they're told to be somewhere all day to gather interviews, they'll ask who they're interviewing, how many people they need to talk to, and if these interviews will go to air. They don't just say yes like a robot. They need to know their work is going to mean something. They value their time.

A consequence of this approach is that a lot of this generation lacks real expertise. How can you really be an expert at something unless you invest an incredible amount of time? It can be argued that not every occasion requires a ton of questions; sometimes you just do it. It's through putting in this time and effort that you gain the knowledge and experience to determine what's worth doing and what's not.

I've also noticed this group doesn't define who they are by what job they have. Their world won't crumble if they're replaced because there's a good chance they already have two or three other things on the go.

Many Cautious Ones I've spoken to have said, "If I'm not doing this job till the day I retire, I don't know what I'll do. This is who I am!"

An Unapologetic One often responds with, "Meh, it'll stink if I get let go, but I have this podcast I want to focus on. Or maybe I'll ask my friend for a hook up at their place of work!"

I understand both of their worlds. Because then there's me and my generation: The In-Betweeners.

I put my head down, pin my ears back, and charge ahead with whatever task I've been assigned. Sometimes I ask why, sometimes I don't.

I feel lucky for how my career has gone, but damn it, I know I made a lot of my own luck.

I don't want to speak too loudly or make requests that could be seen as demands because I'll be labelled "difficult" and "unappreciative"; but excuse me, my experiences and credentials give me every right to command my own space and not be sorry for how strong my voice is.

I think about being replaced, but I don't allow those thoughts to cripple me . . . I love my job, but if it's taken away from me, I know I'll thrive in whatever is next.

You see, this is why it has taken me so long to write this book.

Some will see it as courageous while also thinking I should've stayed quiet.

Others will say that it's about time and to never hold back.

I see it both ways . . .

That's what it's like for The In-Betweener.

Turns out this feeling of being in the middle and understanding both sides has a reason. When I was talking to a friend about how I felt, she said, "For sure you feel that way. It's because you're an Xennial."

I looked it up. It's a thing.

I was born in 1980. Apparently, I'm right in the middle of Generation X and Millennials. Xennials are described as "having an analog childhood and a digital young adulthood. Xennials came of age during a rapidly changing period that was the 1990s."

This term was added to the Oxford English Dictionary in 2020.

Yes, my generation came of age during a technological boom. It wasn't until high school that I got my first email address and needed a computer to do schoolwork. Dial-up took forever, and I didn't have Wi-Fi until I moved out of my parents' house in my twenties.

I went from having no way to find my friends if they weren't home to getting a pager when I was seventeen. But even after getting beeped, I often needed to call collect on the payphone when I didn't have a quarter.

I got my first cellphone in university.

If my generation experienced all these technological changes, you can only imagine the ideological changes we went through.

As mentioned earlier, my parents blurred the gender lines. I was never raised to behave a certain way because I'm a girl, and I was never taught to expect things from boys because they're boys. But that doesn't mean I wasn't exposed to things.

A man paying for dinner is very nice. But it's ok to go Dutch or pick up the tab myself. I grew up assuming the big bosses of companies were men, but I was taught to believe that I too could be a boss one day.

I grew up seeing only women taking maternity leave to society finally accepting men taking paternity leave.

And I've gone from covering the National Hockey League to the Professional Women's Hockey League.

My generation has seen exceptional evolution on many fronts during our most pivotal years, our most influential years — our teens and twenties.

Xennials. The In-Betweeners.

## CHAPTER 40

# CHANGING MEDIA LANDSCAPE

It's been over thirty years since I was first exposed to this industry in 1994, shadowing Libby Znaimer and Laura Di Battista at Citytv News.

Citytv was the cool kid on the block in the '90s, and the way they did news challenged the establishment.

Their main anchors were Gord Martineau and Anne Mroczkowski, and they didn't sit at a desk. They roamed the newsroom. They did walk-and-talks. They would be sitting on desks or standing in a place where people were walking behind them and doing work. I was present for one of these broadcasts, and as a fourteen-year-old, I was in complete awe of all the movement and chaos.

In 2023, during one of my guest-hosting appearances on *Breakfast Television*, Gord Martineau was a guest. I felt like a kid again, getting to meet him officially all these years later. I asked him about those broadcasts, and his eyes lit up. He knew Citytv News was doing something different and pushing the envelope. And not just when it came to how the news was shot.

David C. Onley was the first on-air reporter with a visible disability. It was very eye-opening for a young kid like me to see a person in a wheelchair reporting on the news.

Jojo Chintoh was the station's first Black reporter, and I loved his raspy Ghanaian accent.

I had no clue what a videographer was until I saw Audra Brown. I was amazed at her ability to hold two cameras at the same time and I thought her stand-ups that she shot through side mirrors on a car were the coolest ever.

And who could forget *Speakers Corner*? It was Facebook before Facebook was a thing. People piling into a sidewalk video booth to record a video and share things about themselves: what they did that week, a joke, a gripe, or a love story. The network would compile the videos and play them as a show. It was must-watch TV.

Leafs TV had some innovations of their own. They had *Leafs in 30*, which would cut down the regular two-and-a-half-hour game into thirty minutes, allowing fans to watch the valuable parts of the game. We eventually started airing *Leafs in Six* because one of our producers had read an article in *GQ Magazine* about the attention span of readers. It said that if an article takes longer than six minutes to read, people won't read it. I believe the exact example given in the magazine was the average time a man spends on the toilet is six minutes, so the article shouldn't surpass that reading time. He transferred that theory to television and made editors cram the best parts of the Maple Leafs games into six minutes to retain a viewer's attention.

When I joined *Hockey Night in Canada*, I hosted the iDesk. The segment was all about bringing viewers highlights and storylines from other games around the league. With the invention of social media and fans gaining access to goals and saves and big hits as they happened in real time, there was no need for viewers to wait until intermission to see them.

I've seen this industry go from long-form viewing to short, snippy highlight packs. I've seen journalists hand out their demo tapes on VHS tapes to USB keys to now just providing a link to a video. I remember watching TV, and certain networks would still shut things down between midnight and 1 a.m. Seriously, they would go off the air. No programming; nothing. Bars and tone or fuzzy static would come up on the screen, and shows wouldn't start again until around 6 a.m.

News was the first to go 24/7.

Even though sports networks loop their highlight show overnight, the world of social media keeps people on their toes 24/7. And if there's a big tournament happening somewhere in the world that requires a Canadian network to be live on the air all night, then so be it. My first Olympics hosting job in Sochi had me on the air in Canada between midnight and 6 a.m. ET. There were also a few soccer games I covered when kick-off was midnight eastern time and others that started at 5 a.m. ET.

I've seen wonderful changes in this industry, like women becoming play-by-play and colour analysts and BIPOC communities being better represented. I've seen a world where there were only men's professional leagues become one where there are now many women's pro leagues. And I've seen traditional television challenged by technology and the ever-growing digital world.

Before, your content could only air on a network. Now, there are so many platforms to display your work.

Unless you had state-of-the-art camera equipment and lighting and audio, you couldn't produce something that was network-worthy. Now, you can attach a camera to your head or film something on your phone, bring a ring light and use wireless lavalier microphones that transmit audio right to your phone. Boom. You've just created content that can air on multiple platforms.

Crazy how far we've come.

When I was still at Leafs TV, we were considered a specialty channel. You had to purchase Leafs TV separately from your cable package. Diehard Leafs fans had no problem subscribing. Every year, the channel would retain a handful of Leafs games to air on the network. This was before the Rogers and Bell takeover. This upset a lot of hockey fans who didn't have LTV. You see, Leafs TV wasn't a streaming app, it was a specialty channel offered on linear TV.

I remember being confused by some of the reactions because, around this time, a lot of people were frustrated with cable. They felt they were paying too much and were getting way too many channels they didn't care about. The buzz phrase at the time was "a la carte." People wanted to be able to pick and choose their channels and not just be handed bundles by the cable providers.

And then people started talking about Netflix — a true streaming app. It launched in the United States first and three years later in Canada, its first international market. A streaming app, unlike a specialty channel, meant you didn't need a TV at all. People started giving up their cable packages: "cord cutting."

There were some people who, upon hearing what I did for a living, would say, "Sorry, I don't watch TV anymore. I only subscribe to apps."

And then they would proceed to brag about how much money they were saving. I couldn't blame them. Who doesn't want to save money? But it also upset me because the industry was making massive cuts due to revenue loss. A lot of good people, a lot of people who were my friends, were losing their jobs because people were cord cutting.

Eventually, more streaming services joined Netflix. Now you have Crave, Amazon Prime, Apple, etc. I knew it wouldn't take the industry long to correct itself. It's not that I'm a genius or a prophet, it's just common sense. I remember telling people: If you were one of the first to cut the cord, then you saved money. But be prepared because now that networks have figured out the digital world, they're going to splinter off, and you're going to have to purchase all these apps in order to keep watching the shows or news or sports that you want.

Cue the present day. Just about every network has a traditional linear channel and a digital channel for which they charge extra. And all these networks have the rights to different things. You want to watch a certain show or movie? Gotta have the app they're on. Wanna watch soccer? Gotta have about four different apps for that.

Amazon, Apple, DAZN, Netflix, OneSoccer, YouTube, and FuboTV are some of the main digital platforms already in the sports game. Sometimes, networks will air certain games and tournaments strictly on their digital platforms instead of on their linear channel. Examples of this are ESPN+ and NBC's Peacock.

I know this is frustrating, especially since a lot of people haven't let go of traditional cable but are still investing in streaming services. I get it. I'm a consumer too. The bills add up.

Managing your sports apps is like managing your bank accounts.

However, the networks are starting to understand the struggle of consumers. And there seems to be some acknowledgment by these online streamers that viewers are feeling scattered and pinched financially. In the United States, there was a proposed sports-focused streaming service that would have seen networks traditionally in competition for viewership, join forces. The proposed name was Venu Sports. The likes of ESPN, Fox Sports, and TNT Sports would have offered up the games to leagues to which they have the rights in a bundle that would've seen consumers having to pay just one subscription fee. Concerns were raised by other TV networks and streamers about how this could unfairly impact competition in the market. Ultimately, Venu Sports died on the vine. The point I'm trying to make is that there has been some recognition that viewers feel like they're being asked to subscribe to a bunch of apps, and they're seeing their bills rise again. Venu, upon first impression, appeared to be bringing back the cable model but in a digital form.

I know this may still be little consolation to people who prefer to sit on their couch and channel surf, but those people are becoming the minority. The reason why more and more sports are migrating to the streaming world is because that's where the fans are going. The fans are dictating the market; they are the ones consuming their content through online apps. Before the start of the 2024–25 NFL season, commissioner Roger Goodell did an interview with CNBC and was asked why some NFL games are strictly being shown on streaming services. He responded, "The bottom line is you have to go where your fans are, and our fans are moving off onto streaming platforms."

Despite some of the headaches that come along with adjusting to a new way of consuming sports content, it's still very exciting times for viewers. More sports than ever before are available for viewing. And if you're a fringe sports fan whose sport is traditionally ignored by the larger networks, you now have an app you can subscribe to that will satisfy your fandom.

And for Canadians who work in the sports industry, both in front of and behind the camera, there are more opportunities for employment. The more networks that own league rights, the more jobs being created.

When OneSoccer launched in 2019, it created a bunch of new jobs for people, and it gave many former players a platform to share their knowledge of the game while covering the domestic Canadian Premier League and national team broadcasts.

Amazon is another great example of more work being created. In 2024, when they took over Monday night NHL hockey in Canada, they hired a whole new crew of people.

The streaming world isn't the future way of consuming content — it's the present, the here and now. Change is always scary, but when it's done right, it can also be incredibly amazing.

## CHAPTER 41

# [THANKS FOR TUNING IN. I'LL SEE YOU NEXT TIME.]

On all my broadcasts, I sign off by saying," Thanks for tuning in. I'll see you next time."

Not the most catchy or clever tagline, but the words speak the truth. I am thankful you decided to watch the show, and I truly do look forward to seeing you next time. I may not physically be able to see you the same way you can see me on your television screen or monitor, but I'm aware that you've welcomed me into your home, and for that, I am grateful.

My hope is that those of you reading this book will be left with a better understanding of the divide in the treatment of men and women that still exists in sportscasting. If I've encouraged just one person to challenge the unfair judgment of women in the industry, then *Just Call Me Andi* will be a success.

More importantly, my wish is that young women aspiring to become sportscasters will recognize that there are many incredible people in the business who *will* support them; women don't just belong in this space, we helped create it.

Throughout my career, I've dealt with my fair share of hard times — the majority of which simply occurred because I'm a woman — but I've mostly been having the time of my life. I pinch myself when I think I was just fourteen when I first shadowed a reporter. At forty-five, I now have young reporters shadowing me. Time flies when you're having fun.

My confidence and perseverance began with the support I received at home. My parents and my family never tried to put me in a gender box. My husband's strength has created a foundation that allows me to shine.

There are wonderful men in this industry who recognize the worth and power of women; they are incredible allies.

The sisterhood in broadcasting continues to grow. More and more veterans are taking young women under their wings, and more young women seek out their mentorship. We are stronger together.

And finally, to all the amazing sports fans: I hope you feel the love I have for sports every time you see me interviewing an athlete or analyzing a game. My gender should be a non-factor. My passion for and knowledge of sports, as well as many other women's passion and knowledge, should be all that matters.

So, I say from the bottom of my heart: Thanks for tuning in. I'll see you next time.

# ACKNOWLEDGEMENTS


"There is a stubbornness about me that never can bear to be frightened at the will of others. My courage always rises at every attempt to intimidate me."

— Jane Austen, *Pride and Prejudice*

My family is my rock. Nothing would be possible without them. My biggest thanks go to them.

Thank you to my literary agent, Brian Wood, who tracked me down and convinced me this was a book worth writing. Writing a book is like throwing a party and wondering, *Will anyone show up?* Hopefully people do read this book, but either way, it was cathartic writing it: Thank you, Brian.

To ECW Press, thank you for taking a chance on my book. A special shout-out to Michael Holmes and Victoria Cozza for combing through every line, making sure every story was told with clarity, and ensuring the words on the page still belonged to me. You encouraged me to share my experiences and opinions and to do so unapologetically.

Thank you to all the incredible people I've worked with over the years. There are so many wonderful humans who work behind the scenes and are the real reason any programming makes it to air: Thanks for letting me take the glory!

Thank you to my good friend, James Duthie, for writing the foreword. He jokes, but I know how busy he is and how hard he works. But he didn't hesitate to say yes when I reached out to him.

To my husband, Jon, you know I'm strong enough to fight my own battles but you're always at the ready when I need you. Having you in my corner gives me great strength.

To the women who dare to command their space and uplift other women: Your strength is infectious.

**ANDI PETRILLO** is an award-winning sports broadcaster. In 2016 she became the first woman in Canada to win the Canadian Screen Award for Best Sports Host, and she's gone on to win this award multiple times. In 2022, she became the first woman to be recognized by Sports Media Canada in the Outstanding Sportscaster category. Andi continues to present major sporting events for CBC Sports such as the Olympics and World Championships. She is a mainstay of Canadian hockey and soccer coverage, and currently hosts shows for Prime Hockey and OneSoccer.

Andi grew up in Maple, Ontario, the only child of Italian immigrants, Eva and Joe. She currently lives in Toronto, Ontario, with her husband, Jon, and two dogs, Pepper and Ginger.

**Entertainment. Writing. Culture.**

ECW is a proudly independent, Canadian-owned book publisher. We know great writing can improve people's lives, and we're passionate about sharing original, exciting, and insightful writing across genres.

**Thanks for reading along!**

We want our books not just to sustain our imaginations, but to help construct a healthier, more just world, and so we've become a certified B Corporation, meaning we meet a high standard of social and environmental responsibility — and we're going to keep aiming higher. We believe books can drive change, but the way we make them can too.

Certified B Corporation

Being a B Corp means that the act of publishing this book should be a force for good — for the planet, for our communities, and for the people that worked to make this book. For example, everyone who worked on this book was paid at least a living wage. You can learn more at the Ontario Living Wage Network.

This book is also available as a Global Certified Accessible™ (GCA) ebook. ECW Press's ebooks are screen reader friendly and are built to meet the needs of those who are unable to read standard print due to blindness, low vision, dyslexia, or a physical disability.

The interior of this book is printed on Sustana EnviroBook™, which is made from 100% recycled fibres and processed chlorine-free.

FSC
www.fsc.org
MIX
Paper | Supporting responsible forestry
FSC® C103567

ECW's office is situated on land that was the traditional territory of many nations, including the Wendat, the Anishinaabeg, Haudenosaunee, Chippewa, Métis, and current treaty holders the Mississaugas of the Credit. In the 1880s, the land was developed as part of a growing community around St. Matthew's Anglican and other churches. Starting in the 1950s, our neighbourhood was transformed by immigrants fleeing the Vietnam War and Chinese Canadians dispossessed by the building of Nathan Phillips Square and the subsequent rise in real estate value in other Chinatowns. We are grateful to those who cared for the land before us and are proud to be working amidst this mix of cultures.

ecwpress.com